Owen Barfield's Poetic Philosophy

Bloomsbury Studies in Philosophy and Poetry

Series Editors: Rick Anthony Furtak, Colorado College, USA, and James D. Reid, Metropolitan State University of Denver, USA

Editorial Board:

Daniel Brown, University of Southampton, UK
Kristen Case, University of Maine Farmington, USA
Hannah Vandegrift Eldridge, University of Wisconsin–Madison, USA
Cassandra Falke, University of Tromsø, Norway
Luke Fischer, University of Sydney, Australia
John Gibson, University of Louisville, USA
James Haile III, University of Rhode Island, USA
Kevin Hart, University of Virginia, USA
Eileen John, University of Warwick, UK
Troy Jollimore, California State University, USA
David Kleinberg-Levin, Northwestern University, USA
John Koethe, University of Wisconsin–Milwaukee, USA
John T. Lysaker, Emory University, USA
Karmen MacKendrick, Le Moyne College, USA
Rukmini Bhaya Nair, Indian Institute of Technology, India
Kamiyo Ogawa, Sophia University, Japan
Kaz Oishi, University of Tokyo, Japan
Yi-Ping Ong, Johns Hopkins University, USA
Anna Christina Soy Ribeiro, Texas Tech University, USA
Karen Simecek, University of Warwick, UK
Ruth Rebecca Tietjen, University of Copenhagen, Denmark
Íngrid Vendrell Ferran, Goethe University Frankfurt, Germany

Bloomsbury Studies in Philosophy and Poetry explores ancient, modern, and contemporary texts in ways that are sensitive to philosophical themes and problems that can be fruitfully addressed through poetic modes of writing and focused on questions of style, the relations between form and content, and the conduciveness of literary modes of expression to philosophical inquiry.

With a keen interest in the intertwining of poetry and philosophy in all forms, the series will cover the philosophical register of poetry, the poetics of philosophical writing, and the literary strategies of philosophers.

The series provides a home for work on figures across geographical landscapes, with contributions that employ a wide range of methods across academic disciplines, and without regard for divisions within philosophy, between analytic and continental, for example, that have outworn their usefulness. Featuring single-authored works and edited collections, curated by an international editorial board, the series aims to redefine how we read and discuss philosophy and poetry today.

New Titles:

***Maurice Blanchot on Poetry and Narrative** Ethics of the Image* by Kevin Hart
***Philosophy of Lyric Voice** The Cognitive Value of Page and Performance Poetry* by Karen Simecek
***Heidegger and Poetry in the Digital Age** New Aesthetics and Technologies* by Rachel Coventry

Owen Barfield's Poetic Philosophy

Meaning and Imagination

Jeffrey Hipolito

BLOOMSBURY ACADEMIC
LONDON • NEW YORK • OXFORD • NEW DELHI • SYDNEY

BLOOMSBURY ACADEMIC
Bloomsbury Publishing Plc, 50 Bedford Square, London, WC1B 3DP, UK
Bloomsbury Publishing Inc, 1359 Broadway, 12th Floor, New York, NY 10018, USA
Bloomsbury Publishing Ireland, 29 Earlsfort Terrace, Dublin 2, D02 AY28, Ireland

BLOOMSBURY, BLOOMSBURY ACADEMIC and the Diana logo
are trademarks of Bloomsbury Publishing Plc

First published in Great Britain 2024
This paperback edition published 2025

Copyright © Jeffrey Hipolito, 2024

Jeffrey Hipolito has asserted his right under the Copyright,
Designs and Patents Act, 1988, to be identified as Author of this work.

For legal purposes the Acknowledgments on p. xv constitute an extension
of this copyright page.

Series design: Ben Anslow
Cover image: *Yellow-Red-Blue* (1925), Wassily Kandinsky
(Contributor: Mariano Garcia / Alamy Stock Photo)

All rights reserved. No part of this publication may be: i) reproduced or transmitted
in any form, electronic or mechanical, including photocopying, recording or
by means of any information storage or retrieval system without prior permission in
writing from the publishers; or ii) used or reproduced in any way for the training,
development or operation of artificial intelligence (AI) technologies, including
generative AI technologies. The rights holders expressly reserve this publication from
the text and data mining exception as per Article 4(3) of the Digital Single
Market Directive (EU) 2019/790.

Bloomsbury Publishing Inc does not have any control over, or responsibility for,
any third-party websites referred to or in this book. All internet addresses given
in this book were correct at the time of going to press. The author and publisher
regret any inconvenience caused if addresses have changed or sites have
ceased to exist, but can accept no responsibility for any such changes.

A catalogue record for this book is available from the British Library.

ISBN: HB: 978-1-3504-2028-1
PB: 978-1-3504-2032-8
ePDF: 978-1-3504-2029-8
eBook: 978-1-3504-2030-4

Series: Bloomsbury Studies in Philosophy and Poetry

Typeset by Deanta Global Publishing Services, Chennai, India

For product safety related questions contact productsafety@bloomsbury.com.

To find out more about our authors and books visit www.bloomsbury.com
and sign up for our newsletters.

In Memory of Jane Hipolito, 1942–2019

Contents

Foreword	x
Acknowledgments	xv
List of Abbreviations	xvi
Introduction	1
1 On the Dolphin's Back: Poetics	7
2 The Texture of Thought: The Evolution of Consciousness	51
3 The Antecedent Unity: Metaphysics	75
4 The Door to Eternity: Anthroposophy	107
5 A Coinherence of Selves: Ethics and Politics	137
6 Mysterious Potency: The Burgeon Trilogy	163
Appendix	215
Notes	219
Bibliography	231
Index	241

Foreword

Before Jeffrey Hipolito and I first met in person we engaged over a period of four years in a mutually enlivening correspondence on the subject of philosophical poetics. When Hipolito initiated this exchange he shared that his "current project is a book on Owen Barfield as a thinker and creative writer, trying to do equal justice to both." For reasons of length, this manuscript has since been divided into two complementary books. The present one is weighted toward Barfield as a thinker and the other toward his creative writings, but in keeping with the ultimate indivisibility of Barfield the poet from Barfield the philosopher, both books integrate Barfield's poetics and thought. Along with his initial email Hipolito attached a draft of the first chapter of *Owen Barfield's Poetic Philosophy*. On reading this I was immediately convinced that Hipolito was the leading contemporary scholar of Barfield. As my first impression still rings true, I will quote part of my reply from 2018:

> I have greatly enjoyed reading your truly excellent chapter on Barfield's poetics. The chapter is lucid, illuminating, and finely written. It also gave me a more detailed knowledge of the debates Barfield was engaged in prior to completing *Poetic Diction* and *History in English Words*. The way in which you contextualise Barfield within European/American Modernism is significant not only for our understanding of Barfield but also for a reevaluation of the subsequent history of English poetry and criticism, whose effective history continues to shape the present. In my estimation, (as much as I admire Eliot's poetry, especially the *Four Quartets*) Barfield emerges (in your account) as offering a more comprehensive account of the problems of modernity (and their solutions) . . . as well as a vindication of Romanticism.

While, as Hipolito details in his book, Eliot was a great admirer and a publisher of Barfield's writings, there are fundamental disagreements (especially in the 1920s) between their positions on poetic tradition, Romanticism, and Modernism. Despite Barfield's international standing as an important and original poet-philosopher, his influence on twentieth-century and twenty-first-century poetics and poetry is minor compared to Eliot's. My initial response to Hipolito registers a sense that the cultural history of the twentieth century and our present moment would be significantly different and, importantly, better, had the reception of Barfield been comparable in magnitude to that of Eliot. This claim is likely to seem an exaggeration. How can it be justified?

In the first chapter of *Owen Barfield's Poetic Philosophy* Hipolito frames Barfield's position as the higher third between the historical determinism and traditionalism of Eliot, on the one side, and the ahistorical, mystical sensualism of Lawrence, on the other. For the Eliot of "The Waste Land" Western culture is inevitably in decline--"a heap of broken images"--and there is little that the individual can do to resist this disintegration. Lawrence, in contrast, recommends as the remedy for the alienation of the modern individual the immediacy of sensuous experience as a form of communion with the cosmos. For Barfield, Lawrence's position holds too little reflection and Eliot subsumes the individual under a kind of historical fatalism. Lawrence forgets the meaning of history, and Eliot sees only the meaning (or loss of meaning) of history.

As Hipolito clearly illustrates, Barfield's vehement rejection of the anti-romanticism of Eliot and Pound had largely to do with his deep conviction that the true remedy for our historical predicament was discovered by the Romantics, namely the power of the individualized poetic imagination, which, among the British Romantics, was most profoundly theorized by Coleridge. Imagination, if we learn to exercise it in the appropriate way, is nothing less than an agent of spiritual renewal and cultural evolution.

The spark of a future culture and civilization cannot be found anywhere "outside" ourselves; while we must learn from history, appealing to tradition or a past culture cannot suffice to show the way forward. The spark of the Phoenix is buried within the individual spirit, waiting for us to breathe it into life, so it can fuse in a new gestalt that which has come asunder: self and world, spirit and nature, the individual and the collective. We must look into the speculative mirror and realize that the ruins of modernity--alienation, division, destruction--are our own reflection and that cultural evolution is dependent on whether and how we activate ourselves. Forms of historical determinism that subsume the individual under supra-individual forces are thus part of the very problem of nihilism. They inhibit us from seeking the buried ember.

According to Barfield, however, things have not always been so and this is part of the reason why shapes of consciousness that were realized by past cultures cannot provide a sufficient model for the future. At the same time Barfield rejects the naivety of Lawrence's ahistoricism. In order to develop an adequate conception of the past and its relation to the present--and vice versa-- we need to grasp what Barfield calls the "evolution of consciousness." While this expression might at first be mistaken as referring exclusively to the way in which human consciousness has evolved, it designates the whole evolution of nature and the human mind and their shifting relation to one another. I will not repeat here Barfield's compelling arguments--and Hipolito's illuminating reconstructions--rather, as a brief indication I will only say that in contrast to the naturalist view that the human mind emerged as an epiphenomenon out of a mindless nature, Barfield illustrates that we must assume an original unity of "mindnature" or "spiritnature" (my terms) from which consciousness did not miraculously emerge but rather from which "mind" and "nature" gradually divided from one another, in a way that bears a resemblance to the chemical division of water into hydrogen and oxygen, though, by contrast, it entails the contradistinction of an "exterior" (nature) and an "interior" (mind) that remain co-constitutive of one another.

The process of division and respective consolidation of nature and mind slowly occurred over immense periods long before any external historical records. Nevertheless, historical documents--when perceived in the correct light--present evidence of this process, of which they are moments. In ancient Greek philosophy one cannot find any doctrine that faintly resembles Cartesian dualism. Why is this the case? Because the "natural attitude" of the ancient Greeks involved an experience of nature and mind, which did not yet entail the great rift between them that first emerged in the early modern period. Moreover, if we look back to the period prior to philosophy (in Greek as well as in other cultures) we find mythology in its place. For Barfield, mythology is nothing other than a form of thinking or dreaming, which can at the same time be described as nature thinking in us. Or, more specifically, as the thinking of "the gods"--the creative and destructive forces that underlie nature and human culture. In earlier forms of human society, one similarly finds nothing comparable to the modern divide between the individual and the collective.

The upshot of this evolution of consciousness for Barfield is the emergence of individual self-consciousness and the possibility of freedom. However, its negative consequences include the expulsion of all "soul-like" qualities from nature--the vision of nature as an inanimate, lifeless mechanism that has become predominant in modernity--and the experience of alienation--alienation of the individual from the cosmos and alienation of individuals from one another. To understand ourselves today, we must grasp how the evolution of consciousness has led to our current world outlook. At the same time, the way forward cannot involve a return to a past stage of consciousness, a reabsorption of the individual into "the one."

The structure, conditions, and requirements of modern consciousness are different from those of the past. While figures such as Eliot and Heidegger also sought a renewal--or another beginning--for contemporary culture, both Eliot and Heidegger retain an element of nostalgia (in Heidegger, a nostalgia for the cosmos of pre-Socratic Greece) that is in part reactionary. A pertinent aspect of Barfield's story is that in the process of the introversion of mind from nature, the creative principle (of nature and mind) became entwined with human individuality. This creative, evolutionary principle evinces itself, for example, in the way in which an individual poet in the process of forging a metaphor christens a new meaning in language and thus enlivens and transforms the language. In short, in the active, individualized imagination we find the vital power of spiritual evolution and cultural renewal.

The earlier text is only a schematic outline of what Hipolito brilliantly realizes on a large canvas in the present book. Here I only want to add a few words about what Barfield at times describes as "systematic imagination." With this expression, Barfield has a couple of related things in mind. First, it implies that beyond the momentary creative insights of the poet at work on language or the pioneering scientist intuiting a new hypothesis, the imagination can be applied in a systematic manner as an organ of focused research. In the realm of natural science, Goethe's studies of optics and comparative morphology (in the domains of botany and anatomy) are models for Barfield. Goethe's "higher empiricism" that employs "exact sensorial imagination" and leads to a form of spiritual identity between the knower and the known, the mind and natural phenomena, realizes this potential of the imagination for systematic application. Barfield holds the conviction that there is no better example of how the poetic mind can enable a profound knowledge of nature than the empirical studies of the great German poet.

The second crucial example for Barfield of the capacity of the imagination to be developed systematically is the spiritual research of the Goethe scholar, philosopher, and founder of Anthroposophy, Rudolf Steiner. In his early career Steiner was an editor of Goethe's natural-scientific writings and authored a number of philosophical works that articulated a Goethean theory of knowledge, the evolutionary theory of Ernst Haeckel, an account of Nietzsche's philosophy, and his own *Philosophy of Freedom*. Building on Goethe's scientific approach to nature, Steiner later (in his theosophical and anthroposophical works) demonstrated how the imagination could be employed in a systematic fashion in the study of psychological, mental, and spiritual phenomena (as well as to natural phenomena in the manner of Goethe). Beyond what he names

Imagination, Steiner outlines two further stages of cognitive development that transcend the subject-object dualism of modern intellectual consciousness; these he calls Inspiration and Intuition, which can be roughly described as ever deeper forms of union between the knower and the known, thinking and being. For these reasons, Barfield saw in Steiner the fulfilment of the promises for the imagination that he found in British and German Romantic writers, including Shelley, Coleridge, Wordsworth, Blake, and Novalis.

It was not only the place of cognitive imagination as the starting point for healing the ills of modernity that drew Barfield to his appreciation of Steiner's poetic philosophy, it was also the fortuity of the emergence of his own theory of the evolution of consciousness--on the basis of the study of diachronic semantics--and his discovery of Steiner's vastly elaborate version of the same (which has antecedents in the philosophies of history in German Idealism and Romanticism, as well as in the late Enlightenment, including those of Lessing, Herder, Schiller, Hölderlin, Novalis, Schelling, and Hegel).

The reception of Steiner within academia and in public intellectual discourse has been marked by a scant familiarity with his immense oeuvre--the *Gesamtausgabe* currently numbers more than 400 volumes--and the ways in which it advances the traditions of German Idealism and European Romanticism (including their esoteric undercurrents, such as Böhmean theosophy). Unfortunately, this has also been a limitation of much Barfield scholarship. One of the many merits of Hipolito's groundbreaking book is the illuminating and impartial manner in which it articulates the connections between Barfield and Steiner.

There is still time for the twenty-first century to learn from Barfield what the twentieth century failed to learn. In recent years there has also been a noticeable growth in the reception of Barfield. It is thus an ideal moment for the publication of Hipolito's book, which sets a new standard for Barfield scholarship and will be a crucial resource for future research.

With the interpenetration of agile imagination, philosophical insight, and critical discernment required to comprehend Barfield's corpus, Jeffrey Hipolito elucidates the indispensability of Barfield's poetic philosophy. This landmark in Barfield scholarship counters Heidegger's resignation that "only a god can save us," as each individual holds the key in the poetic imagination.

—Luke Fischer, July 2023, Sydney

Acknowledgments

I have been able to write this book only because I have been acquiring the debts that made it possible across my lifetime. Foremost is my debt to Owen Barfield himself, who was selfless and patient in playing games with me when I was a small boy during a very memorable vacation together and in answering my stammered undergraduate questions as we played a game of correspondence chess in the last years of his life. I must also thank Barfield's grandson, also named Owen Barfield, for his kindness, encouragement, and permission to quote freely from his grandfather's published and unpublished writings. Thanks also to *Journal of Inklings Studies, VII* and *The Coleridge Bulletin* for permission to reprint material that appears in the first and second chapters of this book. Tom Kranidas taught me a great deal about Barfield the man during a memorable flight together; his kindness and good humor are a continued inspiration. Graham Davidson and Gareth Polmeer also offered encouragement that buoyed me when my energy flagged. My father, Terry Hipolito, offered helpful suggestions. Hazard Adams suggested thirty years ago that I write this book. I was unready to do so then, but his prompt was a seed that sprouted in its own time. Wendie Hipolito offered indispensable help in the early stages of this project. I have benefited from conversation, feedback, and encouragement from many people. None compares, though, to the generosity, acumen, and unfailing goodwill of Luke Fischer—without his help I could not have brought this book to completion. Fred Dennehy offered helpful feedback on Chapter 6. Anouk Tompot made countless sacrifices and offered daily love and support; I wrote the words, but this book is truly a joint production. Michael Hipolito showed great patience and understanding when I secreted myself away, though he would rather have read one more book together. I dedicate this book to the memory of my mother, Jane Hipolito; her love and help feel as energetic now as ever.

Abbreviations

ABS	*A Barfield Sampler*
HEW	*History in English Words*
HGH	*History, Guilt and Habit*
PD	*Poetic Diction*
RCA	*Romanticism Comes of Age*
RM	*The Rediscovery of Meaning*
SA	*Saving the Appearances*
SM	*Speaker's Meaning*
TEDP	*This Ever Diverse Pair*
UV	*Unancestral Voice*
WA	*Worlds Apart*
WCT	*What Coleridge Thought*

Introduction

This is the first book to offer an overview that is at once comprehensive and introductory to the philosophical thought of Owen Barfield, who was to England what Gaston Bachelard was to France—a genre-defying polymath and culture critic with equal talent for mastering diverse fields and synthesizing them into larger unities. If anything, however, Barfield exceeds Bachelard (or Walter Benjamin or Martin Heidegger) because he was as much a poet, dramatist, and novelist as he was an intellectual force. Though there have been notable and excellent studies of different aspects of Barfield's thought, none have yet attempted to demonstrate its unity, and understandably so. Simply to keep up with Barfield's thinking and reading is a trial—A. D. Nuttall is certainly correct that Barfield was a "pathologically well-read" author (Diener 13) whose corpus has "a progressive, evolving coherence" (Diener 14) and that "the sheer quality and complexity of Barfield's ideas has not received the attention it deserves" (Diener 13). One goal of this book is to bring out the quality and complexity without losing sight of its evolving coherence and while giving some small sense of Barfield's reading. Barfield's career as a writer extended to more than seventy years, during which he made meaningful and unique contributions in a variety of fields, including poetics, philology, semiotics, epistemology, historiography, philosophy of science, metaphysics, ethics, theology, and social theory. The bibliography of his published works alone extends to over fifty pages, and there is a substantial body of work that remains unpublished. His work includes books and essays in all the above fields and more as well as highly accomplished lyric and epic poems, short stories, several plays, two novellas, a novel, and several works of genre-defying fiction that constitute a genre-defying trilogy. Barfield, in other words, was both a prophet and a practitioner of the imagination.

This book attempts to do justice to the complexity of Barfield's work by bringing into view at least a part of its depth and unified richness. Northrop Frye, who would later read Barfield's *What Coleridge Thought* with admiration,[1] began his review of Hugh Kenner's *The Poetry of Ezra Pound* by saying that "Ezra Pound is not exactly unread or even neglected, but he is, so to speak, unidentified" (Frye 29, 99). Barfield, too, though hardly unread, remains unidentified, and like

Kenner I hope to highlight the "intelligible order" in the rich variety of Barfield's work in order "to help as many people as possible to read [it] for themselves" (Kenner 13). To do so is to discover works and ideas that have retained their potency and relevance.

The wide range, complexity, and relative unavailability of Barfield's work is the main reason it is not better known today, but he has had "a fit audience, though few" at all times. At the beginning of his career, to choose one notable example, he quickly attracted the attention of T. S. Eliot, who published his short story "Dope" in 1923 in the *Criterion* and encouraged him to submit more work. Eliot was then instrumental in the publication of *Poetic Diction* by Faber & Gwyer in 1928, kept Barfield before the public in his role as director at Faber & Faber, and in 1962 defended Barfield's profitless presence in their catalogue by saying, "of course he is difficult to sell but he will make his mark in the long run. I myself have a high regard for his work" (Eliot 2009 5, 101n). Barfield was "of course . . . difficult to sell" for the same reason he deserves a wider reception today—he demands serious concentration from his readers, most of whom were unable to offer it while he was alive. And yet, that concentration pays dividends, as much now as then. During his lifetime Barfield attracted the sympathetic and interested attention of an eclectic range of intellectuals beyond Eliot and Nuttall, including, in no particular order, J. R. R. Tolkien, Gabriel Marcel, W. H. Auden, Walter de la Mare, Joseph Campbell, Philip Wheelright, Hazard Adams, Harold Bloom, C. S. Lewis, Theodore Roszak, Norman O. Brown, John Lukacs, Henri Corbin, Howard Nemerov, Robert Funk, Richard Wilbur, Kathleen Raine, Northrop Frye, Hayden White, and David Bohm. To ask what unifies this group is to begin to grapple with the diversity of Barfield's thought. Barfield once said in conversation that he would be understood seventy years after his death. This book is a companion volume to a study of Barfield as a poet, novelist, and playwright. My hope is that together they will take a small step toward remedying his relative neglect and shortening the seventy years of misunderstanding envisaged by Barfield.

Barfield is perhaps most well known at present as the "fourth Inkling," alongside C. S. Lewis, J. R. R. Tolkien, and Charles Williams. It is true, as has been recently claimed, that "the literary status of both Tolkien and Lewis and, to a lesser extent, Williams, Barfield, and the other Inklings, is undergoing rapid ascent as academic courses and mature literary criticism focused upon their work blossom around the world" (Zaleski & Zaleski 9). I have given Barfield's role in the Inklings relatively little attention, in the hopes that by gaining a proper understanding of the broad reach of his thought and reading, the question can be revisited. Instead, I focus on the writers and thinkers whom Barfield engages most energetically in his writing—contemporaries like T. S. Eliot, D. H. Lawrence, Isaiah Berlin, Martin Heidegger, and Jean Paul Sartre, with whom he tended to disagree; those like R. G. Collingwood, Ernst Cassirer, Gabriel Marcel, and Erich Auerbach whom he considered his "friends" in the broad sense; and Romantic figures like J. W. Goethe, Novalis, Percy Shelley, William Blake, and Samuel Taylor Coleridge who resonate through the whole of his work. Though this book is not about Barfield's influence on others, I hope to spur readers to consider why writers as different as W. H. Auden, Saul Bellow, and Howard Nemerov were deeply impressed and affected by his thought and why Eliot wrote to Barfield in 1960 that he not only had a "very high opinion" of *Saving the Appearances* but also that it made him "proud to be a director of the firm which publishes [it]."

The story of Barfield as a literary artist belongs to a different book but is worth being aware of. Relatively few of Barfield's readers know that in addition to his strictly intellectual work, he was a creative writer. His first published work, in 1917, was a poem, and his last one, in 1993, was a selection of his poetry and short fiction. In the many decades between them, Barfield wrote three very different long poems: *The Tower*, *The Unicorn*, and *Riders on Pegasus*. Eliot, again acting as gatekeeper, rejected two of them for publication, though not for lack of merit; Barfield himself rejected Eliot's suggestion that he pursue having Virginia Woolf's Hogarth Press publish *The Tower*, and did not vigorously pursue publication of *The Unicorn* or *Riders on Pegasus*, perhaps because they were too far out of step with their time. All three poems were finally published for the first time in 2020, along with two of Barfield's three plays. Barfield's only novel, *English People*, which he completed in 1929, still languishes among the Barfield papers at the Bodleian Library. None of these works, including *Orpheus*, the Burgeon trilogy, or the late novellas, have been discussed at any length elsewhere. Only the trilogy will be considered in this study. The picture that emerges is that Barfield was a sophisticated artist, a nuanced reader of his contemporaries into his eighties who developed a distinct form of Romantic Modernism. His philosophy may also be considered a form of Romantic Modernism. It is Romantic in its commitment to the view that poetic thinking is interwoven with, and ultimately the fulfilment of, discursive reason. It is Modernist, though, in its full engagement with phenomenology, existentialism, logical positivism, behaviorism, and a host of other modern movements.

Barfield unfolded the different dimensions of his poetic philosophy mostly simultaneously, but the process was preceded by his development of a sophisticated and historically important poetics. The first chapter of this study explores the largely pre-philosophical formulation and articulation of his poetics. He showed remarkable self-confidence, sharpness, and originality as he defended a unique form of Romantic Modernism. It was the fruit of his deep immersion in the literary and critical polemics of 1920s London, as he sought to supplement and correct the various arguments of Eliot, Lawrence, Graves, Murry, Smith, and others. This chapter reads his early forays into phenomenology and hermeneutics as preparations for *Poetic Diction* and *History in English Words*, which focus on the relation of poetic diction to meaning. They belong to sharply contested debates among the Modernists and are prominent examples of the attempt, which Barfield shared with Richards, Graves, Murry, Eliot, and others, to establish a science of criticism. They also present in nascent form what he would later defend as his historiography and metaphysics, without losing sight of its origin in his poetics. The second chapter focuses on the theory of the evolution of consciousness, which Barfield considered at times to be the master theme of his work. This chapter places Barfield's argument in the context of the contemporaneous views of C. S. Lewis, A. O. Lovejoy, Isaiah Berlin, and R. G. Collingwood. It argues for the originality and depth of Barfield's historiography, its roots in his poetics, and its metaphysical implications. The next chapter, on metaphysics, unpacks the metaphysical assumptions and implications of Barfield's theory, in conversation with some of the philosophers most congenial to him, including S. T. Coleridge, Rudolf Steiner, and Ernst Cassirer. It shows that for Barfield a complete metaphysical deduction of the Absolute or the imagination was impossible, but that at the far end of philosophical thinking one faces the need to use the imagination to create a poetic cosmology. Chapter 4 follows the implications of Barfield's leap into poetic cosmology. In particular, it explores Barfield's lifelong immersion in and elaboration of Steiner's philosophical and poetic system of "spiritual science" as the most compelling poetic cosmology of our time. Chapter 5 extends to the practical upshot of the preceding chapters for ethics and politics, in dialogue with Isaiah Berlin, Immanuel Kant, David Hume, and others. It shows that here too, Barfield developed an original moral and political philosophy that parallels Heidegger in uncanny ways even as it parts from him, responds to alternatives like Sartre and Berlin, and incorporates diverse thinkers like the Russian philosopher Vladimir Solovyov. The final chapter, on the Burgeon trilogy, is the only one that considers Barfield's work as a creative writer. It affords a glimpse of the integral and irreducible role of the poetic in the dramatization and articulation of his poetic philosophy. It includes an articulation of his metaphysics and poetic cosmology, within the context of their dramatic unfolding, so that the reader does not merely think about them but is led into a direct imaginative experience of them. A full exploration of Barfield's creative work as poet, dramatist, and novelist belongs to a different study, but no consideration of his philosophy can be complete without some consideration of it.

I have written this book in the conviction that Barfield was not only one of the most incisive, vital, and brilliant thinkers of the twentieth century but also an unjustly neglected literary artist of beauty and depth. He did not find his true standing during his lifetime, but any cultural history of the twentieth century is incomplete without an account of him. The time has come for Barfield to make his mark. Perhaps one benefit of his potent thought being overlooked during his era is that during ours it may burst more forcefully into life in the minds of his readers.

1

On the Dolphin's Back

Poetics

Owen Barfield began his career as a poet, novelist, and combatant in the battles among the Modernists over the nature and significance of poetry. These were waged in the pages of *The New Statesman*, *The Criterion*, and other magazines, as he developed the theory of metaphor that is the seed of his later thinking about historiography, metaphysics, and ethics, and that informs his later conviction that in the end philosophy must give way to cosmology. According to Ronald Schuchard, *Poetic Diction* was quietly championed and shepherded into print at Faber & Gwyer by T. S. Eliot, who wrote the blurb as well, though much of Barfield's argument is an implicit rebuke of Eliot's poetics.[1] *Poetic Diction* has been cited approvingly by Max Black, Paul Ricoeur, and other prominent thinkers about metaphor. Barfield looms large in Aileen Ward's *The Unfurling of Entity*, an important history of the theory of metaphor up to 1950, and Black reprinted Barfield's essay "Poetic Diction and Legal Fiction" (1947) in his popular collection *The Importance of Language* (1962). My focus in this chapter is on the theory of meaning, which Barfield developed during the 1920s, culminating in *History in English Words* (1926) and *Poetic Diction* (1928), and on the way that those books resolve fundamental challenges of anti-historicism and skepticism that his own early articles pose to him. By the time he wrote *History in English Words* and *Poetic Diction*, Barfield had sorted out not only his theory of poetry and its relation to his theory of the evolution of consciousness, but also his orientation to his Romantic and Victorian inheritance, to such older contemporaries as Sir Walter Raleigh, W. B. Yeats, and Logan Pearsall Smith, and to his Modernist peers, who include not only the Bloomsbury set[2] but also I. A. Richards, Robert Graves, T. S. Eliot, and many others.[3] To paraphrase a comment Eliot once made about F. H. Bradley, the unity of Barfield's thought is not the unity attained by a man who never changes his mind. As Barfield began to explore the relation between poetry and consciousness, he saw that it was inseparable from a study of the evolution of consciousness that runs, like Alph the sacred river, beneath the history of language; and, that the Romantic legacy from which he drew as he formed his ideas about poetry, consciousness, and language had crucial resources to offer at a time of massive social and cultural dislocation. These three themes are intertwined vines, each growing into and out of each other, that climb the lattice of Barfield's thought in such a way that they cannot be fully separated without killing all three, and that cannot be excised from his parallel growth as a poet and novelist.

1. Early Critical Writings

Our beginning is in our end: Barfield recalls his earliest critical essay, "Form in Poetry" (1920), in one of the last forays in his seventy-five-year career as a writer, the afterword to a collection of his fiction and poetry, *A Barfield Sampler* (1993). Barfield notes that he was negatively inspired by Clive Bell's proposal of "significant form" as the only reliable indicator of aesthetic merit. "This led to a lot of nonsensical suggestions" when applied to poetry, Barfield says.[4] Representative among those proposals is that of another member of the Bloomsbury set, Roger Fry: "as poetry becomes more intense the content is entirely remade by the form and has no separate value at all" (Woolf 183). It will soon become clear why this is "nonsensical" for Barfield, but for now let us follow Barfield to the heart of his recollection:

> I thought I detected a fallacy behind all this, and the first prose piece I ever published was an article entitled "Form in Poetry" in the *New Statesman* in August 1920, wherein I pointed out that the "form" created by poetic language exists, not on the printed page, but in the consciousness of the reader or hearer. Of course the same thing might have happened later in any event, but this was in fact the occasion of my beginning to contemplate human consciousness as a field, a category, a thing to be thought about and studied in its own right. From there the step was a relatively short one to the evolution of consciousness, which has always been my major theme. (*ABS* 173)

For many readers, the most striking feature of this statement must be Barfield's claim of the "relatively short" step to "the evolution of consciousness" from a first musing on the nature of poetic form. I suspect that for many readers today, even having been directed to it by Barfield, the step is neither obvious nor compelling. Some might also pause on the contention that poetic form is a property of consciousness, not of "the printed page." We can see in this recollection the three themes of Barfield's early years: that Barfield developed his ideas as a kind of contentious conversation with his contemporaries about the cultural significance of aesthetic experience, that this conversation centered from the start on the relation of language to consciousness, and that from the beginning this was inseparable from an appreciation of the history of language as revelatory of an evolution of consciousness.

"Form in Poetry" is also a riposte to the ascendant view that the Romantic impulse had had its day. An anonymous March 1920 review in the *Times Literary Supplement* of Eliot's *Ara Vos Prec* is typical:

> The death of Swinburne marked the end of an age in English poetry, the age which began with Blake. It was impossible for any poet after Swinburne to continue the romantic tradition: he carried his own kind of versification and the romantic attitude as far as they could be carried, and both died with him. Now our poets have to make another beginning, to find a method of expression suited to their different attitude; and of this fact they are almost over-conscious. (Brooker 2004, 26–7)

Barfield's entire career takes up the provocation of this review by staking both his creative and his critical writings on the continued relevance of Romantic thought and artistic practice, as represented primarily by Blake, Coleridge, Wordsworth, Shelley, and Keats among English poets, and by Goethe and Novalis among German authors. For Barfield, embracing the Romantic tradition involves following Pound's injunction—itself a free translation of a Chinese precept—to "make it new" (Pound 1934).

"Some Elements of Decadence," another early article in the *New Statesman*, sets the tone. Barfield rejects "gentle modern criticism" as a symptom of "decadence," comparing it unfavorably with the "at least violently sincere" criticism that was typical of the Romantic age. Barfield concludes from the mere existence of Shelley's *Adonais*, Byron's *Vision of Judgment* and *Don Juan*, and other poems responsive to contentious criticism, that "the narrow criticism of the age sprang in some way from the same serious, compact soil as its greatest literature. It was symptomatic" (Barfield 1921e, 244–5). Barfield's article proceeds in similarly vigorous fashion to take on well-established writers like John Masefield, who would be Poet Laureate by the decade's end and yet according to Barfield "sets out ... in a little boat in search of Beauty, [but] he has lost whatever hope he may have once had of finding her" (Barfield 1921e, 244). Even Yeats faces oblique criticism. His mystical exploration *Per Amica Silentia Lunae* (1918), which anticipates the first version of *A Vision* (1925), is the target of Barfield's satirical (and, it must be said, unfair) suggestion that:

> he may lay out himself, and his remembered selves and his anti-self on paper with a view to disinterested inspection, comparing himself with his fellows, and their work with his, with all the assurance of approbation. He may call in the aid of doctors and scientists . . . in a dream world of art for art's sake. (Barfield 1921e, 244)

But it is not only acclaimed older writers whom he targets. He holds up for polemical ridicule Eliot, Pound, and other alleged connoisseurs of chaos:

> you will hear him asking you earnestly if you think "all the established verse-forms are exhausted," or evolving elaborately mechanical theories on the correct shape of the novel. Then, perhaps, he will set to work himself, with his carefully fretted fragments, only to discover when it is too late that jig-saw puzzles are made of wood. (Barfield 1921e, 244)

In the previous year, Pound had infamously described Western civilization as an "old bitch gone in the teeth" (Pound 1952, 200) and Eliot, beyond following Pound in composing "carefully fretted fragments," had a few years earlier in his infamous essay on *vers libre* (also originally published in *The New Statesman*) dismissed blank verse as "the inevitable iambic pentameter" before adding with typically elegant malaise: "As for the sonnet I am not so sure" (Eliot 2021 1, 516). Barfield also seems to single out Eliot for his energetic embrace of spiritual exhaustion, "that cowardice of a premature spiritual old age, which reveals itself in the eagerness to detach literature from life, form from matter" (Barfield 1921e, 245). Indeed, Eliot's persona Gerontion (1920), "an old man in a dry month," is itself a symptom "of premature maturity and hollow wisdom; for it was not spiritually old enough for . . . those things" (Barfield 1921e, 245).

Eliot earned Barfield's lifelong and sometimes unfair invective because he was foremost among those who led the charge against Romanticism.[5] Eliot offered a succinct single statement in 1923: "With Mr. Murry's formulation of Classicism and Romanticism I cannot agree; the difference seems to me rather the difference between the complete and the fragmentary, the adult and the immature, the orderly and the chaotic" (Eliot 2021 2, 460). Or, as Eliot put it a few years earlier: "the generation after 1830 preferred to form itself upon decadence, though a decadence of genius: Wordsworth; and upon an immaturity of genius: Keats and Shelley; and the development of English literature was retarded" (Eliot 2021 2, 79). These charges were part of a running dispute between Eliot and J. Middleton Murry in the pages of *The Criterion* and *The Adelphi* about the relative merits of the Classic and the Romantic.[6] Robert Graves weighed in with his own definitions:

> Classical is characteristic and Romantic is Metamorphic; that is, though they are both expressions of a mental conflict, in Classical poetry this conflict is expressed within the confines of waking probability and logic, in terms of the typical interaction of typical minds; in Romantic poetry the conflict is expressed in the illogical but vivid method of dream-changings. (Graves 1922, 73–4)[7]

Graves steps away from Eliot's formal equation of the Classical with the complete, the adult, and the orderly and of the Romantic with the fragmentary, the immature, and the chaotic; instead, he sees them as representative of dynamic and productively polarized states of mind. As we shall soon see, by the time Barfield came to write *Poetic Diction*, he had recast the Classical/Romantic dichotomy along the lines Graves suggests, as one between discursive reason and the "irrational" and "dream-changing" metamorphosis of the very concepts out of which one shapes reasonable judgments. Barfield will rename the Classical and the Romantic as the rational principle and the poetic principle, respectively, will argue that the two together are necessary to attain any new knowledge, and will imply that the whole debate recapitulates one that took place within Romanticism itself in the complex interactions of "the prolific and the devouring" in Blake's prophetic books, Coleridge's "two forces" and distinctions of "fancy" from "imagination" and "reason" from "understanding," and Shelley's "two classes of mental action."

And yet, it would be a distortion to say that Barfield's tone and intent in this early essay is simply polemical; his combative style is in service to a larger cultural diagnosis. He sees beneath all this restless experimentation a quest for beauty that is "as unconscious as it is inevitable" (Barfield 1921e, 244)—one thinks again of Pound's Mauberley, who "strove . . . to maintain 'the sublime' / In the old sense" (Pound 1952, 197). Barfield finds elements of "the common intellectual attitude of to-day" as it tries again and yet again to find the roots of beauty:

> Sceptical with Hume and Voltaire, impersonal with Mr. Bernard Shaw, or dilettante with the Platonists and George Santayana. Thomas Hardy has apparently monopolised the only personal dogma which a powerful intellect can hold, without needing to be ever up in arms to defend it with fierce, brilliant paradoxes and overwrought mysticisms. The Western world is like Pope's *Essay on Man*: it knows much, but it has not felt what it knows. (Barfield 1921e, 245)

The allusions that open and close this passage make Barfield's point clear: the contemporary scene dominated by Wells, Shaw, Hardy, Yeats, and the rest is a decaying enlightenment, prevented from apprehending the beauty for which it longs due to "premature maturity" and "an exaggerated fear of looking foolish" (Barfield 1921e, 245). This is true not just of Shaw[8] and Hardy,[9] for whom Barfield had little use, or of Yeats the brilliantly paradoxical, overwrought mystagogue, of whom he could have made better use, but also of Pater (then the most famous dilettante Platonist) and Santayana, of whom he was otherwise an admirer.[10]

What is missing from the contemporary scene, then, beneath a commonly understood sense of cultural and spiritual catastrophe, is a proper engagement with Romanticism; in fact, the spilt religion of the immature, sentimental Romantics was blamed implicitly and explicitly for the ruins everyone recognized but none could see their way clear of. Those who should know better, like Eliot (or Matthew Arnold before him), "will answer foolish critics who are afraid of Shelley's ethics and Shelley's politics with the still more foolish reply that Shelley's ethics and politics do not matter" (Barfield 1921e, 245). Barfield's other early essays, culminating in *Poetic Diction* and *History in English Words*, are forays into this contested cultural sphere that Richard Sheppard describes well as a crisis of language:

> To use Pound's metaphor, many modern poets have felt that the god is locked inside the stone. For the essential powers of language and the person . . . are encrusted by the excessive cultivation of the will and the conscious powers of the mind which technological society requires. Cut off from the "primal source," modern poetry is permeated by a sense of homelessness. (Sheppard 327)

Barfield was sharply aware of this predicament. The reconnection of people with themselves, each other, and the world around them—the survival of civilization itself—seemed at stake, and the debates over the Classical and the Romantic, the true nature of poetry, and the relation of our "sense of homelessness" to our alienation from language were the core of the crisis.

What was needed, in addition to a criticism that faced the challenge of its time by integrating the poetic, the philosophical, and the ethical, was a proper science of criticism to replace the soft appreciations that were still common, though it took Barfield some time to find his way to his fully mature positions. A few months before Eliot's unflattering comparison of the Classical and Romantic appeared, Barfield called for "a new kind of criticism" (Barfield 1923c, 525). This in itself was not unusual—J. Middleton Murry was able to begin *Aspects of Literature* (1920) with the reflection that "it is curious and interesting to find our younger men of letters actively concerned with the present condition of literary criticism. This is a novel preoccupation for them and one which is, we believe, symptomatic of a general hesitancy and expectation" (Murry 1). Barfield, one of the younger critics to whom Murry refers with benign condescension, echoed the younger intellectuals for whom Murry's writings were "a frenzy of insincere sincerity" (Collis, quoted in Goldie 10). At the time, Barfield was put off by what he took to be Murry's "irritating unction," though a few years later he noted Murry's "valiant attempt" to defend Romanticism "in his *Adelphi*" (*RCA* 6).

In any event, the title of Barfield's ambitious review essay, "Milton and Metaphysics," helps to crystallize the special urgency of this need, as a response to the equally urgent need for a new picture of literary history expressed in Eliot's own ambitious and notorious (and now much-anthologized) review essay "The Metaphysical Poets." Eliot there argues for the existence of a "dissociation of sensibility" as characteristic of the conventional modern mind. Frank Kermode points out that Eliot was not alone in this—near the same time, for example, Yeats and Hulme located during the Renaissance the loss of "some golden age when the prevalent mode of knowing was not positivistic and anti-imaginative" (Kermode 143), and in *Fantasia of the Unconscious* (1923) D. H. Lawrence put forward the imaginative picture of the fully integrated sensibility on ancient Atlantis, joining Ezra Pound, Richard Aldington, R. G. Collingwood, Aldous Huxley, and Virginia Woolf in proposing alternative theories of a pristine unity of consciousness that somehow, sometime, fell apart.[11] As we will see in later chapters, for Barfield this was symptomatic of a universal human longing to restore an archetypal Golden Age that reflects the perceived loss of "the antecedent unity underlying apparent or actual fragmentation" (*RM* 4).

Once again, Eliot's conjecture became paradigmatic: "the ordinary man's experience is chaotic, irregular, fragmentary" because he "falls in love, or reads Spinoza, and these two experiences have nothing to do with each other, or with the noise of the typewriter or the smell of cooking; in the mind of the poet these experiences are always forming new wholes." This is an indication of "something which happened to the mind of England between the time of Donne . . . and the time of Tennyson and Browning":

> The poets of the seventeenth century, the successors of the dramatists of the sixteenth, possessed a mechanism of sensibility which could devour any kind of experience. They are simple, artificial, difficult, or fantastic, as their predecessors were; no less nor more than Dante, Guido Cavalcanti, Guinicelli, or Cino. In the seventeenth century a dissociation of sensibility set in, from which we have

never recovered; and this dissociation, as is natural, was aggravated by the influence of the two most powerful poets of the century, Milton and Dryden. (Eliot 2021 2, 380)

Eliot lays at the feet of Milton and Dryden the exacerbation of chaotic fragmentation and romantic sentimentality in the modern sensibility; indeed, the "second effect" that Milton and Dryden had on the age was to help instigate the revolt "against the ratiocinative" because they "felt by fits, unbalanced." Nor did the romantics offer much help: in Shelley and Keats there are only "in one or two passages . . . traces of a struggle toward unification of sensibility" (Eliot 2021 2, 381).[12]

Barfield's essay is an extended, subtle critique of Eliot's argument, though as Ward showed, the views of Barfield and Eliot also share affinities (Ward 292). In place of Eliot's loose formulation that "something happened to the mind of England," Barfield proposes that "human consciousness evolves" (Barfield 1923c, 524) in ways that can be studied in precise detail; and, rather than place at the feet of Milton the inward alienation of thoughts from feelings and each other, and of people from their thoughts and feelings, Barfield uses the history of Milton criticism itself as a case study for "the history of our own minds" (Barfield 1923c, 524). He discovers therein the emergence of a dissociation: "the eighteenth century, which still 'accepted' his theology, had foresworn his curiosity and enthusiasm, and that is what makes Johnson's *Life* such a queer lopsided affair" (Barfield 1923c, 524). Today, the theology along with the enthusiasm have been shed. The dissociation that becomes evident as one explores the history of Milton criticism also reveals what Milton's work needs and has not found, "serious, philosophical criticism" (Barfield 1923c, 524):

> Criticism and metaphysics are alike in this, that they both require a complicated machinery in which to objectify themselves. . . . Indeed, this is true of every outward expression of human consciousness. You have only to sit down at this moment and attempt to put into words how you feel towards the world, and you will realise at once the awful unwieldiness of the machinery—or rather, the many machineries—which you are compelled to employ. Language itself is only a scrapheap of ancient mythologies and metaphysics, and if in your zeal for accuracy you allow your researches into the true "meaning" of any word to wax historical, you will find the word and its meaning, and with it the whole queer structure of our speech and consciousness, floating away into thin air. (Barfield 1923c, 524)

It is not difficult to see why, for Christopher Norris, Barfield is too close to the late Heidegger's anti-realism (Norris 120–7). Barfield seems to imply here, in an early example of the "linguistic turn" identified by Richard Rorty, that because metaphysics and inner experience are contingent on language, and language is "only a scrapheap of ancient mythologies and metaphysics,"[13] any starting point we choose in any critical endeavor must be capricious. Indeed, "you would very soon find it necessary to select one definite Machinery as the nodus round which your metaphysical imagination might harden" (Barfield 1923c, 525). This makes the critical enterprise itself an example of metaphysical conceit in the limited literary sense: Eliot's proposal to substitute Donne for Milton and to redefine literary history on that basis is like comparing lovers to fleas rather than roses. The capricious sentimentality Eliot complains of belongs to himself, an example of a common vice in critical practice that Barfield will call "logomorphism" in *Poetic Diction*:

> To project our own way of thinking into the past, when we are attempting to explain and criticise its writers, will explain to us neither the past nor the present. The incorrigible habit of doing this is the weakness . . . of the late nineteenth and the twentieth centuries. . . . We can do what is worth very much more—and that is to incorporate their finest perceptions, their state of consciousness, into our own consciousness. The past is a symbol of the present in the history of a mind. The important thing is . . . what *Paradise Lost* means to us now. (Barfield 1923c, 525)

The continual shift in the meanings of words ensures that "we can never really enter into Milton's mind" (Barfield 1923c, 525), which compels Barfield in 1923 to embrace hermeneutic humility, if not outright skepticism. We cannot really know whether Milton or Donne perceived thought as a fragrance, as Eliot would have it. We can know, though, that we have lost the confident metaphysical and theological passion of Milton's earliest readers, and having no critical method to compensate for the loss have little idea what *Paradise Lost* might mean for us. Barfield's hermeneutic humility has the more limited goal of understanding what states of consciousness hold at a given time, based on the common meanings of words as used at that time, and attempts on that basis to discern what *Paradise Lost* means to us now.

Barfield does not reject Eliot's claim for a "dissociation of sensibility." In fact, Eliot is on the verge of recognizing an evolution of consciousness and does not go far enough, so Barfield seeks to deepen Eliot's hypothesis by inquiring more closely into the relation of poetic language to metaphysics. In *Poetic Diction*, Barfield will describe this dissociation as "a separation of consciousness from the real world [that] is only too conspicuous alike in philosophy, science, literature, and normal experience" and will add that "there [is no] remedy for this state of affairs but that experience of truth, or identification of the self with the meaning of Life, which is both poetry and knowledge" (*PD* 143). In this early essay, Barfield's goal is limited: to supply a more secure sense that "the human mind evolves," though his own vertiginous sense that the mind floats away on shifting breezes of language leaves him unsure how to accomplish it.

Thus far we have seen that the article on "Decadence" argues that contemporary cultural ills arise from our inability to fully meet the Romantic imperative and that the article on "Milton and Metaphysics" brings us to the cusp of recognizing an "evolution of consciousness" that might help us to address at least one of those ills, the dissociation of sensibility; we still need some account of the relation of poetry to consciousness. That is the thrust of Barfield's first articles: "Form in Poetry," "The Reader's Eye," and "The Silent Voice of Poetry."

"Form in Poetry" ends on the same note of qualitative skepticism present in "Milton and Metaphysics." In this case, there is no queasy awareness of "the whole queer structure of our speech and consciousness floating gently away into thin air," or that "we can never enter into the mind of anyone who lived more than a few years ago" (Barfield 1923c, 524–5). Barfield instead places another limit on criticism:

> But words change their meanings. They are changing all the time as surely and imperceptibly as men are changing their skins. Art critics begin to put the word "form" into inverted commas; soon it comes to mean something slightly different.... It is through these readjustments that criticism gradually approaches nearer to the truth. It can never go all the way; but definitions, generalisations, epigrams containing half-truths are all like so many searchlights playing upon an airship at night. The airship can never be seen as clearly as in the daytime; its upper half can never be seen at all. Nevertheless, the more searchlight the better, for if the latest beam falls on a spot already illuminated, then that spot is made a little brighter; ... we are one step nearer to perfect appreciation. (Barfield 1920a, 501–2)

This is not a Pyrrhonian skepticism that avoids any truth claims, but rather a pragmatic, almost Peircean, recognition that because the meanings of words change, do what we may, we can never go all the way to a perfectly (that is to say, eternally) precise definition of any word, though such perfection is a horizon toward which we must strive. Barfield places this caution at the end of his article to set a limit on essentialist discussions of form by himself as much as by those, like Clive Bell, who push the idea of "significant form." Crediting Pater for "cutting ... a new path through the wilderness of sentimental criticism" (Barfield 1920a, 501) by positing that "all art aspires to the condition of music," the focus of the essay is not only on the "form" of poetry in consciousness, but also on dismantling the division between form and content, music, and meaning.

Barfield begins by asking what in poetry might parallel form in painting—can there be pure, nonrepresentational "lines" in poetry when language, not paint or sound, is the medium? Barfield contends, using associationist vocabulary that he absorbed from Wordsworth and early Coleridge but would soon abandon, that words of their nature are "the final objective record for each person of the whole series of thoughts or sense-impressions received by him every time he has spoken or heard that word." He adds that "it is just this blending and harmonising of remembered impressions that constitutes true form in poetry" (Barfield 1920a, 501). This definition of form suggests that it is inseparable from meaning, or content, for that is what one blends or harmonizes in the act of constituting poetic form by reading a poem.

This is not to say that form is reducible to content. The "music" of a poem, as instantiated by "the actual mechanical rhythm, poetry's primitive foundation, is a *sine qua non*" and "indispensable part" of a poem's "whole aesthetic appeal" (Barfield 1920a, 501). In other words: no music, no poem. A poem cannot *simply* be musical, though—Barfield rejects that there can be "pure" nonsense verse. Shakespeare's songs, for example, are not "musical nonsense" because "their music is their sense and has its own effect on the arrangement of the memory, dealing perhaps with the subconscious rather than with the conscious associations" (Barfield 1920a, 502). For Barfield, when it comes to poetry, there is no form without content and no content without form. This is true even at the level of the surprising epithet. Blake's "rural pen" is remarkable to Barfield for its salvaging of a "vapid, colourless word" through its quasi-metaphorical juxtaposition with "pen" (Barfield 1920a, 501). Barfield arrives at the end of his argument, having dismantled the division between form and meaning—no wonder there is so much "nonsense" written about it—but with the meanings of both terms having shifted in the process. He has taken the first step toward a proper "science" of criticism.

In the companion essay that followed a few months later, "The Silent Voice of Poetry," Barfield deepened the analysis begun in "Form in Poetry" by uniting it with the insight that consciousness inevitably evolves and takes on a linguistic form, but in an extraordinarily subtle way. He begins with the axiomatic claim that "in literature to 'say what you mean' is nothing less than to impart your whole state of mind." Distinguishing between literary prose and verse, he adds that literary prose is "the rhythm of [a] whole life and thought" and in poetry it involves "a kind of elusive discrepancy between two rhythms" (Barfield 1921a, 448). The discrepancy is caused by the slippage between "some rigidly regular metrical form" on the one hand, and on the other hand "a soft fabric of words already woven in a rhythm of their own" (Barfield 1921a, 448). In this respect poetry is unlike music:

> The analogy is a false one, for the voice of poetry is a silent voice, and its silence is ever deepening with the development of language and civilization. This is not to say that the voice is less melodious or less insistent than before; on the contrary its silence is nothing but a sinking further and further into the soundless depths of imagination. (Barfield 1921a, 448)

The "voice" of poetry, then, though like all literature expressive of a "whole state of mind," is ultimately "silent" because it creates its music from what Keats called (and Barfield was fond of recalling) the unheard melodies that are sweeter than the audible tones of the conventional form and distinct speech patterns of the poet (Keats 1978, 282). It may be worth noting that at the time Barfield was working his way to this view, Yeats and Pound were describing exquisite aesthetic sensitivity as "listening to incense" (Longenbach 44–5)—another sign of Barfield's attunement to, and distance from, the leading currents of his time.

One consequence of this curious and complex state is that the "whole implausible music" of the blank verse of *Paradise Lost* causes the reader to follow the "tortuous central path between these two extremes" toward "the vanishing point, where their whole impalpable music lies" (Barfield 1921a, 448). Having already established to his satisfaction that "the fundamental base-music of poetry is heard best in blank-verse" (Barfield 1921a, 448)—thereby making iambic pentameter "inevitable" in a positive way—Barfield concludes that its powerful effect comes from its polar tension with the breaks of form and the idiosyncratic rhythms and idioms that belong to individual poets and readers. As with the critical and hermeneutical limits we saw in earlier essays, here too there is a phenomenological limit, a "vanishing point" where the "silent voice" of poetry becomes an "imaginary voice" (Barfield 1921a, 448)—that is to say, a voice heard only in and by means of the imagination. Here too a problem arises for the reader regarding the tension between their prosaic inner monologue and the language of poetry, one that Barfield only resolves, or at least more fully addresses, in *Poetic Diction*.

The final major point of this early essay is the crucial role of the imagination as it relates both to the function of poetry and to the evolution in Western civilization of our experience of it. For readers falling on this side of the birth of print culture, "the 'form' of a line of poetry . . . cannot be properly grasped, unless the whole line is flashed on the mind at once. Eye and ear must hear and see the last word in the line, even while they are resting on the first" (Barfield 1921a, 449). Though poetry is born of oral and aural culture, and meets us now "through both eye and ear . . . its history is a gradual march towards greater reliance on the latter" (Barfield 1921a, 449). This correlates with the way that the "silent voice of poetry" is "ever deepening with the development of language and civilization." And that is as it should be for us, because "by reading a poem (if it is already familiar to me) I find that I get the fullest perception of its beauty and the keenest enjoyment from it" (Barfield 1920b, 327).

We derive a maximum of pleasure from the silent reading of a familiar poem because:

> the function of poetry . . . is to produce a state of mind compact of imagination and emotion—that the stimulus must arrive at the imagination *through* the senses, but that the sooner it can get through, and the less disturbance it causes in its passage, the better. . . . For imagination, after all, is the salt of appreciation—in music no less than in poetry—"Imagination" in Coleridge's sense of the word—not a series of tangible thoughts or images in the brain, but a certain high consciousness, diffused, of the universal issues that are suggested by the artist's presentation. (Barfield 1921a, 449)

It is the modern mode, Barfield suggests—in the first of many references throughout his career to Coleridge's theory of the imagination—to cultivate by means of the imagination what Coleridge describes as "a translucence of the Special in the Individual or of the General in the Especial or of the Universal in the General. Above all by the translucence of the Eternal in and through the Temporal" (Coleridge 1972, 30). This of course is why the "imaginary voice" is also silent: it is that vanishing point where the universal shines through the particular, but does not have a voice of its own. The wordless space in poetry is where the meanings of words transform.

2. *Poetic Diction*

Poetic Diction is an attempt to transform and rehabilitate the Romantic tradition as it stood in the century's first three decades. More than once Barfield lamented "the tragedy of the Romantic Movement" (*RCA* 117), in particular that in "the state of Romanticism as it exists today, we see the tragic consequences that followed" the inability of the Romantics or their modern followers to ask of "the visionary Grail of the human imagination . . . 'Of what is it served?'" (*RCA* 39). For Barfield in the 1920s, the Romantic legacy had devolved into Lawrence's anti-intellectual sensualism, the Bloomsbury set's cult of beauty and Fabianism, Yeats's "private store of 'wisdom' in a castle," and Walter de la Mare's wise but limiting decision to remain "speculative, doubtful, liking questions better than answers" (Barfield 1956b, 8) in order to preserve his "clear child-vision" (Barfield 1920e, 141). Middleton Murry and Richards are themselves limited in their defense of Romanticism by their conviction that they must "bring all phenomena, aesthetic and otherwise, to the test of immediate personal experience," which renders them vulnerable to "the obviously superior breadth of Mr. Eliot's culture" (Barfield 1930c, 10). *Poetic Diction* sees Barfield move in a quite different direction. Like Murry, he relies on his own "immediate personal experience," while he also offers, like Eliot, a richly informed cultural vision. Barfield is able in this way to meet in surprising and deep ways Eliot's criteria of wholeness, maturity, and order while also finding a place for Murry's inclusion of the full personality of the individual.

Poetic Diction is written in the same combative mood as his early articles: "To a considerable extent . . . it was preoccupied with those whom I will call 'enemies' for short, though I am not aware of much personal animosity" (*PD* 212). Barfield had Modernist London in mind, not C. S. Lewis alone, when he chose as an epigraph one of Blake's Proverbs of Hell: "Opposition is true friendship." This should not come as a surprise. As early as 1921, "Barfield began 'desultory reading' for his B.Litt. thesis on 'Poetic Diction'" (Adey 4), and by 1922—at the age of twenty-four—parts of what he would later integrate into his book began to appear. In fact, the first of those pieces to be published, an etymological study of the word "Ruin," is not only a meditation on the history of that word but also a finally hopeful commentary on the feeling of helpless, ironic collapse that preoccupied the postwar period, and that Barfield reflects in early short stories like "Seven Letters" (1922), "Dope" (1923), and "The Devastated Area" (1924).

Poetic Diction also tries to make good on Barfield's call for a "new kind of criticism." The prevalent and sterile variety he describes in this way:

> The non-creative critic can never be the interpreter proper; . . . he can only be the *collector*. As time passes and the dammed springs of poetic impulse which first impelled him to criticism dry up, his criticism becomes no more than a hunting for subtle sensations and high flavours, and then a nice classification

of these according to similar sensations and flavours enjoyed in the past. He invents proper epithets like *Dantesque, Dickensian, Shavian*, to save himself the trouble of interpretation; and these become less and less significant as they are drawn from more and more minor artists; till at last his work tells us nothing about the subject-matter and too much about its author. (*PD* 169)

This is the "gentle" decadent criticism of the previous generation, masking its lack of method and insight with euphemistic and academic vagueness, a "cat and dog business" that must "peter out into expressions of personal taste" for lack of "fresh air" and a "ground-plan" in "theorizing on the problems of poetic diction . . . [and speculating] as to what was or was not beautiful or justifiable in the poetry of the past" (*PD* 59). This "fresh air" would come in the form of a "poetic" criticism, a "kind of criticism . . . that attempts to know, by sharing in, the poetic process itself" rather than "the fastidious sort which can only moon aimlessly about the room with its hands in its pockets" (*PD* 132).

In other words, Barfield aims for *Poetic Diction* to be the objective, methodologically self-aware criticism he thought the time demanded, while also being "poetic" in its own right. We have already seen that Barfield considered Robert Graves's *On English Poetry* (1922) a step in this direction. No less notable, and of considerably greater impact in the emerging field of critical theory, was the work of I. A. Richards. Richards and C. K. Ogden together wrote *The Meaning of Meaning: A Study of the Influence of Language upon Thought and of the Science of Symbolism* (1923). Richards's *The Principles of Literary Criticism*, a landmark volume because it was "the first book in English that attempted to develop a comprehensive theory of criticism" (Searle 693), sought the curtailment of the "chaos of theories." Richards attempted to study poetic language by using insights derived from Behaviorism to adequately explain how "every element in a form, whether it be musical form or any other, is capable of exciting a very intricate and widespread response" (Richards 157). Barfield dismissed this as "Behaviorist nonsense" (Barfield 1930c, 10), a view he came back to in his preface to the second edition of *Poetic Diction* (1951) as he challenged Richards for having "sought no less than to define imagination in terms of a philosophy of Behaviourism—when it is precisely the fact of imagination which makes Behaviourism at once untrue and dangerous" (*PD* 34). More importantly in this context, Barfield takes Richards and Ogden to task for writing a book about meaning without accounting for metaphor and "without having practiced the gentle art of *unthinking*"; as a consequence, "they are absolutely rigid under the spell of those verbal ghosts of the physical sciences, which today make up practically the whole meaning-system of so many European minds" (*PD* 134). They have written about the "science of symbols" without recognizing that "linguistic symbols have a *figurative* origin" (*PD* 134).[14]

The inability of Richards to see that any theory of meaning, and any methodologically sound literary criticism, must give a central place to the "figurative origin" of linguistic symbols had a corollary for Barfield that seems to align him with Eliot: "the perfect poet is also the perfect critic" (*PD* 170). This of course is a direct reference to another of Eliot's landmark essays, "The Perfect Critic," which was the lead essay in *The Sacred Wood* (1921), and which ends by recalling that "the poetic critic is criticizing poetry in order to create poetry" (Eliot 2021 2, 270). Eliot's essay begins with a (for Barfield) promising reference to Coleridge as "perhaps the greatest of English critics" (Eliot 2021 2, 262) but we soon learn that this comparative greatness is due to the poverty of English criticism in general. Coleridge had "natural abilities" that were "probably more remarkable than any other modern critic" but his intelligence "cannot be estimated as . . . completely free" due to "the pernicious effect of emotion" (Eliot 2021 2, 268). This is a somewhat more measured description than one offered by Eliot a year earlier, of "the wakeful and wasteful mind of Coleridge which wasted its metaphysical sleep on Highgate Hill" (Eliot 2021 2, 79). Eliot contrasts Coleridge's bathetic squandering of his talent with Aristotle, who, though no poet, is the perfect critic of the essay's title because his precise yet systematic intelligence is undiluted by emotion or prejudice. He "looked solely and steadfastly at the object; in his short and broken treatise he provides an eternal example—not of laws, or even of method, for there is no method except to be very intelligent, but of intelligence itself swiftly operating the analysis of sensation to the point of principle and definition" (Eliot 2021 2, 267). Intelligence may not have a method but it consists of several things at least: first, of recognizing the "manifest fact of the existence of two types of mind, an abstract and a concrete." The concrete mind apprehends through the senses, while the abstract mind apprehends through the intellect. Furthermore, "there are two ways in which a word may be 'abstract'" (Eliot 2021 2, 266). The first is simply to have "a meaning which cannot be grasped by appeal to any of the senses"—Eliot holds up the experience by Pascal and "Mr. Bertrand Russell" of mathematics as an example of this understanding—and the second is "the tendency of words to become indefinite emotions" (Eliot 2021 2, 266), with Hegel's "dealing with his emotions as if they were definite objects which had aroused those emotions" being the chief philosophical transgressor. The latter is a "corruption [that] has extended very far" beyond Hegel, though, such that "you will observe that words have changed their meanings. What they have lost is definite, and what they have gained is indefinite" (Eliot 2021 2, 266–7). Thus Eliot calls for critics to overcome the merely "appreciative" and "imprecise style" in order to produce "true generalizations" upon "a structure" of perceptions: "criticism is a statement in language of this structure; it is the development of a sensibility" (Eliot 2021 2, 270). In this way, the poetic critic has true insights about poetry to offer its practitioners, and critical poets can pass along their own insights, through their practice, to poets and critics alike.

Barfield offers a different picture of the way in which the perfect poet is also the perfect critic:

> Surely, if criticism is anything worth while, it must be a sort of midwifery—not, of course, in the Socratic sense, but retrospectively. It must try to alter the state of mind of the artist's audience, from mere wondering contemplation of an inexplicable *result*, towards something more like sympathetic participation in a process. And in poetry, as far as it is merely semantic, and not dramatic, or sentimental, or musical—this process is the making of meaning. What kind of criticism, then, is dilettante: that which attempts to know, by sharing in, the poetic process itself, or the fastidious sort which can only moon aimlessly about the room with its hands in its pockets, till the infant is nicely washed and dried and ready for inspection? (*PD* 132)

Because "the *raison d'être* of all criticism" is "to increase appreciation" (Barfield 1920a, 501), and appreciation increases most readily when we participate in "the making of meaning," that is to say in "the poetic process itself," the critic's task is to transform reading from an "absolutely rigid" reception, into a "sympathetic participation in a process." This is not to confirm the fears of Christopher Norris that for Barfield the critic is a proto-Heideggerian vatic vessel, or Eliot's possible fear that Barfield has invited the chaos of indefinite emotion through the critical back door. Barfield envisions a different kind of gentleness, born of insight, in a critic with "a controlled and fundamentally sane consciousness, a gentle sympathetic imaginative understanding, not only of 'human nature' in the ordinary sense, but of the nature of inspiration and of its function in human evolution" (*PD* 170).

The idea that criticism is a controlled creative or poetic activity begins with the Romantic poets, and Barfield's new science of poetic criticism owes a great deal to Coleridge and Shelley. For example, near the end of *Poetic Diction* Barfield rehabilitates Coleridge's time-worn concepts of fancy and imagination and stresses their urgent contemporary importance:

> the distinction between Fancy and Imagination is one which ought to be particularly emphasized in an age like ours, divorced from reality by universal abstraction of thought, and in which the fanciful poetry of "escape", as it is sometimes called, is so popular.... [I]t is a tragedy of art in our time that most of those who—whether they desire it or not—are regarded as the living representatives of the poetic, are under the spell of a Kantian conception of knowledge, or, worse still, a popular conception of "Science". (*PD* 202)

It may not be immediately obvious how Coleridge's desynonymizing of fancy and imagination remedies our contemporary "divorce from reality," our collectively dissociated sensibility, so it is worth bringing freshly to mind Coleridge's perhaps too-famous distinction. Fancy, one recalls, is "no other than a mode of Memory emancipated from the order of time and space . . . [and] equally with the ordinary memory it must receive all its materials ready made from the law of association" (Coleridge 1983 1, 305). In the same passage Coleridge makes for the only time in his writings a further distinction between primary and secondary imaginations: the primary imagination Coleridge defines as "the living Power and prime Agent of all human Perception, and as a repetition in the finite mind of the eternal act of creation in the infinite I AM" (Coleridge 1983 1, 304). The secondary imagination is that which: "dissolves, diffuses, dissipates, in order to re-create; or where the process is rendered impossible, yet still at all events it struggles to idealize and to unify. It is essentially *vital*, even as all objects (*as* objects) are essentially fixed and dead" (Coleridge 1983 1, 304).

In Barfield's view, there is an urgent need for a revitalized interest in Coleridgean fancy and imagination because they offer an antidote to the felt perception that we are surrounded by spectral appearances and divorced from things in themselves. This mostly unexamined assumption undergirds almost all of the major and lesser writers, thinkers and artistic movements of the time, like the "definite objects" that Eliot assumes lie undisturbed and undiscerned at the back of Hegel's "emotions." Coleridge, by contrast, suggests that only our way of thinking can become fancifully "fixed and dead"—that is to say, to redeploy Eliot's critical terminology, classical. Instead, Coleridge offers a vitalist, dynamic, and Romantic system that assumes "two contrary forces, the one of which tends to expand infinitely, while the other strives to apprehend or *find* itself in this infinity" (Coleridge 1983 1, 297). In this picture of self-consciousness, there is nothing from which to be divorced, only the fanciful means of convincing oneself that one is. Bringing Coleridge's distinction and his "two forces" before the public is important to Barfield, then, because only something like them will help to heal the manifold psychological and social ills that underlie our condition of being "divorced from reality by universal abstraction of thought" (*PD* 202). For Barfield, Richards and Eliot are prime examples of what goes wrong when the metaphysical presuppositions that support our critical reflections go unexamined. Coleridge proposes that behind individual, subjective consciousness—standing over against me as "not me"—is more consciousness. Adducing Rudolf Steiner's philosophical writings, Barfield underscores this by saying that "it is not justifiable, in constructing a theory of knowledge, to take subjectivity as 'given' . . . [b]ecause, if we examine the thinking activity carefully . . . we shall find that in the *act* of thinking, or knowing, no such distinction of consciousness exists" (*PD* 208).[15]

Barfield would make major contributions to the study of Coleridge, but Andrew Welburn is correct that *Poetic Diction* is "remarkably Shelleyan in much of its thought" (Welburn 225, n. 28). Besides using lines from *Prometheus Unbound* to exemplify poetic diction, Barfield credits Shelley with recognizing that "a proper study of poetic diction is inseparable from the study of language as a whole" (*PD* 58) and with grasping that the earliest forms of language are invariably figurative. He quotes with approval Shelley's own approving nod to Francis Bacon's description of metaphor as "the footsteps of nature" and makes qualified but regular use of Shelley's claim that "metaphorical language marks the before unapprehended relations of things and perpetuates their apprehension, until the words which represent them become through time signs for portions or classes of thoughts, instead of pictures of integral thoughts" (Shelley 653). So too, Barfield contends that as an effect of metaphor "my own consciousness had been expanded" (*PD* 55). He applauds Shelley's "piercing gaze" in appreciating the distinction between "the mood of creation and the mood of appreciation" (*PD* 105) and endorses Shelley's definition of the poet (*PD* 135): "to be a poet is to apprehend the true and the beautiful, in a word the good which exists in the relation, subsisting, first between existence and perception, and secondly between perception and expression" (Shelley 654). Choosing as an example Shelley's song "My soul is an enchanted boat" from *Prometheus Unbound*, Barfield finds "the image contains so much truth and beauty that henceforth the eyes with which I behold real boats and waves and swans, the ears with which in the right mood I listen to a song, are actually somewhat different" (*PD* 55). Thus, Barfield finds in Shelley-the-critic a proper means to appreciate and articulate the "truth and beauty" of Shelley-the-poet, thereby confirming that Shelley is among the select few perfect critics.

Most importantly, though, Shelley offers Barfield the distinction between the "rational principle" and the "poetic principle," το λογιζειν and το ποιειν. Barfield relies upon it throughout *Poetic Diction*. For Barfield, the "subtle interaction of the two principles ... is implied in the mere existence of language" (*PD* 109); in considering "man ... as knower, we shall find that he always knows by the interaction within himself of these poetic (ποιητικός) and logistic principles" (*PD* 139). Without the existence and interaction of these "principles," in other words, neither knowledge nor language could exist. One may even go further: "in the whole development of consciousness ... we can trace the operation of [these] two opposing principles, or forces" (*PD* 87).

Let us begin with the "logistic principle" since for Barfield "the natural progress of language, if left, as it were, to itself, is a progress from poetic towards prosaic" (*PD* 152). Without entering the long and vexed critical history that surrounds Shelley's distinction of the rational and poetic principles or of his definition of the poet, it is worth recalling Shelley's description of το λογιζειν. It is for him "mind contemplating the relations borne by one thought to another, however produced"; it is the "principle of analysis, and its action regards the relations of things, simply as relations; considering thoughts, not in their integral unity, but as algebraical representations which conduct to certain general results." It is also "the enumeration of quantities already known." Finally, "Reason respects the differences ... of things [and] is to Imagination as the instrument to the agent, as the body to the spirit, as the shadow to the substance" (Shelley 651–2).

Barfield retains much of Shelley's account. "The το λογιζειν of Shelley's *Essay*," he says, is "the force by which ... simple meanings tend to split up into a number of separate and often isolated concepts" (*PD* 87). Considered as the "absolute rational principle" it "is that which makes conscious of poetry but cannot create it" (*PD* 103). As with Shelley, for Barfield it "can clear up obscurities, it can measure and enumerate with greater and ever greater precision ... but in no sense can it be said ... to *expand* consciousness" (*PD* 144).

Though Barfield acknowledges the need for the rational principle, his additions to Shelley's account emphasize its malign effects. It consists of "death-forces" (*PD* 168) that "would kill, alike the given Meanings of which language, at its early stages, still retains an echo, and the meanings which individual poets have inserted into it later by their creative activity in metaphor" (*PD* 179). It carries out its Jovian function in two ways, by creating abstractions and by locking language into sclerotic regularity. The latter produces the former. To say:

> that words lose their freshness through habit ... will do well enough, as long as we remember that "habit" is itself only a familiar name for the repetition of the identical, and that the repetition of the identical is the very essence of the

rational principle—the very means by which the concrete becomes abstract—the Gorgon's head. (*PD* 115)¹⁶

This negative picture of abstraction is fundamentally different from Eliot's—for Eliot, it is "indefinite emotions"; for Barfield, it is "the repetition of the identical." The entropic drift to rigid fixity, the shriveling of imagination into fancy, is evident not only in the evolution of grammar toward the increasingly logical and abstract (*PD* 154), and the increasing fixity of word order (*PD* 148), but also in the efforts by contemporary logicians like Bertrand Russell to develop arcane systems of symbolic logic in order to wrestle words into pinned submission:

> The Logician . . . in his endeavor to keep [words] steady and thus fit them to his laws, is continually seeking to *reduce* their meaning. I say seeking to do so, because logic is essentially a compromise. He could only evolve a language, whose propositions would really obey the laws of thought by eliminating meaning altogether. (*PD* 131n)

For Barfield, then, it is not Hegel but Russell who best exemplifies how to drain meaning from language. The logician who achieved the dream of a totally closed formal logic would have to completely excise meaning because meaning cannot be wholly abstract. In fact:

> A purely abstract term—which, with the possible exception of numbers, can nowhere exist—is a mark representing, not a thing or being, but the fact *that* identical sensations *have been* experienced on two or more occasions. It is in fact a *classification* of sense-perceptions. Purely abstract thinking, carried to its logical conclusions, is thus—counting; as was realized by Hobbes, who described all thinking as addition and subtraction. (*PD* 185)

We are reminded again that for Shelley and Barfield alike the rational principle is essentially enumerative. In the Empiricist lineage begun by Hobbes and adopted in Barfield's day by Russell, meaningful thinking reduces to stasis, as if the essence of language were the abstract noun.

Between Hobbes and Russell, though, lie "Locke, Kant and the post-Kantian subjective idealists" (*PD* 212) whom Barfield singles out for critique. Barfield focuses on Locke because of his historical importance and his "limpid clarity" in articulating "a very important step in the development of those intellectual premises (they are premises *now*) which make it so difficult for Western thought to grasp the true nature of inspiration" (*PD* 62, 184). Throughout the book, Barfield places Locke at the beginning of what he calls the "Locke-Müller-France way of thinking" (*PD* 75) that is founded on two convictions: first, that "the full meanings of words ... appear as solid chunks with definite boundaries and limits, to which other chunks may be added as occasion arises" (*PD* 75); and second, "the conception of language as the prime material of logical constructions" (*PD* 62).

Locke articulates particularly well a pervasive assumption in the Empiricist tradition that the primary function of words is to denote discrete things and the causal or logical relationships that bind them. This view is itself founded on an anti-historicist epistemology. "The chief end of language," for Locke, "is communication" (Locke 247). Thus our goal as users of language is to clarify our meanings as much as possible. Words are, and always have been, "signs of internal conceptions" that "stand as marks for the ideas within [one's] own mind" (Locke 205). Since words are affixed to generalizations, I must form a generalization (that is to say, an idea) before I can give it a name; and, before I can form an idea, I must have experienced and synthesized a variety of sensations. That is to say, imperceptible particles (indescribable except in terms of the "primary qualities" of solidity, mobility, etc.) constitute objects that impinge through one or several of my sense organs, thereby giving rise to a "simple idea" within me. Having experienced a number of these sensations, I combine them to form a "complex idea." Language then becomes possible, and necessary not to thought but to communication. Having synthesized from the experience of tall and leafy "simple ideas" the abstract generalization "tree," I coin the term and apply it to the other tall and leafy simple ideas that impinge upon my senses so that I can communicate with others about them.

It is not difficult to see behind this simple picture many of the complex theories of the origin of language that preoccupied linguists like Müller as well as the efforts of Russell and his followers in the 1910s to polish descriptive language to a gleaming ideal of mathematical purity. Its shadow also hangs over Eliot's description of the poet's relation to language in the essay on the metaphysical poets already discussed:

> our civilization comprehends great variety and complexity, and this variety and complexity, playing upon a refined sensibility, must produce various and complex results. The poet must become more and more comprehensive, more allusive, more indirect, in order to force, to dislocate if necessary, language into his meaning. (Eliot 2021 2, 380)

Barfield agreed with Eliot that poets need to respond to the complexity of modern life, but behind Eliot's violent description of forcing and dislocating an unwilling language to suit the needs of a complex time there lies an instrumentalist view of language as a mere tool that is an echo of "Locke's picture of Adam at work on the synthetic manufacture of language" (*PD* 206). It is also telling and inevitable for so discerning a thinker and poet as Eliot that he recognizes that language is incorrigibly resistant to coercion, though for Barfield he missed the lesson available in its stubborn refusal to be tamed.

Because Eliot is beholden to the rational principle that produces to an unhealthy degree "full waking consciousness" (*PD* 152), he is tormented by acute self-awareness. For Eliot, each of us in our modern subjectivity is "each in his prison / Thinking of the key, each confirm[ing] a prison" (Eliot 2015 1 71); for Barfield, the mind-forged prison is a byproduct of the "rational principle" and "nothing but the rational, or logistic, principle can endow him with this subjective—*self*—consciousness" (*PD* 103). Nevertheless, this view of language, and of Eliot's dilemma, is similar to the one Barfield invokes in "Milton and Metaphysics," with "the whole queer structure of our speech and consciousness floating away into thin air" (Barfield 1923c, 524). Barfield's answer to his own challenge lies in the "poetic principle" as it is anchored in the "living unity" of primordial figurative language that arises from human nature itself. Speech and consciousness cannot finally float away, but can only seem to, because both language and consciousness are rooted in the antecedent unity of nature.

The contrary of the prosaic principle, and the other half of "man as knower," is the "poetic principle." Here too it is helpful to begin by recalling Shelley's description. το ποιειν is synonymous with the Imagination and is "mind acting upon . . . thoughts so as to colour them with its own light, and composing from them as from elements, other thoughts, each containing within itself the principle of its own integrity." It is the "principle of synthesis, and has for its objects those forms which are common to universal nature and existence itself." Finally, it is "the perception of the value of those quantities" that Reason manipulates (Shelley 651–2).

Unlike the use Barfield makes of Shelley's account of the "rational principle," Barfield dissents from much of what Shelley says about the "poetic principle." Barfield agrees that the imagination or poetic principle (like Shelley, he uses the terms interchangeably) makes possible our perception of value, universal nature, and existence itself, and he agrees that these are three aspects of the same thing. But Barfield does not agree that the "poetic principle" is a "principle of synthesis." As Barfield puts it, "synthesis, as well as analysis, is not a poetic, but a discursive function, operating *within* the sphere of the rational principle" (*PD* 190). This is so because synthesis, like analysis, already implies abstraction. Synthesis and analysis form what Blake called a "negation," the contrary to which is what

Barfield terms "concrete thinking." A mere synthesis of abstract fixities—once again, Coleridge's "fancy" is not far in the background—"can only come *after*, and *by means of*, a certain discrimination of actual phenomena—a seeing them as *separate* sensible objects" (*PD* 191). So, while a need for synthesis will "direct me to *look out* for a possible real resemblance between apple-blossom, pear-blossom, and roses," the same act as "intuited in actual observation, becomes poetic knowledge (*inspiration*), and will then react, as wisdom, on my further experience in observation (*recognition*), so that I shall truly see or 'read' the flowers with different eyes" (*PD* 190).

Barfield's "poetic principle," then, differs from Shelley's because it precedes synthesis and analysis alike. Synthesis and analysis are two aspects of a single rational principle that is contrary to a precedent poetic principle:

> The poetic principle was already operative before such discrimination took place, and, when it continues to operate afterwards in inspiration, it operates *in spite of* that discrimination and seeks to undo its work. The poetic conducts *an immediate conceptual synthesis of percepts*. Brought into contact with these by its partial attachment to some individual human brain and body, it meets—through the senses—the *disjecta membra* of a real world, and weaves them again into the one real whole; whence it was called—not perhaps very happily—by Coleridge *esemplastic*. (*PD* 191)[17]

Eliot also uses "concrete" as the equivalent of the "poetic" in his critical writings of the 1920s.[18] If the "concrete" mind is the same as the "poet's mind" that he evokes in "The Metaphysical Poets" a year later, it "is constantly amalgamating disparate experience ... [and] always forming new wholes" (Eliot 2021, 2 380). It is similar to Barfield's "concrete" thinking, which "conducts an immediate synthesis of percepts." At any rate, whereas the rational principle is either "a synthesis of *ideas* already abstract" or an analysis of synthesized ideas, the poetic principle "is always a direct conceptual linking of percept to percept, or image to image" (*PD* 189). In the terms Barfield would use three decades later in *Saving the Appearances*, concrete thinking is "final participation," that is, self-aware figuration free of meddlesome and alienating alpha-thinking.

The rational principle consists of "death-forces" that would pin meanings to the wall of language; the "very poetic itself" is "the genesis of meaning ... the making of meaning" (*PD* 132). This "making" is "not some fantastic 'creation out of nothing', but the bringing farther into consciousness of something which already exists in unconscious life" (*PD* 112). This "unconscious life" is the life of nature, from which language and consciousness emerge:

we find given us, to start with, as the nature of language itself at its birth. It is the principle of living unity. Considered subjectively, it observes the resemblances between things, whereas the first principle marks the differences, is interested in knowing what things *are*, whereas the first discerns what they are not. Accordingly, at a later stage in the evolution of consciousness, we find it operative in individual poets, enabling them (τὸ ποιειν) to intuit relationships which their fellows have forgotten—relationships which they must *now* express as metaphor. Reality, once self-evident, and therefore not conceptually experienced, but which can *now* only be reached by an effort of the individual mind—this is what is contained in a true poetic metaphor; and every metaphor is 'true' only in so far as it contains such a reality, or hints at it. (*PD* 87–8)

The "poetic principle" intuits "living unity" and is the pre-rational vehicle by means of which that unity gives itself forth in language. It would be difficult to form a greater contrast with the Locke-Müller-France school that by giving precedence to the "rational principle" saw the origin and function of language in purely instrumental terms. Indeed, in answering the question of why language becomes more figurative the further back in its history one goes, Müller had been forced to posit a race of "mighty poets" who stocked its literal meanings with metaphors. Barfield takes the simpler route of proposing that "these poetic, and *apparently* 'metaphorical' values were latent in meaning from the beginning" (*PD* 85). Thus, *pneuma*—to take a common example also used by Barfield—had originally a single meaning of both "spirit" and "wind" and "afterwards, in the development of language and thought, these single meanings split up into contrasted pairs— the abstract and the concrete, particular and general, objective and subjective" (*PD* 85). The so-called "primitive" mind is not a blank slate grasping clumsily for proto-scientific understandings of otherwise meaningless experiences; it is "literally resounding with all manner of meaning, with meaning such that, if he could but communicate it to us, we should be listening to poetry" (*PD* 86).

Mythology too, in Barfield's account, is not a disease of language or series of mistaken guesses about natural and human causation. Rather:

> myths, which represent the earliest meanings, were not the arbitrary creations of "poets", but the natural expression of man's being and consciousness at the same time. These primary "meanings" were *given*, as it were, by Nature.... Not man was creating, but the gods—or, in the psychological jargon, his "unconscious". (*PD* 102)

In this era before the full emergence of the rational principle, "mythology is the ghost of concrete meaning" in which "connections which are now apprehended as metaphor, were once perceived as immediate realities" (*PD* 92). One thinks of Shelley's famous declarations that "poetry is connate with the origin of man" (Shelley 652) and that "every original language near to its source is in itself the chaos of a cyclic poem" (Shelley 654). One can see, in this long view, just how much is lost in the "dissociation of sensibility"—all intuited coherence, all apprehension of meaning, thins into a cadaverous tissue of imprisoning abstractions. In the face of this predicament one has a first sense of why Steiner's cosmology will hold lasting appeal for Barfield.

Barfield distinguishes his position sharply from Eliot's, then, but it is not a simple opposition. A better representative of such opposition is D. H. Lawrence, who in the introduction to his *New Poems* (1920) tries to move as far from analytic abstraction as possible. Lawrence pauses to appreciate, if that is the word, Eliot's classical perfection, his ideal of maturity, in "all that is complete and consummate . . . conveyed in exquisite form: the perfect symmetry, the rhythm which returns upon itself like a dance where the hands link and loosen and link for the supreme moment of the end" (Lawrence 1956, 85). To this sterile perfection Lawrence opposes "another kind of poetry" that instead celebrates and captures "life, the ever-present, [which] knows no finality, no finished crystallization . . . the very white quick of nascent creation" (Lawrence 1956, 85). What for Eliot is an endless, dispassionate preoccupation with the infinite closed sphere of tradition, for Lawrence is "the stiff neck of habit" and "shackles and death" (Lawrence1956, 88). Lawrence celebrates instead a "rare new poetry" that focuses on the "one great mystery of time [that] is *terra incognita* to us: the instant," within which lies "the most superb mystery we have hardly recognised: the immediate, instant self" (Lawrence 1956, 89).

The form suited to the rhapsodic individualist mood of this "rare new poetry" is of course free verse. Lawrence, though, places himself at antipodes from Eliot's *vers libre*. He dismissed his buttoned-up iconoclasm as merely "to break the lovely form of metrical verse, and to dish up the fragments as a new substance, called *vers libre*" (Lawrence 1956, 88). Just as Eliot has ignored his poetic ancestor Whitman, he has also missed that freedom is a verb, as it were, an "insurgent naked throb of the instant moment" in which "the utterance is like a spasm, naked contact with all influences at once. It does not want to get anywhere. It just takes place" (Lawrence 1956, 88).

There is much in Lawrence for Barfield to celebrate. In an era of abstraction, Lawrence is an apostle of reunion with the surging processes of life from which we spring. For Barfield, too, the modern self is stranded "in the network of its own, now abstract, thoughts" and "having awoken, it is as helpless as any other new-born thing without the life of the mother-Nature from which it sprang" (*PD* 143). This divine maternal parent, the "living unity" from which we are born and toward which we strive, is not just the nature that we murder to dissect, but "that experience of truth, or identification of the self with the meaning of Life, which is both poetry and knowledge" (*PD* 143). Barfield thinks of "primitive man," man outside of history, in a manner somewhat similar to Lawrence's idealization, with the difference that for Barfield he is not only a series of throbs and surges, but is also, as we have seen, "literally resounding with all manner of meaning, and moreover, with meaning such that, if he could but communicate it to us, we should be listening to poetry" (*PD* 86). Here is the return to immediacy, to "the old, instinctive consciousness of single meanings" (*PD* 95), and the shedding of the "ghastly tissue of empty abstractions" (*PD* 135) that passes for thinking in modern life. Barfield describes this being present to presence as "pure poetry.... It is the momentary apprehension of the poetic by the rational, into which the former is forever transmuting itself—which it is itself for ever in the process of becoming" (*PD* 178).

Barfield nevertheless was as leery of Lawrence as he was of Eliot. He saw Lawrence as speaking to "the peculiarity of our age . . . that it is possessed with a desire to become more conscious of . . . fundamental and hitherto unconscious impulses. . . . Men feel that the impulses, less conscious as yet, are more real. Hence the popularity of, for instance, D.H. Lawrence" (Barfield 1940a). It does not surprise Barfield that Lawrence was frustrated in his travels by the effort to find people living unmediated by abstract thinking, because he was "an intellectual reacting against intellectualism" (Barfield 1962, 17–18) with an "unsatisfied desire . . . for depths, dark, unconscious quiet depths—with less talk of this fussy little intellect, and this fiddling little 'personality' we hear so much about" (Barfield 1930a, 76). In short, as Barfield wrote in an essay published in Eliot's *Criterion*, Lawrence valorizes "sensation without intellect, and indeed [is] rather hostile to intellect" (Barfield 1930b, 616). Most importantly though, and again consistent with Eliot's own position, Lawrence is "a metaphysician *malgré lui*, and a very bad one" because "without . . . an underlying body of ideas, the artist has no medium in which he can *communicate*, except on a purely superficial level, with his fellow-men. Consequently, . . . his energy is prone to be dissipated in the exhausting effort to *create* such a medium" (Barfield 1930c, 9).

Put another way: Lawrence's pure sensation is no less conditional than Eliot's "ratiocinative" principle. He attempts to live by what Barfield calls the "absolute poetic principle," regardless that this principle in its absolute purity "is that which creates poetry but cannot [be] conscious of it" (*PD* 103). Lawrence tried to will himself into "primal" consciousness by uprooting himself from the traditions that birthed him and about which he wrote hundreds of pages of commentary, and unsurprisingly earned frustration for his effort. He tried to enter by force Blake's born condition (as judged by Eliot) of lacking "a framework of accepted and traditional ideas" (Eliot 2021 2, 190–1). For Barfield, though Eliot is incorrect in his assessment of Blake he is right that individual talents necessarily participate in the traditions from which they spring. Eliot is also wrong, though, in thinking of tradition as a kind of web in which individual talents are bound, and which they make tremble only by their endlessly defeated efforts to escape their own personalities.[19] It is worth reminding ourselves that for Barfield, "man as knower" requires the presence of the poetic and rational principles alike, even if modern culture gives too much weight to the latter while would-be modern prophets often make plain their misapprehension of the former.

Barfield's "concrete thinking" is a contrary to the negation exemplified by Eliot and Lawrence. And, echoing both Lawrence and Eliot, Barfield affirms that "the modern poet is in some sense... in the position of having to fight *against* words" because "[the] poetic principle is dying out of language" (*PD* 107). The remedy, though, is not to pair total immersion in the "rational principle" with rigid adherence to traditions chosen *ad hoc* or to throw despised intellect overboard in a rush to sensation. Instead, while "the primitive bard was carried forward on... meanings like Arion on the dolphin's back," the modern poet must look "nowhere but in himself" because "the same creative activity, once operative in meaning without man's knowledge or control... is now to be found within his own consciousness. And it calls him to become the true creator, the maker of meaning itself" (*PD* 107). This "making," which as we have seen is a rediscovery, is for modern poets a cyclical process:

> Provided, then, that we do not look too far back into the past... it does indeed appear historically as an endless process of metaphor transforming itself into meaning. Seeking for material in which to incarnate its last inspiration, imagination seizes on a suitable word or phrase, uses it as a metaphor, and so creates a meaning. The progress is from Meaning, through inspiration to imagination, and from imagination, through metaphor, to meaning; inspiration grasping the hitherto unapprehended, and imagination relating it to the already known. (*PD* 141)

This is a creative hermeneutic circle, what Paul Ricoeur, with whom Barfield has affinities, described in the somewhat different context of mimesis as a "temporal form inherent in experience and the narrative structure [that] is not a lifeless tautology. We should see in it . . . a 'healthy circle'" (Ricoeur 76). In this case, the "healthy circle" begins with the passage from the "living unity" that is original, undivided meaning, identical with the "footsteps of nature." One passes then through "real inspiration, the expression of first-hand spiritual experience, [which] breaks through the shell of poetic posturings embodied in the fashionable diction of the moment" (*PD* 162). This is the unselfconscious moment of creativity, analogous to the "throb" idealized by Lawrence or the "original participation" experienced by ancient bards (to once again anticipate the nomenclature of *Saving the Appearances*), but found today by the poet in the unreflective apprehension of the pulse of living language. Moving around the circle, Barfield implies that imagination involves self-awareness and at least a hint of the "sense of homelessness" that typifies modern consciousness in its striving to find itself within the expanding infinity that surrounds us. The modern poet, against the backdrop of alienated self-consciousness, returns us via a "true poetic metaphor" to "reality, once self-evident, . . . but which can *now* only be reached by an effort of the individual mind" (*PD* 88).

It is worth comparing this image with the one used by Eliot to describe the "mythical method" in his famous review of *Ulysses*:

> In using myth, in manipulating a continuous parallel between contemporaneity and antiquity, Mr. Joyce is pursuing a method which others must pursue after him. . . . It will simply be a way of controlling, of ordering, of giving a shape and a significance to the immense panorama of futility and anarchy which is contemporary history. It is a method already adumbrated by Mr. Yeats. (Eliot 2021 2, 478)

Read in the light of Barfield's different picture, which is itself informed by Shelley and Coleridge, the "immense panorama of futility and anarchy" is Shelley's ever-expanding circumference and Coleridge's "tendency to expand infinitely," which for Barfield becomes the "living unity" into which the artist, "using myth," might expand. The "parallel between contemporaneity and antiquity" is for Barfield the "archaism" that, because of the "progress of language . . . from poetic towards prosaic" (*PD* 152), creates "something like an echo of just those rhythms . . . by externalizing as fully as is possible in words his own first-hand experience beyond them" (*PD* 158, 160). Eliot assumes that the mythical method is suitable for satirical purposes alone, that for us there is nothing more to be found in modern life than futility and anarchy; Barfield, certainly, is aware that "the Meaning of life is continually being dried up . . . and left for dead in the human mind by the operation of a purely discursive intellectual activity, of which language . . . is a necessary tool" (*PD* 179), but this and the anarchic futility it creates belong to a much larger evolutionary process that is still unfolding, of which we are living parts, and in which the poet actively intervenes through just this healthy creative circle. The "gradual loss of ancient meaning" is part of a larger "sequence of loss and recovery" (*PD* 116).[20]

The relatively uninspired reader plays a crucial role in this process. After all, "no poet . . . can be the creator of all the meaning in his poem" (*PD* 50), not only because the poet inherits and must work with given meanings but also because "in order that 'poetry', strictly so called, should exist, an appreciating imagination, in which aesthetic experience can light up, is of course as necessary as the creative activity of the poet" (*PD* 105). The fruit of this reception, which mirrors the healthy circle of creativity, is a cyclical receptive movement from a precedent "mood of appreciation" through an "expansion of consciousness" on encountering a true metaphor, and the increase of knowledge as "the ability to recognize significant resemblances and analogies" that "considered as a *state*, and apart from the effort by which it is imparted and acquired, I shall call *wisdom*" (*PD* 55). The passage from appreciation through expansion and knowledge to wisdom, and finally back to increased appreciation, mirrors the creative cycle from the "living unity" of meaning through inspiration and imagination and, via metaphor, back to meaning. Taken together, these two circles are properly gentle forms of Blake's prolific and devouring, of Shelley's two principles at work with the dilating center and circumference, and of Coleridge's fancy and imagination operative within the polarity of infinite expansion and self-knowledge within that expansion.

There is a mystery at the boundary where these cycles intersect. Recall that the "true voice" of English-language poetry for Barfield is in the unheard tension in the gap between the baseline of iambic pentameter and the poet's personal idiom. Writ large, the same is true of "meaning" both as it is made and as it is received. The modern poet in the act of creation recapitulates the evolution of language from the figurative to the literal, the concrete to the abstract, with "dazzling rapidity," and "not only from one day or hour to another is there alternation of mood: his whole consciousness oscillates while his pen is poised in the air, and he deliberates an epithet" (*PD* 110). It is the mission of the modern poet to accelerate this movement such that "the frequency of these oscillations may have increased to infinity; at which point at last the poet shall be creating out of full self-consciousness" (*PD* 110). This infinite vibration of reception and creation, prosaic and poetic, within the individual modern poet mirrors the fecund infinity of the "living unity" out of which she works, for "there really is no end to the secrets hidden behind the meanings of single words" (*PD* 132). Barfield will later call this "clairvoyance" and make the leap into poetic cosmology on its warrant.

Between these two spinning infinities, the "felt change of consciousness" that indicates the experience of meaning emerges in the margin that joins them; and it too proves an elusive possessor of its own infinity. With the very question of meaning "one is brought face to face, on the threshold, with the whole mystery of creation—and even of incarnation." Meaning resists direct declaration; a meaningful statement in Barfield's sense is paradoxical because it arises within concrete thinking, which is not abstract: "a concrete definition is an impossibility" (*PD* 187–8). Consequently, meaning is only "indirectly expressible in metaphor and simile." It is "suggestible" and "every individual must intuit [it] for himself" (*PD* 133). It is an "endless process" (*PD* 140) that "lights up" when "a kind of gap is created" and the "discursive activity [that] is inseparable from human *self-consciousness*" is "interrupted" (*PD* 179). One is reminded of the paradox of time: that we are only aware of the past and the future, which are not present, and not of the present, which is all that is. Meaning is infinitely abundant yet can be grasped by "man the knower" only in the gap between, or through the interaction of, the rational and poetic principles that pass beneath consciousness; like the creator god in many mythologies, it "hovers, for ever unable to alight" as it broods over "the perpetual evolution of human consciousness, which is stamping itself upon the transformation of language" (*PD* 181).

3. *History in English Words*

"It is a curious age," wrote Edmund Blunden (whom Barfield gave a tepid review) in 1921, "that finds so many minds living a century or centuries ago. Research is in the air" (Blunden 19). So it was with Owen Barfield in the mid-1920s. Along with his many articles, stories, poems, reviews, and the thesis that became *Poetic Diction*, he was also at work on a history of the English language that applied the theoretical work he was doing. *History in English Words* is a detailed, practical account of just how the stamping by the hovering spirit of meaning unfolded over the course of time. It is a polar complement to *Poetic Diction*, offering an extended empirical justification of Barfield's theory that metaphor drives semantic change. Its method is carefully pragmatic in the popular sense, "proceed[ing] from the known to the unknown," and it is inductive insofar as it does not "put forward theories" (*HEW* 20–1). It anticipates Barfield's own later call for an "approach [to] the history of meaning free from all assumptions based on biological theories of evolution" that instead takes the Goethean approach of "a faithful study of the *nature* of language" that is not "seduced into such arbitrary surmises" (*SA* 122).

It also has a different tone from the contrarian spirit of *Poetic Diction*, one captured kindly and well by his friend C. S. Lewis. "No one can fail to get the feeling you had when you wrote it," Lewis wrote to him, "or feel windows opening in all directions" (Lewis 2007, 1498). The mood of open exploration, of new planets swimming into his ken, was seemingly inspired by the spiritual kinship and gentle mutual regard that Barfield felt for Logan Pearsall Smith. In the afterword which Barfield added for the 1954 edition published by Faber & Faber (at a time, once again, when Barfield's work was championed by T. S. Eliot—Faber had published a second edition of *Poetic Diction* in 1951 and would publish *Saving the Appearances* in 1957), Barfield fondly recalls the benign, formative influence of Smith's *The English Language* (1912) and *Words and Idioms* (1925). He notes not merely that it remains "very difficult to speak too highly" of Smith's books but also the "more direct and personal help which I have been fortunate enough to receive from time to time from this distinguished writer" (*HEW* 217). *History in English Words* lacks a dedication, but it could easily have gone to Smith, and unlike Barfield's dedication of *Poetic Diction* to Lewis, their friendship would not have been memorialized as opposition. Barfield seems to have kept this regard for the whole of his life, recommending Smith's books to an audience of Coleridge scholars almost fifty years after the first appearance of *History in English Words* and nearly thirty years after Smith's death (Barfield 1974, 204). Barfield himself could have written the last sentences of *The English Language*:

> The change of thought from one generation to another does not depend so much on new discoveries as the gradual shifting, into the centre of vision, of ideas and feelings that had been but dimly realized before. And it is just this shifting from the background to the centre of thought, that is so important and yet so elusive, which is marked and dated in the history of language. When anything becomes important to us it finds its name; and in the history of these names in the English language can be traced many changes in English life, many developments of thought, which would yield a rich reward to patient and careful study. (Smith 1912, 250–1)

Barfield found in Smith, if not a mentor then at least a very close fellow traveler, who for a time was further along the same path as himself.

This is not to suggest that Barfield's account is derivative. Smith's claim in *The English Language* is that:

> language can give the most important aid to history; if we know what words were current and popular at a given period, what new terms were made or borrowed, and the new meanings that were attached to old ones, we become aware, in a curiously intimate way, of [the] interests of that period. (Smith 1912, 216)

For Barfield, this is true, but insufficient: the "curiously intimate" connection of thought to language reveals a deeper evolution of consciousness. Barfield builds upon Smith's efforts, and maintains the basic structure of Smith's fundamental book; but, he also supplements it with his own interest as a working poet and novelist in the connection of consciousness to poetry in general and to metaphor in particular.

History in English Words gives the impression of having had its planks planed and masts raised on the shores of a tropical harbor far from the choppy Atlantic seas of the "violently sincere" critical battles in which Barfield was engaged in the mid-1920s; but, Barfield developed some of the rudimentary insights of his book in his essays and reviews of the time. These include some of the essays, like "Ruin," which found their way into *Poetic Diction*. They also include a review of Smith's *English Idioms* (1923), in which Barfield describes Smith's earlier *The English Language* as "combining solidity with lightness" (Barfield 1923a, 370), a quality Barfield aimed for in *History in English Words*. Barfield's review, published a month before his dystopian postwar story "Dope" appeared in Eliot's *Criterion*, claims that "the average man has a miserably limited vocabulary and the miserably vague and watery consciousness which that implies" (Barfield 1923a, 368). The main focus of the review, though, is on the moment when "fresh" language becomes "dead," and the importance of continually refreshing the springs of language, so that the "average man" might have his lot improved.

Barfield takes a first step toward *History in English Words* in an earlier review of a collection of ballads edited by Hyder Rollins (whose greatest fame today is from his still-authoritative edition of Keats's letters). Barfield notes that ballads are more important than "the historical facts" if one wishes to truly understand the era in which they were written: "in them we have the spirit behind dates and genealogical trees. They are a cross-section of the history of a region—part of humanity's reaction to the Universe—and the cross-section marks every detail of the growth to that point" (Barfield 1920c, 702). In their very simplicity, they reflect that poets were once "capable of reacting directly to nature" (Barfield 1920c, 701). This is of course a Romantic cliché, at least as old as Friedrich

Schiller's distinction of naïve from sentimental poetry, but it is Barfield's first step, as an aspiring poet above all, toward a comprehensive picture of the significance of the history of poetry and of language behind it.

A year later, in a review of "Fourteenth Century Verse and Prose," Barfield asserts for the first time that with "no imaginative grasp" one cannot take hold of an earlier era like the English middle ages. Exercising this imagination, Barfield distinguishes as characteristic of that period that "in those days all philosophy and all knowledge lay enclosed in a simple framework of religious faith and could be grasped (with application) by one man in a lifetime" (Barfield 1921d, 78). More importantly, Barfield observes that:

> in the thirteenth and fourteenth centuries, the poetry that clustered thick about the Virgin became the core of a new attitude towards women.... There was a strange conflict of desires and a new word, "love-longing". We are so accustomed to the idea of a religious emotion in the sex-relationship that it is difficult to imagine a time when this was a new thing. (Barfield 1921d, 78)

Barfield was impressed enough by this revelation that he returned to it explicitly in *History in English Words*: "if there are occasions when a single word seems to throw more light on the workings of men's minds than a whole volume of history or a whole page of contemporary literature, the Middle English *love-longing* is certainly one of them" (*HEW* 125). As we shall see, this triumphant discovery by the medieval imagination is for Barfield one of the key moments in the history of the English sensibility and its evolving inner world.

Finally, in a review of a biography of James Boswell, Barfield sees the Scottish author as emblematic of the modern sensibility. Unlike, say, the authors of medieval ballads, "Boswell knew himself," not with an intuitive awareness of his spiritual essence but as a self-aware performance of "Boswell" (Barfield 1921c, 520). He was a "man who, being often fatuous, can yet appreciate and even enjoy his fatuity" (Barfield 1921c, 520). Hume famously described the mind as an empty stage across which impressions strolled to and fro; so too, "Boswell has dished up Boswell with supreme art" (Barfield 1921c, 520). Boswell is on the cutting edge of enlightenment modernity in being a supreme artist of self-aware self-dramatization.

History in English Words is of an altogether different order than these scattered impressions, systematic and complete where they offer hints and indications, though the hints find their way into the book. It is organized in two sections, "The English Nation" and "The Western Outlook," both of which cover the whole period from the Aryan invasion (as it was then called)[21] to the present. This structure copies Smith's *The English Language*, which also has two parts that offer two complete cycles from the first recorded language to the present, but Smith has an alternative vision that helps make clear where Barfield differs from his mentor. For Smith, the first part detailing external history is "its formal aspect" and its second part, recapitulating that history from within the histories of words, deals with "the thought of which . . . the English language . . . is the expression, and which fashions it for its instrument" (Smith 1912, 126). This is true for Barfield as well, but he makes two additions that subtly shift his account away from Smith's: first, he identifies metaphor as the essential catalyst in semantic change; second, he works with Coleridge's two tendencies—the "outer" world that expands infinitely and the "inner" world that seeks itself in the midst of that expansion—in his elaboration of the evolution of consciousness. Smith amasses a great deal of information regarding semantic change but lacks an explanation for it, and as a result is not able to describe very precisely what it is. He proposes that there is a "mysterious power which creates and changes language" that has been "vaguely defined, by the name of 'the Genius of Language'" (Smith 1912, 27). Vague or not, Smith accepts the phrase; one senses Schopenhauer's shadow brooding over Smith's description of it as "not a conscious or deliberate, but a corporate will" that is "often capricious in its working" and "illogical and childish" (Smith 1912, 26). Though Barfield too uses at one point the phrase "genius of the English language" (*HEW* 49), we shall see that he finds coherence, if not teleology, in the unfolding of the forces that drive the history of language as it shapes and reflects the underlying evolution of consciousness.

Barfield says in the first chapter of Part One that "language has preserved for us the inner, living history of man's soul. It reveals the evolution of consciousness" (*HEW* 14). In the first chapter of Part Two, Barfield confesses his dissatisfaction with the word "consciousness," preferring the German "Weltanschauung." Consciousness will do, he says, provided that it "is taken not simply in its finite sense, as 'the opposite of unconsciousness,' but rather as including a man's whole awareness of his environment, the sum total of his intellectual and emotional experiences as an individual" (*HEW* 86n). Perhaps with Weltanschauung in mind, Barfield also offers "outlook" as a way to capture the flickering quiddity, the evolution of which is evident in the fossil record of language:

> Like consciousness, this word must be taken here in its very widest, metaphorical sense, as of a human ego "looking out" upon the world through the windows of memory, recognition, the senses, etc., and of the cosmos it "sees" through those windows. It is obvious that the *outlook* of every individual will be slightly

different from that of every other, also that there will be a great difference between the average *outlook* of broad contemporary classes.... The widest gulf of all is likely to be that between the average outlooks of different historical periods. (*HEW* 83n)

Beyond fleshing out what Barfield means by "consciousness," this passage returns to the hermeneutic skepticism of "Milton and Metaphysics," where Barfield first asserts that consciousness evolves. Barfield is still wary of making the passage between individuals or eras too smooth—from center to circumference, every "outlook" is unique—but the *sine qua non* of language is that meanings, and therefore the horizons of outlooks, must be shared to some extent. "The very nature of language," he would later write, "makes a 'word-for-word correspondence' impossible" (Barfield 1961b, 73). Barfield retained skepticism about "word-for-word" translation throughout his life, but he gave up the more resolute skepticism of "Milton and Metaphysics" as he deepened his study of semiotics and linguistics. He still maintains that the relation of thought to language is "fluid and flickering" and that "it is impossible to fix a point in time, and then to cut a kind of cross-section, and define the exact relation between language and thought at that particular moment" (*HEW* 86). Even so, this recognition is balanced by Barfield's choice of "cosmos" rather than "universe" to represent the "outer," infinitely expanding world. For most people they are synonyms, but:

> as the words are used in this book ... we should say that there is only one *universe*, but as many *cosmoses* as there are individuals. In this way the word *cosmos* becomes a sort of tool with which we can detach, and objectify for the purposes of inspection, the purely subjective *consciousness* or *outlook*. (*HEW* 101n)

"Cosmos" is the circumference of which "consciousness" or "outlook" is the center; or, if you like, the meaning of which consciousness is the form; each responds to and molds the other—including, in our mechanomorphic age, the fiction of a "universe" wholly independent of our consciousness but nevertheless identical with it.

The "metaphorical sense" we must bring to both "outlook" and "consciousness" is a property of all semantic change. This is how one realizes the unknown in terms of the known:

> The English-sounding word, *spoil*, comes to us from a Latin term which once had no other meaning than to "strip a conquered foe of his arms". By entering with our imaginations into the biography of such a word, we catch glimpses of

civilization in primitive Rome. Agriculture and war, we feel, were the primary businesses of life, and it was to these that the Roman mind instinctively flew when it was casting about for some means of expressing a new abstract idea—of realizing the unknown in terms of the known. Not often could the warlike city afford to beat her swords into ploughshares, but she was constantly melting both implements into ideas. (*HEW* 35–6).

The rotting fruit, robbed of its riches, is a fallen warrior in a field. It is one of many examples in the book that remind us of "the simple yet striking truth that all knowledge which has been conveyed by means of speech to the reason has travelled in metaphors taken from man's own activities and from the solid things which he handles" (*HEW* 183–4). In the modern era, for example, much of our understanding of the body is laden with incorrigible mechanical metaphors—the heart is a "pump," the nerves send electrical "signals," the legs are "pistons," and so on—and just as we live by such metaphors, so too do we form new understandings by introducing new metaphors:

> We think by means of words, and we have to use the same ones for so many different thoughts that, as soon as new meanings have entered into one set, they creep into all our theories and begin to mould our whole cosmos; and from the theories they pass into more words, and so into our lives and institutions. (*HEW* 184)

Beyond the mechanomorphic way we think about our own bodies, Barfield offers many examples of how we think about our interpersonal relations, our societies, and our thinking. These changes are often due to the efforts of a "small" band of creative speakers (one thinks again of Coleridge's "clerisy" and Shelley's "unacknowledged legislators"). So, it was "the scientists who discovered the forces of electricity [who] actually made it possible for the human beings who came after them to have a slightly different idea, a slightly fuller consciousness of their relationship with one another. They made it possible to speak of the 'high tension' between them" (*HEW* 13). Likewise, "the language which is used by the theologians, philosophers, and scientists of Europe was the gradual creation of the thinkers of ancient Greece; and . . . without that language, the thoughts and feelings and impulses which it expresses could have no being" (*HEW* 36). This extends to the metaphorical terms in which we think of our societies, from "checks and balances" in the Constitution of the United States, to thinking of that document as "living."

Barfield himself makes liberal use of organic metaphors—language and thought are themselves alive. Bacon's *Advancement of Learning* is a harbinger of "the coming metamorphosis" (*HEW* 146) in English thought. "Language never ceases growing" and the Old Testament is "like a cross-section of its stem"

(*HEW* 111). In considering the transition from mythological to intellectual thinking, Barfield finds that "in a word here and a word there we trace but the final stages of a vast, age-long metamorphosis from the kind of outlook which we loosely describe as 'mythological' to the kind which we may describe equally loosely as 'intellectual thought'" (*HEW* 84). One could go on. Oswald Spengler's epoch-making *Decline of the West* appeared in English translation in the same year that Barfield published *History in English Words*. With its massive erudition and governing metaphor that civilizations are organisms, it is no wonder that Barfield revised *Poetic Diction* at a late stage in the light of Spengler's "profound and alarmingly learned study of the *historical* . . . relation between the prosaic and the poetic" (*PD* 12–13).

And yet, Barfield's historical vision, morphological though it may be, is unlike Spengler's because it does not necessarily include a death-stage or any qualitative evaluation of the different evolutionary stages of Western civilization. "We must remember," says Barfield:

> that the semantic histories of words merely inform us of changes which have actually occurred in a large number of minds or "outlooks". They tell us of what is earlier and what is later, but not of truth and error. In this direction all that a knowledge of them can do is to equip us a little better for forming opinions of our own. (*HEW* 181)

Barfield's vision of the evolution of Western consciousness is an anticipatory response to Spengler, countering in advance his sense of unavoidable doom with an opportunity for deeper self-knowledge and an enlivening of our capacity to imagine a health-bringing future. In this way, it responds—proleptically, once again—to a request Eliot made in *The Criterion* in June and August 1927, the year after *History in English Words* appeared:[22] first, in June 1927 Eliot writes that we "cannot altogether accept so Spenglerish a point of view . . . [and] assume as axiomatic the statement that *tout est foutu*" (Eliot 2021 3, 100). Again, in August, with Spengler and others in mind, Eliot called for "a small number of intelligent persons" to work toward:

> the reaffirmation of the European tradition. It will be helpful, certainly, if people will begin by believing that there is a European tradition; for they may then proceed to analyse its constituents in the various nations of Europe; and proceed finally to the further formation of such a tradition. (Eliot 2021 3, 156–7).

Barfield answers this call in a deeper way than Eliot invites, by locating national traditions at the cellular level of individual words and their histories, tracing their emergence and evolution for the help that they can give "to equip us a little better for forming opinions of our own."

A detailed account of *History in English Words* would require a study in itself. But, the chapter titles to Part Two help us to understand that Barfield sees the unfolding history of Western consciousness as being like the self-division of a cell. First, there is the "living unity" of "myth," which then divides into its inner and outer aspects as "philosophy" and "religion"; this in turn further divides, the "inner" pole deepening into "devotion" as the "outer" one morphs into "experiment." These deepen still further into "personality" and "reason," respectively, with a final polarity of "imagination" and "mechanism" at the end. It is not difficult to see in this what Barfield calls in *Poetic Diction* the poetic and prosaic principles: the two principles, relatively undifferentiated in myth, then work progressively from philosophy to imagination via devotion and personality on one side, and from religion to mechanism via experiment and reason on the other. In short, it charts the division of the "living unity" of myth into the increasingly separated "outlook" and "cosmos." Let us now examine briefly a few aspects of this scheme, focusing on "myth," "devotion," "mechanism," and "imagination" in particular.

Barfield's treatment of "myth" gives us a prototypical picture of his method. In Chapter One of the book he gives the "external" view of Aryan invaders as having "something dynamic, some organic, out-pushing quality" (*HEW* 22). Among their hobbies are "brutality" and "mead" (*HEW* 25). We begin to see shelters take shape:

> The connection of the word *bed* with the Latin stem "fod-" (fodio), "to dig", should prevent us from forming an unduly voluptuous image of the final stages of this prehistoric pastime. If we call up before us a roof and walls of wood or wattles . . . lit only by a draughty hole in the roof—an arrangement which the Teutons were evidently trying to express when they afterwards dubbed it a "wind's eye" or *window*—we have a picture which will serve. (*HEW* 26)

In this way, across hundreds of words, Barfield presents a picture of the "external" unfolding of European civilizations, as evidenced in the development and adaptation of words to new technologies and cultural developments.

More germane, though, is the "inner" picture that he builds in Part Two of his book. In the corresponding chapter on "myth," for example, Barfield explains that the period in which the Aryans form their brutal yet dynamic culture is also one in which "the farther back language as a whole is traced, the more poetical and animated do its sources appear, until it seems at last to dissolve into a kind of mist of myth" (*HEW* 83–4)—one thinks again of Shelley's "chaos of a cyclic poem." In this misty but unified consciousness, "the beneficence or malignance—what may be called the soul-qualities—of natural phenomena, such as clouds or plants or animals, make a more vivid impression at this time than their outer shapes and appearances. Words themselves are felt to be alive and to exert a magical influence" (*HEW* 84). As the Aryans built their "wind's-eyes," they "looked up to the blue vault [and] they felt that they saw not merely a place, whether heavenly or earthly, but the bodily vesture, as it were, of a living Being" (*HEW* 85).[23] We cannot know exactly when "the thought of 'sky' may have been quite separated in the average Aryan mind from the thought of 'God'" (*HEW* 85–6) but that moment marks emblematically the first split of "living unity" into spirit and matter, inner and outer, center and circumference.

Barfield's chapter on "devotion" explores a further development of the experience of divinity, even as subject and object move farther apart. It begins with a long excerpt from Shelley's "Defence" that offers a highly compressed account of the origin, essence, and effects of the Courtly Love tradition. It is the product of "huge shadowy movements [that] were taking place deep down in the wills and imaginations of men," as reflected in "the meanings and associations of all those Latin words which were subsequently to come into our language" (*HEW* 119–20).[24] Take "conscience" as an example:

> It is particularly interesting to note the appearance of *conscience* in the thirteenth century. In classical times the Latin "conscientia" seems to have meant something more like "consciousness" or "knowledge"; it was generally qualified by some other word ("virtutum, vitiorum"—"consciousness of virtues, of vices," ...), and its termination, similar to that of *science, intelligence*, ... suggests that it was conceived of by the Romans more as a general, *abstract* quality, which one would partake of, but not actually possess—just as one has knowledge or happiness, but not "a knowledge" or "a happiness". Used in ecclesiastical Latin and later in English, *conscience* seems to have grown more and more real, until at last it became that semi-personified and perfectly private mentor whom we are inclined to mean today when we speak of "my *conscience*" or "his *conscience*".
> (*HEW* 128)

I quote so long a passage because it is a good illustration of Barfield's method, and because it pinpoints what was for Barfield a pivotal moment in the evolution of Western consciousness. This moment marks, on the one hand, the development of "individualism," of a knowable and worthwhile inner space, that did not exist in the same way in the ancient world; and reflects, on the other hand, the influence of Mariology and the tenderness that extended to women and children:

> Just as lyrical devotion to the Virgin Mary and to the infant Jesus had helped to evolve a vocabulary which could express, and thus partly create, a sentiment of tenderness towards all women and young children, so we seem to feel the warmth of human affection, as it were, reflected back into religious emotion in such creations as Coverdale's *lovingkindness* and *tender mercy*, Tindale's *long-suffering, mercifulness, peacemaker*, and *beautiful* (for it was he who brought this word to general use). (*HEW* 126–7)

This new appreciation of women and children, and the personal possession of a conscience, are themselves related to the "religion of love," part of a "new element [in] human relationships, for which perhaps the best name that can be found is 'tenderness'" (*HEW* 125). In the thirteenth and fourteenth centuries, this was a "new region of the imagination which the poets . . . of Europe were just discovering; we might call it the region of devotional love" (*HEW* 123).

Barfield's description of the emergence of "courtly love" is notable not only as a reminder of why Lewis dedicated *The Allegory of Love* to Barfield as "the best and wisest of my unofficial teachers," and not only for the greater sensitivity to tender interiority and the birth of romantic love; the felt sense of the alienation or dissociation of subject and object, word and meaning, is also coeval with it. It is not complete, but it has begun: the heavens were no longer felt actually to be the Divine itself, but "the stars and the planets were also living bodies; they were composed of that 'fifth essence' or *quintessence*, which was likewise latent in all terrestrial things, so that the character and the fate of men were determined by the *influences* (Latin 'influere', 'to flow in') which came from them" (*HEW* 137). Thus, "in spite of that strong and growing sense of the individual soul, man was not yet felt, either physically or psychically, to be isolated from his surrounding in the way he is today" (*HEW,* 135). Likewise, the debate between the Realists and the Nominalists had indeed begun, with the Nominalists coming to maintain not only that "universals had no separate or previous existence" but also that "these universals did not exist at all, that they were mere intellectual abstractions or classifications made by the human mind—in fact, 'ideas' in the sense in which, owing to them, we use the word today" (*HEW* 131). This debate, in other words, is the beginning of the process that runs from Ockham to Locke, and on to Müller and the triumph of Russell's "logical atomism." In *Poetic Diction*, Barfield again returns to this medieval debate and says he "would fix on the prominence in men's minds of the metaphysical problem of 'universals'" as the moment in which "the ascending rational principle and the descending poetic principle . . . are passing one another" (*PD* 94).[25] By the end of the Middle Ages, then, we can see an inner world opening up for discovery even as the outer world recedes into otherness:

> When we reflect on the history of such notions as *humour, influence, melancholy, temper*, and the rest, it seems for the moment as though some invisible sorcerer had been conjuring them all inside ourselves—sucking them away from the planets, away from the outside world, away from our own warm flesh and blood, down into the shadowy realm of thoughts and feelings. There they still repose; astrology has changed to astronomy; alchemy to chemistry; today the cold stars glitter unapproachable overhead, and with a naïve detachment mind watches matter moving incomprehensibly in the void. At last, after four centuries, thought has shaken herself free. (*HEW* 138)

Barfield fills out the picture of our experience of the world today in his chapters on "mechanism" and "imagination." The flowering of the prosaic principle into contemporary ubiquity means that we view the body as a machine and the quantifiable as the true. We live now in a "new cosmos—a complex of matter and forces proceeding mechanically from spiral nebula to everlasting ice" (*HEW* 192). And yet, concomitant with the reduction of cosmos to machine is the "curious" fact that "the erection within men's imaginations of this severely mechanical framework for themselves was accompanied by, and may have been partly responsible for, an increase in their sense of self-consciousness. The more automatic the cosmos, apparently, the more the vital ego must needs feel itself detached" (*HEW* 192). We have returned, once again, to our beginning: the postwar recognition that the Western world had arrived at universal catastrophe, the sense of homelessness, Pound's toothless old bitch, Eliot's anarchic futility, Lawrence's lost Atlantis, and the rest. Before the war, Logan Pearsall Smith had painted a similar picture of modernity as experiencing a "growing sense of individuality and self-consciousness" (Smith 1912, 249) while finding that "our modern universe is a vast process of ordered change and regular development . . . formed in a moment out of nothing, and destined to end as suddenly as it began" (Smith 1912, 231).

Barfield's account of contemporary consciousness focuses on moral vocabulary. The sense of devotional love is mostly gone, replaced by the new reality that "we are hardly conscious at all of being *human*, more so of being *humane*, more still of being *humanitarian*, and very conscious indeed of *humanitarianism*" (*HEW* 193). The irony built into the triumph of nominalism is that as "universals" become shadowy specters, the only terms in which the alienated individual can reflect on itself are precisely the most abstract terms available; meanwhile, the individual—stripped of all terms denoting essence—cannot give up a felt sense of vulnerable yet inalienable integrity. The term "self-respect" is born, but "the Christian vocabulary of the human and social virtues—*charity, lovingkindness, mercy, pity* and the like" begin to fade as "now more of a *political* autonomy" takes over, built around such words as "*humane, humanity,* and *humanitarian*" (*HEW* 195). "We are constrained to ask a little sadly," says Barfield, about "what had become of a certain sunny element, a suppressed poetic energy, a wonder and wild surprise, which lurks in the former words, but somehow—with all respect for them—not in the latter" (*HEW* 195).

The draining of the "wild surprise" of meaning from our experience of moral vocabulary is a great contemporary danger, which helped to convince Barfield that the Romantic impulse must be renewed:

> Let us remember that every time we abuse these terms, or use them too lightly, we are draining them of their power; every time a society journalist or a film producer exploits this vast suggestiveness to tickle a vanity or dignify a lust, he is squandering a great pile of spiritual capital which has been laid up by centuries of weary effort. (*HEW* 153)

We are back to the "crisis of language," the god locked in the stone. Our insensitivity to the power in words like "beauty" (the subject of Barfield's invective in this passage) or "mercy" parallels the need that gave rise to the courtly love tradition. Just as there opened a "new region of the imagination" that disclosed things like "tenderness" and "lovingkindness" so too is there a new need today for a rich vocabulary to express individual creative capacities. As Lawrence appreciated in his search for "dark depths," the Romantics "brought up to the surface of consciousness that vast new cosmos which had so long been blindly forming in the depths. It was a cosmos in which the spirit and spontaneity of life had moved out of Nature and into man" (*HEW* 212).

This is why Barfield makes "the semantic development of two more words . . . *fancy* and *imagination* . . . the last examined in this book" (*HEW* 208), just as he ended *Poetic Diction* by emphasizing that Coleridge's "distinction between Fancy and Imagination . . . ought to be particularly emphasized in an age like ours" (*PD* 202). We are on the cusp of discovering within ourselves the vast creative power that we once experienced in the god-sky that used to bend above us; the Romantics discovered that "this re-animation of Nature was possible because the imagination was felt as *creative* in the full religious sense of the word" (*HEW* 213). Here too Barfield steps aside from Smith, for whom the Romantics were more remarkable for "the growth of a romantic and sentimental attitude towards bygone ages" as reflected in the "romantic glamour" that surrounds "these words of the Romantic revival—*chivalry, chivalrous, minstrel, bard*, etc." (Smith 1912, 229). For Barfield, on the contrary, the Romantic practice of reviving "that despised habit of looking at life through the spectacles of the old Romances, the mysterious faculty of superimposing on Nature a magical colour or mood" is a revival in modern form of Vico's *sapienza poetica*, "of Nature impassioned by any effluence arising from within" (*HEW* 211).

Imagination is "the power of creating from within forms which themselves become a part of Nature" (*HEW* 211)—the tendency to find oneself in the midst of infinite expansion itself becomes the infinite expansion in which one finds oneself. The distinctively modern form of the old instinctive consciousness is that "the perception of Nature—that is to say of all in Nature that is not purely mechanical—depends upon what is brought to it by the observer. Deep must call unto deep" (*HEW* 211). We must bring up into consciousness from Lawrence's dark depths the "spirit of poetry" that hovers "above language," but with a "throbbing, feathery warmth" within "our startled souls" (*PD* 181).[26] The solution to the sense of homelessness is to recognize that "home" is a verb, and to speak it. As Barfield finished his first phase as a critic and his first major poem, *The Tower*, he made his first step in appreciating and advocating for the divinity of nature, of overcoming our dissociation from it, ourselves, and each other; of awakening and recognizing "the god within the stone" in the form of our enlivened, concrete thinking; and of finding there the "holy awe" with which we "must now set out to explore this world" (*HEW* 216).

2

The Texture of Thought
The Evolution of Consciousness

In the decades that followed the development by Barfield of his poetics, he put serious effort into clarifying and deepening its implications for the evolution of consciousness, metaphysics, Anthroposophy, and moral-political philosophy. His work as a poet and novelist was crucial to him as he developed his poetic philosophy, and his philosophy must be understood as an integrated whole. One cannot adequately explore Barfield's understanding of the evolution of consciousness, which late in life he called "my major theme" (*ABS* 173), without considering its metaphysical underpinnings and its fuller realization in the poetic cosmology he developed out of it. Nor can we consider these topics in arid abstraction, as they crystallize in urgent practical issues of social and political concern. For example, Barfield's definitions of "evolution" and "consciousness" necessarily involve metaphysical discussions of the self, ideas, continuity, temporality, and so on. Likewise, Barfield stressed repeatedly that for those wishing "to move on from history of ideas and into evolution of consciousness" there is as yet "nowhere to go outside the works of Rudolf Steiner" due to his "full treatment of the subject, both extensive and intensive, clearly based on his actual *knowledge* of it" (*HGH* 65–6). The goal of this chapter is to explore how Barfield's understanding of the evolution of consciousness deepened in the decades after *History in English Words* as he grew to better understand the philosophical context and implications of the concept "evolution of consciousness."[1]

When Barfield noted in 1923 that "human consciousness evolves" (Barfield 1923c, 524), he may not have realized that nearly seventy years later he would pinpoint this as "*the* theme" (Schenkel) of his works. We have already seen how important it is to his theory of meaning, though Barfield would later say, with too much humility, that *History in English Words* was a "slight attempt" (*SM* 25).

As we saw in the previous chapter, Barfield introduced the phrase "evolution of consciousness" in that book:

> [T]here is a difference between the record of the rocks and the secrets which are hidden in language: whereas the former can only give us a knowledge of outward, dead things—such as forgotten seas and the bodily shapes of prehistoric animals and primitive men—language has preserved for us the inner, living history of man's soul. It reveals the evolution of consciousness. (*HEW* 9)

Barfield nicely captures here one of the central themes in the books he would write in the decades to follow, even as he points to what makes the idea "evolution of consciousness" difficult to clarify—what is the relation of the "inner" evolution of consciousness to "outward" geological and biological evolution, of consciousness to language, of evolution to history? Are there two evolutions, of consciousness and nature, that develop on different tracks, or a single process with two aspects? If there are two evolutions and they correlate with natural and historical sciences, do those disciplines have methodologies and foundations appropriate to each, or is one a subset of the other? These questions grew in urgency and importance for Barfield with each new decade, and as the twentieth century unfolded he correlated it with another phenomenon: that an increasing number of people could only answer the existential question "Do I exist?" with "uncertainty" and "anxiety" (Barfield 1970a, 54). Paralleling Martin Heidegger's exploration of the problem of technology as it relates to our alienation from the history of Being, Barfield considered the best remedy for the problem of modern industrial and postindustrial humanity's "paralyzing inability" to affirm the integrity of its own existence to be "the study of history" (Barfield 1970a, 57).

One way to approach the topic is to place "evolution of consciousness" at one end of a continuum with "anti-historicism" at the other, and "historicism" and "history of ideas" midway between the poles, historicism placed closer to evolution of consciousness and history of ideas closer to anti-historicism. We will work our way across the spectrum, beginning with those views that Barfield did or would characterize as "anti-historicist"—contemporary New Historicism, C. S. Lewis's broadside attack on "Historicism," and Isaiah Berlin's more subtle critique of historiography as a discipline. We will then consider A. O. Lovejoy's justification of the "history of ideas" and R. G. Collingwood's "idea of history" before finally proceeding to Barfield's argument for why historical study presupposes and requires that the "evolution of consciousness" is a discreet domain of inquiry.

1. Anti-Historicism

Anti-historicist arguments deny or strongly qualify the legitimacy and coherence of historicism and the evolution of consciousness. C. S. Lewis and Isaiah Berlin offer two such arguments, which we will consider in a moment. Contemporary anti-historicists claim that cultural production arises from, and is finally reducible to, the material conditions of its appearance. As H. Aram Veeser puts it, among the "key assumptions [that] continually reappear and bind together the practitioners" of New Historicism is that "every expressive act is embedded in a network of material practices" (Veeser xiv). Indeed, this is so true that every expressive act is not merely embedded in material practices, but is itself an expression of them—for the thoroughly consistent anti-historicist, there is no expressive act that exists apart from, or that is not itself produced by, underlying material practices. This reduction entails that they eschew the vast narrative scope of projects like those of, say, Toynbee and Spengler because all the tiny bits of historical detritus that do not fit narratives like theirs are left out, as is the recognition of the extent to which their own ideological commitments shape their narratives, so we lose a textured appreciation of all the anecdotal, objective features of the periods they cover. In fact, for the New Historicist there are no true "master narratives" because there are no ideas apart from ideologies, which are themselves epiphenomenal by-products of the visceral struggles that animate concrete physical existence. Ernst Behler cogently expresses this fragile, for Barfield doomed, effort to simultaneously embrace and elude materialism:

> What appeared to be the final basis of our structures of knowledge, moral, social, and political activities, and aesthetic creations as well as enjoyments, that is, human reality, transcendental subjectivity, becomes involved in a bewildering sort of questioning and appears to be predetermined by supraindividual and transsubjective constellations of power. These predeterminations devaluate the seemingly primary principle of subjectivity to a completely secondary entity, an incidental effect in the discursive formation of epochs, a predetermined glance at the world which is codified by preestablished sequences in the mobile system of signs, discourses, institutions, and canons. (Behler 1990, 31)

Much recent historical theory implies, when it does not state directly, that one could fully reduce ideas and subjectivity itself to materially conditioned constellations of power if only one pushed one's analyses far enough, but for Barfield such a reduction is impossible, even in theory, because the historical subject (in both senses of the term) vanishes in the process. After all, one cannot describe the social context of Shakespeare's sonnets, Napoleon's invasion of Russia, or Caesar's crossing of the Rubicon (a river not to be found on any map), without referring to ideas as proper subjects of discussion in their own right. And if one cannot do so, then not only can theory and practice not be brought into alignment, but theory itself cannot be made self-consistent. When Barfield says of Wittgenstein's anti-referential "language games" that "one could perhaps point out that the very term 'self-referring' owes any significance it could possibly have to the fact that language is *not* merely self-referring" (*RM* 136-137) one could as easily apply it to the reduction of meaning as a whole to power relations. Constellations of power are only knowable or meaningful from a perspective outside of them. If Wittgenstein invokes "Silence" where the New Historicist invokes "Power," we might add with Barfield that "if there is a silence of sublimity, there is also a silence of idiocy" (*RM* 137).

C. S. Lewis is unlike a contemporary anti-historicist in almost every way, except that his anti-historicism is also vigorous. Lewis is not concerned with reducing historical events to physical conditions or constellations of power, but with demonstrating the inability to infer divine plans from historical events by proving the inscrutability of history itself. Lewis begin his essay "Historicism" (1950) with a distinction similar to one Berlin would later make. The "historian" is a modest inquirer after motives and ideas who will "find causal connections between historical events" and "may certainly infer unknown events from known ones" (Lewis 1967, 125). The Historicist (with a capital "H") is far more ambitious, and dangerously misguided. Historicists adhere "to the belief that men can, by the use of their natural powers, discover an inner meaning in the historical process" (Lewis 1967, 124). The key words in this definition are "inner meaning" and "process." Lewis marshals a number of reasons to oppose the supposed salience of either of them, making accidental common cause with the contemporary anti-historicist, for whom all meanings are "outer" and all processes contingent. So too, for Lewis historical work is based on the inherent and accidental incompleteness of the evidence: inherent because an "inner meaning" requires a totality, and history can only, under the best circumstances, offer a partial picture of the infinite number of the micro-moments that make up the past, and not the totality of human existence that would explain the teleological import of the past with reference to the future; and accidentally, because we have as historical evidence only the contingent fragments that happen to have survived long enough to be haphazardly dug up and brushed clean by our little hands. In the end, we have only "those fragments, copies of fragments, copies of copies of fragments, or floating reminiscences of copies of copies, which are, unhappily, confounded under the general name of *history*" (Lewis 1967, 140).

Barfield responded to Lewis's frontal assault on Historicism in an address to the C. S. Lewis Society of New York. His tone reflects annoyed bemusement, asking "can Lewis seriously believe this?" Barfield's own approach to history, after all, is precisely to explore its inner meaning as a process. Lewis's essay swings a wrecking ball at Barfield's entire career and worldview. What, then, to make of Lewis's frequent claim that he learned much from Barfield—"What exactly *am* I deemed to have 'taught' C. S. Lewis?," Barfield asks. In fact, more pointedly—and in an unwitting echo of Eliot's famous question to Pound—"What did Lewis really believe?" (Barfield 1989, 73), considering that much of Lewis's own work is built upon Historicist foundations, as defined by Lewis himself.

In reply, Barfield refers his readers to R. G. Collingwood, who shows that "the proper study of history is not, as was assumed in the nineteenth century, a branch of natural science but is a parallel discipline, and one not primarily dependent on the inductive method" (Barfield 1989, 69). Lewis's reduction of historical practice to causal inferences makes it something akin to biology. Barfield unfairly aims this accusation at Berlin in a different context, but it hits the mark with Lewis. If paucity of evidence and the incompleteness of time are the reasons historical knowledge is an oxymoron, Lewis has misunderstood the nature of history. More to the point, though, and as Berlin also clearly understood, the collapse of historical study into the natural sciences conceals a deeper epistemological question:

> Is the only reliable knowledge we can claim always of a staccato succession and causality, never of growth and metamorphosis? All really depends on that epistemological issue. It sounds dry enough, and many of his students will perhaps think it only marginally interesting—until I have enumerated some of the other issues with which it is integrally bonded. (Barfield 1989, 77)

The core "epistemological issue" of whether it is possible to have knowledge of "growth and metamorphosis" also arises in the much more nuanced and philosophically subtle "anti-historicist" historiography of Isaiah Berlin.

Considering that Berlin's name is nearly identified with the "history of ideas," it requires some effort to clarify why Barfield considered him "anti-historicist" at all. Barfield singled out Berlin and Trevor Roper as he attempted to isolate the key features of the "new science" of history:

> Surely it is just such a change in the whole concept of time—or the relation between present, past and future—which the "new science" so desperately

> needs before it can come into its own. "Historicism," without it, leads only to one or another kind of determinism. It leads to those procrustean efforts which we have witnessed from one side and another, to fit history into a system of "laws" analogous to the so-called laws of nature. It is this kind of historicism—exemplified in Spengler and Toynbee—which has recently been attacked with caustic vigour over here by Trevor Roper and Isaiah Berlin; and it is the only kind of historicism they can conceive of. Yet Collingwood pointed clearly enough to the requirements of a true historicism. He showed . . . how its first beginnings have been cramped and distorted by the preponderance of the biological theory of evolution and the consequent assumption that "laws," like those of natural science, must apply to the evolution of man. Whereas in fact the science of man and the science of nature are two different branches of knowledge, requiring an altogether different methodology. (Barfield 1958, 8)

As he does with Lewis, Barfield refers to Collingwood as a corrective to the mistaken anti-historicism of Berlin. Barfield may also be guilty of too hasty a reading of Berlin, though he can be excused for not knowing it yet.[2] Berlin wrote what remains the most popular and influential account in English of Giambattista Vico's thought, and Vico first made the distinction between natural and historical sciences to which Barfield believes Berlin is oblivious. Though Berlin rejects the historical methods and assumptions of Spengler and Toynbee, as Lewis did before him, he not only can conceive of Collingwood's historiography, he was Collingwood's most impressionable and talented student. As Peter Skagestad has demonstrated, building on the research of Michael Ignatieff, "Berlin attended Collingwood's lectures on the philosophy of history in 1931, and Collingwood became the single strongest influence, from the student years, on the subsequent development of Berlin's thinking" (Skagestad 99). This influence is especially strong in "Berlin's later preoccupation with the history of ideas" (Skagestad 100), in Berlin's qualified acceptance of Collingwood's "doctrine of history as the reenactment of past thought" (Skagestad 100), and in the "less obvious link" that "in the study of Enlightenment and Romanticism that was the central project of Berlin's life Berlin was in effect practicing the analysis of 'absolute presuppositions' which Collingwood had prescribed as the province of metaphysics" (Skagestad 100).

In presenting Collingwood's claims that "historical knowledge is the only knowledge the human mind can have of itself" and that "at bottom, [the historian] is concerned with thoughts alone," Skagestad finds Collingwood "highly reminiscent" of Berlin's claims in 1960 that historical reasoning involves "the attempt to capture concepts and categories that differ from those of the investigator by means of concepts and categories that cannot but be his own" (Skagestad 102). However, Berlin saw his position as distinct from Collingwood's. For example, in 1983 he attributed to Hegel and Collingwood the idea that "human history is ... solely an account of human experience or stages of consciousness" (Berlin 1990, 64). Skagestad is content to correct Berlin's semantics: Collingwood only says that "all history is the history of human thought," not consciousness. As Skagestad himself shows, though, Collingwood equates "thought" with "mind," and it is not obvious in what nontrivial way "the human mind" and "consciousness" differ for Collingwood. Berlin's careful shift from "the human mind" to "concepts and categories" seems to be part of his effort to avoid what he elsewhere describes as "the quasi-mystical act of literal self-identification with another mind and age of which Collingwood evidently thought himself capable" (Berlin 2000, 119; quoted in Skagestad 104). Skagestad accuses Berlin of showing "an uncharacteristic lack of understanding of his one-time master" (Skagestad 104) in this description, but Barfield would probably find it accurate. Berlin distances himself from Collingwood's lingering idealism, softening his "quasi-mysticism" with the analytical tools developed by friends like A. J. Ayer. For Barfield, the upshot of Berlin's reframing of Collingwood is to rule out of bounds the proper subject of history, consciousness, while also limiting the investigation of "evolution" only to the natural sciences. If one accepts Berlin's reframing of Collingwood, the idea "evolution of consciousness" becomes "quasi-mystical" and specious.

Berlin made all of these distinctions beginning in 1960, though, and Barfield referred to Berlin's "caustic vigour" in 1958. He probably had in mind Berlin's long essay "Historical Inevitability," which began as the first memorial Auguste Comte lecture before being published by Oxford University Press as a slim volume in 1955. Berlin begins his essay by distinguishing two prominent *genera* of historians, those who maintain that historical explanations ultimately reduce to "questions of the character, purposes and motives of individuals" and those who "are committed ... to tracing the ultimate responsibility for what happens to the acts or behaviour of impersonal or 'transpersonal' or 'super-personal' entities or 'forces' whose evolution is identified with human history" (Berlin 2002, 97–8). This is the essentially the same distinction made by Lewis. The thrust of Berlin's essay is that the latter school is not only untenable, but has malign effects in the political and ethical spheres. Berlin traces the roots of this view to the idealistic philosophies of Herder, Schelling, and Hegel.

Barfield would undoubtedly have recognized himself as belonging to the group Berlin targets for his sustained critique. According to Berlin, the holist position is:

> that the world has a direction and is governed by laws, and that the direction and the laws can in some degree be discovered by employing the proper techniques of investigation; and moreover that the working of these laws can only be grasped by those who realise that the lives, characters and acts of individuals, both mental and physical, are governed by the larger "wholes" to which they belong, and that it is the independent evolution of these "wholes" that constitutes the so-called "forces" in terms of whose direction truly "scientific" (or "philosophic") history must be formulated.... Ideas about the identity of these large entities or forces, and their functions, differ from theorist to theorist. Race, colour, Church, nation, class; ... the Human Spirit, the Collective Unconscious, to take some of these concepts at random, have all played their parts in theologico-historical systems as the protagonists upon the stage of history. They are represented as the real forces of which individuals are ingredients, at once constitutive, and the most articulate expressions, of this or that phase of them. (Berlin 2002, 114–15)

Barfield very likely saw his own view reflected here, though in a glass darkly. His argument that individuals emerge out of a background of social or tribal collective consciousness and the "theologico-historical" scheme of *Saving the Appearances*, on which he was working in 1955, require some defense against Berlin's charges. This is especially so because Berlin draws the moral conclusion that his view of history "transfer[s] responsibility for what happens from the backs of individuals to the casual or teleological operation of institutions or cultures or psychical or physical factors" (Berlin 2002, 118). Those who maintain "belief in the primacy of collective patterns" soon find themselves sliding from "benevolent internationalists like Herder" to "ferocious champions of national or racial self-assertion and war, like Gobineau or Houston Steward Chamberlain or Hitler" (Berlin 2002, 100).

Aside from the shadow of fascism that hovers over idealist historiography, Berlin also charges it with maintaining a "teleological outlook" (Berlin 2002, 104), seeing evil as frustrated fulfillment, being "profoundly anti-empirical" (Berlin 2002, 105), appealing to "a timeless, permanent, transcendent reality, 'above', or 'outside', or 'beyond'" (Berlin 2002, 107), and as being too strongly influenced by the natural sciences, insofar as the idealist historian and the natural scientist both maintain that "to explain is to subsume under general formulae" (Berlin 2002, 109). It therefore entails, according to Berlin, a "deterministic hypothesis" (Berlin 2002, 124) that is at odds with freedom, relativity, inductive science, fallibility, and the messy, contingent randomness of much of daily existence. Berlin maintains, against the holists, that "man is, in principle at least, everywhere and in every condition, able, if he wills it, to discover and apply rational solutions to his problems" (Berlin 2002, 62). The work of the historian is to discover what "concepts and categories" were operative at any given time, and understand them in the light of their own. For Barfield, Berlin commits the same fallacy as the animist, in flattening evolving modes of consciousness into a permanent present: for example, do those eras and cultures, as recent in the West as the pre-Socratics, that lack the concepts "concepts" and "categories" make use of them in the same deliberate, self-aware way that we do? Barfield would undoubtedly find "concepts and categories" too meager a substitute for "mind" or "consciousness," for the same reasons that he finds the "history of ideas" a finally inadequate attempt to articulate the "evolution of consciousness." In both cases, an incipient dualism remains, and there is the unstated assumption that because physical existence precedes human existence, consciousness must evolve from matter, which correlates with the assumption that the "poetic" is a parasitic development of the "literal." For another version of dualism, we must turn to A. O. Lovejoy, the founder of the "history of ideas" as a discipline.

2. Lovejoy and the "History of Ideas"

The "history of ideas" is venerable enough that it thrives in its own right as an object of historical interest. Studies of it typically include discussion of the ways in which Lovejoy shaped the methodology of "history of ideas" investigations, even as they note that many of Lovejoy's methods and conclusions have been critiqued or abandoned.[3] Less often explored, however, are the philosophical underpinnings of Lovejoy's innovations—more specifically, the effect on his historical practice of what he calls "the epistemological dualism of the theory of representative perception, and the psychophysical dualism which conceives empirical reality to fall asunder into a world of mind and a world of matter mutually exclusive and utterly antithetic" (Lovejoy 3). Lovejoy's philosophical self-awareness makes him especially useful in clarifying why Barfield's views and practices differ from his own, and why he distances himself from those who study the "history of ideas."

Lovejoy defends dualism with regard to the present object, the past or future object, and the minds of others. So, for example, I cannot have direct knowledge of present objects because my awareness of them can only be by means of my mediating sense organs. Saying that I perceive an object amounts to saying that it is a:

> partial or symbolic reproduction in the awareness of a cognitive organism which is at the same time capable of thinking of some general scheme or order in which

existences have separate and mutually exclusive situations, and of referring attributes to the data of which it is directly aware to external situations in the world. (Lovejoy 316)

Furthermore, for Lovejoy the dualism of the present object applies with still greater force to past and future objects. These have a twofold split, as it were: as formerly or possibly present, they have the duality of present objects, but the intervention of temporal distance further divides them from present, unmediated awareness. The conclusion that each of these supporting points compels is that "ideas" themselves originate as private abstractions from equally private sense data. It is not necessary to review Lovejoy's baroque theory of "unit-ideas" and how they are supposed to hook onto the external world. We need only note that Lovejoy assumes that we form ideas about a "given" world of sensations that must in the long run correspond to it. The dichotomy he presents—either the world is deduced from our postulates or our postulates must conform to the world—leaves no room for a third possibility, embraced by Collingwood and Barfield (though to different degrees): namely, that "empirical reality," our percepts, cannot finally be disentangled from the "postulates," or concepts, we bring to or discover within it. For Barfield, the inability to grasp this third possibility is due to the:

> terribly obsessive, and terribly contemporary, fallacy which supposes that we must only *distinguish* things that we are also able to *divide*. . . . [T]here are many things that, by reason of their interpenetration—I repeat, because of their *interpenetration*—cannot be divided, though they are easily distinguished. . . . [F]or human consciousness as it is today, thinking and perceiving come within that class. (*HGH* 7)

From the perspective of Barfield and Collingwood, Lovejoy becomes entangled because he assumes that we first approach "empirical reality" as sensations, innocent of what Berlin calls the "concepts and categories" constitutive of, and made available by, thinking.

3. Collingwood and the "Idea of History"

Setting Collingwood's alternative notions of "absolute presuppositions" and the "idea of history" against Berlin's "concepts and categories" and Lovejoy's "historiography of ideas" helps to highlight Collingwood's advancement of our understanding of history. Collingwood's main philosophical influences were

Hegel and Croce, thinkers very far removed from Lovejoy's neo-Lockean dualism or Berlin's powerful affinity for logical positivism, complex, highly qualified and nuanced as that is. Historical judgments of any kind, Collingwood says, are different from judgments about nature. Nature consists wholly of "events" while history consists of "acts," the difference being that "in the case of nature, [the] distinction between the outside and the inside of an event does not arise. The events of nature are mere events, not the acts of agents whose thought the scientist endeavours to trace" (Collingwood 1946, 214). The historian, by contrast:

> investigating any event in the past, makes a distinction between what may be called the outside and the inside of an event. By the outside of the event I mean everything belonging to it which can be described in terms of bodies and their movements. . . . By the inside of the event I mean that in it which can only be described in terms of thought. . . . The historian is never concerned with either of these to the exclusion of the other. He is investigating not mere events . . . but actions, and an action is the unity of the outside and the inside of an event. (Collingwood 1946, 213)

We have already seen that Barfield points to precisely this distinction in his objection to Berlin, erroneously believing that Berlin denies it. There is an uneasy tension in Collingwood's views of this subject, though: for while Collingwood wants to maintain an explanatory balance of the "inner" and "outer" portions of the historical act, he also seems to emphasize the inner to the point of excluding the outer. For example, Collingwood argues that:

> thought is therefore not the presupposition of an historical process which is in turn the presupposition of historical knowledge. It is only in the historical process, the process of thoughts, that thought exists at all; and it is only in so far as this process is known for a process of thoughts that it is one. (Collingwood 1946, 227)

The outer half of the event melts away here in the expansion of the history of thought into history as such. This process becomes essentially complete when Collingwood shows that "there are for historical thought no fixed points thus given: in other words, [. . .] in history, just as there are properly speaking no authorities, so there are properly speaking no data" (Collingwood 1946, 227). From this Collingwood concludes that:

> freed from its dependence on fixed points supplied from without, the historian's picture of the past is thus in every detail an imaginary picture, and its necessity is at every point the necessity of the *a priori* imagination. Whatever goes into

it, goes into it not because his imagination passively accepts it, but because it actively demands it. (Collingwood 1946, 245)

It would be unfair to say that Collingwood is simply inconsistent here—everything depends on what he means by the "*a priori* imagination" and the relation of imagination to perception and the "outer" event—though he does seem to insist, as he most famously puts it, and as Barfield was fond of quoting, that "all history is the history of thought" (Collingwood 1946, 115).

And yet, as William Dray has shown, "it is clear that, far from considering an agent's explanatory thoughts as unobservable entities, [Collingwood] regarded them as having no existence at all apart from events in the agent's life, which could be regarded as expressing them" (Dray 39–40). Dray, addressing "the inside-outside metaphor [that] has bothered some critics of Collingwood a great deal" (Dray 38), notes in particular Collingwood's "vigorous attack on what he calls the 'metaphysical' theory of mind—the conception of it as non-physical substance rather than as a complex of activities" (Dray 40). Dray says that Collingwood offers only a "sketch" for a philosophy of mind (one that Dray believes is similar to Gilbert Ryle's), and indeed Dray attempts for good reason to minimize the importance of the "inside-outside metaphor" that is at the heart of "re-enactment." Because for Collingwood it is only when the historian "discern[s] the thoughts which he is trying to discover" that he is able to "re-think them in his own mind," one must conclude that "the history of thought, and therefore all history, is the re-enactment of the past thought in the historian's own mind" (Collingwood 1946, 215). Dray struggles to reconcile Collingwood's apparently functionalist or materialist—in any event, anti-idealist—theory of mind with his claim that the historian does not just simulate or approximate the thoughts of, say, Caesar or Napoleon, but actually thinks the very same thoughts. As Collingwood puts it, "historical knowledge is the knowledge of what mind has done in the past, and at the same time it is the redoing of this, the perpetuation of past acts in the present" (Collingwood 1946, 218). Here we have a straightforwardly idealist, even Platonic, epistemology that Collingwood himself underscores:

> In a sense, these thoughts are no doubt themselves events happening in time; but since the only way in which the historian can discern them is by re-thinking them for himself, there is another sense, and one very important to the historian, in which they are not in time at all. . . . If Mr. Whitehead is justified in calling the right-angled triangle an eternal object, the same phrase is applicable to the Roman constitution. (Collingwood 1946, 217–8)

History is the history of thought, and thoughts, though they exist in time, are timeless and can be re-thought, re-enacted, as well by the historian as by the original thinker. All of this implies a metaphysic that demands that we know, for example, how such thoughts relate to "nature," which has no "inside" and yet seems to unfold in accordance with, and to be governed by, "thoughts" in the form of natural laws that regulate the behavior of physical objects.

In his final years, Collingwood put forward the outline of a metaphysic founded on the concept of "absolute presuppositions" that could resolve the looming threat of dualism. In the *Essay on Metaphysics*, Collingwood argues that metaphysics should be approached not as the search for the nature of reality or being, but instead as an effort to ascertain "absolute presuppositions." We have seen the appeal of this idea for Berlin, no doubt because it seems to promise a metaphysics free of "quasi-mysticism." Indeed, Collingwood defines as pseudo-metaphysics "the kind of nonsense which comes of thinking that (as the logicians say) supposing is one of the attitudes we can take towards a proposition, so that what is absolutely supposed must be either true or false. That kind of nonsense I call pseudo-metaphysics" (Collingwood 1940, 48). In his *Autobiography*, written shortly before his death, Collingwood offers another definition of metaphysics:

> Metaphysics . . . is no futile attempt at knowing what lies behind the limits of experience, but is primarily at any given time an attempt to discover what the people of that time believe about the world's general nature; such beliefs being the presuppositions of their "physics," that is, their inquiries into its detail. Secondarily, it is the attempt to discover the corresponding presuppositions of other peoples and times, and to follow the historical process by which one set of presuppositions has turned into another. (Collingwood 1939, 65–6)

Collingwood claims here that all thoughts are either conditioned or unconditioned, and that the former are conditioned by the questions to which they are answers (all conditioned thoughts are responses to explicit or implicit questions). Unconditioned thoughts are the presuppositions that allow one to form questions at all, and these absolute (because unconditioned) presuppositions are the *ne plus ultra* for the worldview they make possible; they are "absolute" because they cannot themselves be questioned, but are the basis of all questioning. Metaphysics in this view simply is the history of thought, in the form of the presuppositions, the bedrock assumptions, that allow us to think at all. And because this is a metaphysic, it must obviously include our basic assumptions not only about history but also about nature; it is where history and nature, inner and outer, must converge. It is at this point that the "evolution of consciousness" as Barfield understood it is especially relevant.

4. Barfield and the "Evolution of Consciousness"

One indication of Barfield's respect for Collingwood's battle with positivism is his suggestion that "Steiner... alone among modern historians and philosophers of history (though R. G. Collingwood and Berdyaev came near to be exceptions) approached history as science should, and not simply as positivism does" (Barfield 1961a, 90). Barfield brings Collingwood and Berdyaev into the same neighborhood as Steiner, though not to the same place; Barfield mediates between Collingwood and Steiner, lifting the former toward the latter by means of the concept of the "evolution of consciousness." Barfield begins both *Speaker's Meaning* (1967) and *History, Guilt, and Habit* (1979) with extended discussions of Collingwood's view of history, and he finds much with which to agree. He thinks that Collingwood "was laying his finger" (*HGH* 1) on the difference between biological evolution and history when he said that "all history is the history of thought." As Barfield emphasized in a contemporaneous article:

> it is just a fact that history *is* all about the human psyche distinguished from the human soma. No doubt one may not improperly use the word "history" in connection with marble, but the provenance of marble is not in fact history. It is geology. That is what made ... Collingwood, go so far as to say that "All real history is history of thought." (Barfield 1970a, 59)

History, Barfield contends, is "something that imports a consciously directed process" whereas evolution is "an unconscious process." Barfield then immediately qualifies these definitions in a way that brings them into full conformity with Collingwood, saying that evolution is "a natural process" and that history is "a human one" (*HGH* 2). Barfield infers from this that for Collingwood "you cannot study the history of thought without thinking the thoughts whose history you are studying"—and this study is, says Barfield, what we now call the "History of Ideas" (*HGH* 3). At the same time, though, Barfield registers concern about two aspects of Collingwood's position: the sharp separation of natural from historical science, and the doctrine of "re-enactment." Barfield never directly challenges the latter, but he acknowledges "it has been disputed, by historians and others" (*HGH* 3) and he does not try to defend Collingwood from the "uneasy" critics who ask "What on earth does he mean by this 're-enacting'?" (*SM* 23).

It is the former, though—the methodological dualism of natural and historical sciences—that attracts Barfield's critical attention, even as he also, as we have seen, blames Lewis and Berlin for not grasping it well enough. Barfield argues that Collingwood cannot simultaneously maintain that Caesar's thought and the historian's thought are the same thing while also maintaining that "nature has no inside." When he does so, Barfield says, he forgets that "if a concept in my mind is one and the same with the concept in yours, then it clearly cannot be the product of either my organism or yours" (*SM* 108). Thus, when Collingwood:

> posits an unbridgeable gulf between history and science ... he bases that doctrine on the presupposition, which he takes for granted, that man has what he calls an "inside," but nature has no "inside." Thought, of which he says history consists, is the inside of man and his actions. But nature has no corresponding inside—no inside at all. We see that, in denying an inside to nature, he is really still conceiving thought as the product of man's physical organism, although this is quite incompatible with that view of the superindividual essence of thought which he himself has just categorically stated. (*SM* 109)

Barfield suspects that Collingwood has fallen into Lovejoy's dualism despite himself, insofar as the natural person—who, *qua* natural, has no inside—underlies and gives rise to the historical person who, *qua* historical, has an inside the essence of which is to be "superindividual." And, he implies that Collingwood has done so because of his allegiance to the same "absolute presupposition" of the mutual exclusivity of inner and outer, psyche and soma, to which Berlin and Lovejoy also commit themselves.

Collingwood's difficulty in putting forward a fully defensible theory of re-enactment, in other words, can be traced to his history/nature, inside/outside division. Collingwood falls into this error because he has overlooked the history of language, for which these problems do not occur. "However it may be with historical study," Barfield says:

> there is ... one case where we certainly do re-enact—and really there can hardly be a better way of putting it—in the present the thinking of the past ... although we are not often very keenly aware that that is what we are doing. Is it not exactly what we do whenever we speak or write? (*SM* 23)

At a far remove from the hermeneutical humility of his earliest essays, Barfield now maintains that the *sine qua non* of language use is that:

> when we use a word, we re-enact, or adopt, or reanimate, or entertain the thought of previous users of the same word or some part at least of that thought.

It may be a very small part indeed. But we must be doing just that thing to some extent; for otherwise we should not be uttering a word at all, but simply making a noise. (*SM* 23–4)

Because Collingwood did not fully appreciate this point, he belongs in the end to the large number of those who find "that the main difficulty that prevents us from breaking through the idols to the actuality of history, that is, to the evolution of consciousness, lies in the fact that we go on using the same words without realizing how their meanings have shifted" (*SA* 74). Redefining re-enactment via Barfield's "semantic approach to history" (that is, "to study . . . the thought previously expressed from time to time by words in daily use") alleviates the questions that have plagued Collingwood's theory. Such an approach:

> must attempt to penetrate into the very texture and activity of thought, rather than to collate conclusions. It is concerned, semantically, with the way in which words are used rather than with the product of discourse. Expressed in terms of logic, its business is more with the proposition than with the syllogism and more with the term than with the proposition. Therefore it must particularize. (*SA* 90)

Thought shades into perception here, as it often does for Barfield, rendering moot Berlin's "concepts and categories," Collingwood's nature/thought dichotomy, and Lovejoy's "unit-ideas"—they all miss the lesson offered by Vico, and assume that the "outer" world remains the same while concepts, thoughts, and ideas transform. They all assume that concepts and ideas apply to the world, but are not, strictly speaking, parts of it. To study the history of language is to study the histories of both thought *and* perception; in other words, it is to study the evolution of consciousness as the "inside" of the evolution of nature.

Collingwood himself lacks an adequate philosophy of language—the one he puts forward in *The Principles of Art* treats language as "an imaginative activity whose function is to express emotion" (Collingwood 1938, 225). Barfield critiqued theories like this for over fifty years. In *Poetic Diction*, as we have seen, Barfield argues that Max Müller's similar theory is "contrary to every indication presented by the study of meaning" (*PD* 80) because:

> instead of starting from the present and working steadily backwards, the theorist insists on starting, as it were, from both ends at once. He has his idea, or prejudice, concerning the nature of primitive minds—an idea derived from sources quite outside his own study—and somehow or other he is determined to make his history of language coincide with that. (*PD* 78)

Barfield referred to this methodological anachronism in *Poetic Diction* as "logomorphism." In this case, it involves "explaining how grunts or other animal noises somehow or other developed into words" (Barfield 1978a, 6) without taking adequate account of the history of language itself. Barfield's poetics dictates that if one grants that:

> the figurative . . . meaning in the earliest words was really "given," and was not something added to them by an individual speaker (which is what happens when a metaphor is invented), then there must have been going on, not only a different kind of thinking but a different kind of perceiving. (Barfield 1978a, 6)

It follows that:

> if you can grant this, you see language as originating in that participation, so that in the earliest stages of all it would have to be described as nature speaking through man, rather than man speaking about nature; and you see the subsequent development of language as evincing the gradual diminution of that participation as time went on. (Barfield 1978a, 6)

Collingwood roots his picture of the origin of language in an unacknowledged, and perhaps unwitting, assumption of Darwinist premises that serve as absolute presuppositions, even if they cannot, as Barfield maintains, survive analysis. The dualist absolute presuppositions endemic in our time prevented him from carrying to its logical conclusion his core insight that "all history is the history of thought."

Barfield could not accept that the investigation of absolute presuppositions was an adequate approach to metaphysics, as Collingwood might have hoped and as Berlin pursued to some extent, but he did adapt it to his own purposes, and called it "collective habit" or "common sense." So, for example, he notes that "you will sometimes hear people say they have no metaphysics. Well, they are lying. Their metaphysics are implicit in what they take for granted about the world. Only they prefer to call it 'common sense'" (*HGH* 9). As either "collective habit" or "common sense," Barfield's shift of terms makes clear that while Collingwood improves on Lovejoy's "empirical reality" as a metaphysical grounding, he does not go far enough. Barfield's reframing of "absolute presuppositions" as "collective habits" highlights their relatively subconscious nature, their intractable resistance to conscious tinkering, and, hopefully, the possibility after much effort that one might replace or transform them once they have risen to consciousness.

The first fruit of Barfield's idea of "collective habits" is a proper diagnosis of the puzzling question with which we began this chapter: why the concept of an evolution of consciousness remains elusive. Collingwood, Lovejoy, and the other figures we have discussed cannot find their way to the idea "evolution of consciousness" because they remain bound to a dualistic, mechanistic metaphysic, with a Darwinian overlay. The former has distorted our understanding of "consciousness," the latter our idea of "evolution." While Descartes provided "some help" to people to "distinguish so sharply . . . an inner from an outer" and even "to imagine the inner *divided* from the outer," this help "should not be exaggerated" (*HGH* 12). Rather, our great difficulty in having any other experience than that of "the inner divided from the outer" is due not to "any philosophy" but to:

> a collectively and historically hardened *habit* of thought, of which we are no longer conscious. Two very different matters—as any convinced idealist who has just stubbed his toe on a stone will tell you. . . . And it is precisely because of the great difference between these two that there is a difference between history of ideas on the one hand and history or evolution of consciousness on the other. It is these passive habits of thought, not any ideas we are actively entertaining at the moment, that are inseparable from our perceptions; and it is the changes to *these* with which a history of consciousness must deal. (*HGH* 12)

We saw earlier that Berlin criticized Collingwood for imagining he was investigating the "history of consciousness" when he should have limited himself to enumerating and extrapolating concepts and categories. In Barfield's view, the "history of consciousness" is the proper subject of historical inquiry because it is "structurally inseparable from [the] world" that it entails (*HGH* 19). Collingwood does not pursue it far enough because he is trapped in his own "hardened habit of thought," finally limiting psyche to soma, consciousness and thinking to the individual organic unit.

This pervasive dogma has a Darwinian overlay, a temporal accompaniment to the spatial shape of popular Cartesianism—inner/outer, mind/body—that has warped our understanding of "evolution" just as Cartesianism has shriveled our experience of consciousness. Darwinism has been "rivet[ed] on the western mind" as "something like what we call 'common sense,' common sense about the past" (*HGH* 77, 76). It is an important aspect of "how the word 'evolution' came to mean what it does today" (*HGH* 77). Of particular importance in this process were three things: first, from Descartes, "the principle of an absolute dichotomy between matter and mind and of the mechanical constitution of the former" (*HGH* 78); secondly, from Lyell, "the hypothesis that what we today ascertain as the laws of nature have always existed, have never changed, and never will change—'Uniformitarianism'" (*HGH* 78); and finally, "the Darwinian theory of natural selection as not only *a* cause, but the *whole* cause, of biological development through the ages" (*HGH* 78). Uniformitarianism has become a "hardened mental habit" that makes it impossible, for example, to imagine prehistoric earth as anything other than the earth known to contemporary geologists. As a result, "evolution has come to mean phylogenesis conceived in terms of causality; and 'causality' itself [has] . . . come to mean only mechanical causality, only push-and-pull causality" (*HGH* 75). Because "mechanical causality . . . is atomic, staccato" (*HGH* 75), we have lost all sense of its original meaning:

> an unfolding, a gradual and uninterrupted process of change from one form into another, towards which it has been tending from the start—from one form into another through a whole series of intermediary forms, the one imperceptibly merging into the other. A process of transformation, of metamorphosis; and more particularly a change from *potential* form into *actual and spatial* form, the typical instance being a seed or an embryo evolving by growth into an independent plant or animal. (*HGH* 74)

Having lost this sensitivity to ourselves as "evolving by growth" from form to form, from potential to actual, each "imperceptibly merging into the other," Collingwood is unable to escape the "mechanomorphic" picture of the human being and the cosmos.

In fairness to Collingwood, we cannot blame him for failing to escape the "mechanomorphic" gestalt: it nearly defines modern Western consciousness to its roots. Barfield's description in *Saving the Appearances* of how we evolved into it from medieval consciousness—a metamorphosis that is also key to *History in English Words*— is a case study in the evolution of consciousness. Barfield highlights the much-derided "quaintness" of the medieval sensibility and traces it to "their combining and, as we should say, confusing two ways of approaching phenomena; ways which we are accustomed to regard as quite distinct from one another. These are the literal, on the one hand, and the symbolic or metaphorical, on the other" (*SA* 73). Thus, for the proverbial medieval person in the street, "the phenomena themselves carried the sort of multiple significance which we to-day only find in symbols" (*SA* 74). We reject the medieval sensibility as quaint because the hard division of the literal from the symbolic has become an idol for us. We miss thereby the richness of medieval astrology and medicine, failing to appreciate that the logic of microcosm and macrocosm, grounded in the assumed underlying continuity of the literal and symbolic, ensured that the generic medieval man:

> did not feel himself isolated by his skin from the world outside him to quite the same extent as we do. He was integrated or mortised into it, each different part of him being united to a different part of it by some invisible thread. In his relation to his environment, the man of the middle ages was rather less like an island, rather more like an embryo, than we are. (*SA* 78)

The leap into modernity was, then, a leap into literalism. Harvey, for example, was able to demonstrate the circulation of blood because he took literally "talk ... of the heart as 'a piece of machinery in which, though one wheel gives motion to another, yet all the wheels seem to move simultaneously'" (*SA* 80). This led to the clarification of "palpable mechanical errors" even as it "contributed towards the bringing about of an exclusively mechanomorphic view of both blood and heart" (*SA* 80–1). The legacy of this shift is bifurcated meanings for us of both "heart" and "blood," the "mechanomorphic" significance belonging to modern science, and the figurative residue found, for example, in the mixed blessings of "hot blood" and a "bleeding heart." And deeper still is the quintessentially modern assumption that the mechanomorphic meaning is literal and therefore perhaps true while the figurative meaning is at best only indirectly so.

Mechanomorphic modern consciousness presents us with serious existential problems. The "growing prevalence of mental disease" (*HGH* 49) is due in part to the "*collective* mental habit" (*HGH* 49) of our own "cut-offness" or "imprisonment" (*HGH* 48) within a world that is "no longer a world of images, no longer therefore an exterior expressing an interior, but simply a brittle exterior surface, which is however not the surface *of* anything" (*HGH* 48). Thus, many of us come to realize "with something of a shock" that:

> this world of outsides with no insides to them, which we perceive around us and in which we dwell, is not something unshakably and unalterably given, but is largely the product of the way we collectively and subconsciously think. It is correlative to our mental habit. (*HGH* 48)

The fundamental "habit of thought," which Barfield elsewhere describes as being as difficult to overcome as unlearning how to ride a bicycle, is that of the "brittle exterior" with no interior, our sense of self dissolved into hormone surges and neuron firings as we feebly wander an earth on which we are alienated spectators.

Barfield's suggestions for ways to begin to grasp the idea "evolution of consciousness" are the same as his suggested path out of the "walls of [the] prison" (*HGH* 49) in which we find ourselves today. The first step toward the idea "evolution of consciousness" is to fully absorb the interpenetration of thinking and perception. Paradoxically, it is just this interpenetration, this distinction-without-division, that makes our inner alienation seem fated to correlate with outer mechanism. Our collective Cartesian-Darwinian mental habit is difficult to overcome and "structurally inseparable" from the world, for two reasons. First, "what we perceive . . . is inseparable from what we think" (*HGH* 10). As we shall explore more deeply in the next chapter, Barfield embraces the phenomenological axiom of "intentionality," and sees thought and perception as an interpenetrating polarity. It is important to reflect, he says, that:

> consciousness depends on two elements that must always remain distinguishable, though they are never divisible . . . the distinction between "that-which-is-conscious" and "that-*of*-which" it is conscious. . . . This is a distinction which we re-affirm by the very act of denying it; or, putting it another way, that a theory about the brain, or about behaviour, can never (no matter what microscopic details it reduces to) perform the disappearing trick of vanishing into the brain, or into the behavior, about which it is a theory. (Barfield 1970a, 58).

Consequently, any of the absolute presuppositions or inveterate habits that structure and enable our thoughts also affect our most basic perception of the world. The second reason, correlative to the first, is that:

> Consciousness is not a tiny bit of the world stuck on to the rest of it. It is the inside of the whole world. Or, if we are using the term in its stricter sense—excluding therefore the subconscious mind—then it is *part* of the inside of the whole world. (*HGH* 11)

One consequence of fully uprooting the dualistic assumptions about nature and history, as soon as we accept that all history is the history of thought, is that thought is the "inner" or inverse surface, and "outer" nature the obverse surface, of a single sphere. We can never be in a full state of alienation from the "outer" world, or reduce our "inner" world to a null point of bare consciousness, but can only allow ourselves to become convinced that this is so.

Barfield suggests that, as a means to overcome the "residue of unresolved positivism" that lingers in our habitual thought after we have rejected it intellectually, and that makes it difficult to grasp "interpenetration" beyond mere assent, one undertake the dialectical process of mental activity. After one realizes that "our theories are simply different ways of occupying ourselves in prison," one sees that "the first step of all is to realize that mental habit *is* a prison" and that "what matters is our coming to realize that the way we habitually think and perceive is not the only possible way, not even a way that has been going on very long. It is the way we have *come* to think, the way we have *come* to perceive" (*HGH* 50). The second step he suggests, to resolve as an "act of will" to break our "ingrained" habit of alienated mechanistic vision, is "not so easy" because "habit has a will of its own, a sort of frozen, unconscious will that is much stronger than the little bit of will you are consciously exerting" (*HGH* 51). Even so, the particular act of will that Barfield recommends is a return to thinking—no longer the simple recognition that one is "in prison," but the new "habit of thinking *actively*; of choosing to think, instead of letting our thoughts just happen" (*HGH* 52). This practice amounts not merely to a new habit, the exchange of one "prison" for another, but the habit of breaking habits, thereby awakening the thinker—due to "the mind's self-experience in the act of thinking" (*HGH* 52)—to the direct encounter with "a wholly human and inner self... from which we are free, if we prefer, to withhold our attention" (*HGH* 53). This insight has clear implications for Barfield's moral and political thought. An additional result, to round back to the interpenetration of thinking and perceiving, is that we experience the interpenetration that we seek in this act of self-perception within our own thinking. We can then begin to build outward towards the self-aware experience of intentionality in all acts of perception, including those with a moral valence.

Something similar happens when one takes the "semantic approach to history" (*SM* 25) that helps to break down the habitual assumption of "cut-offness." Semantic change is driven by the dynamic interaction of lexical and speaker's meaning—by the way meaning is shaped by the world, and by oneself as an individual. To be self-aware as a speaker in the act of thinking, then, is also to experience a dynamic exchange with the meaning-creating activity of the wider world in the act of asserting one's own slight variance with the baseline of shared understanding.[4] Similarly, as one steeps oneself in the histories of words—which themselves are records of the interpenetration of thought and perception—one reenacts the dynamic shift in the relation of the self to the world, and within the self of the relative activity of thinking and perceiving. One favorite dramatic example of this for Barfield is the semantic history of "subjectivity" itself. The history of the word reveals that "subjectivity is never something that was developed out of nothing at some point in space, but is a form of consciousness that has *contracted* from a periphery into individual centers" (*SM* 113). Its shifts in meaning reveal with particular clarity what the history of language reveals more broadly: the "gradual historical development of an inner or immaterial language out of a material language enabled mankind as a whole to become aware ... of an inner world in contradistinction to an outer one" (*RM* 232). To participate imaginatively in this process—and imagination is simply "thinking with a bit of will in it" (*HGH* 54)—is to experience oneself as something other than a brittle surface without depth, stuck onto a barren world that is also surface all the way down. It is to become aware both that "the single experience we call 'consciousness'—our inwardness at any moment—is not composed either of perceiving alone or of thinking alone, but of an immemorial and inextricable combination of the two" (*HGH* 45) and that "consciousness is not a tiny bit of the world stuck on to the rest of it. It is the inside of the whole world" (*HGH* 11).

That is a beginning to the rehabilitation of "consciousness," but what of "evolution?" It is the temporal dimension to the same problem of alienation, the dull round we walk in our prison of hardened mental habits. Its original "etymological suggestion" is "a vegetable growth, an unfolding from the centre outwards" (*HEW* 185); and, as we have seen, it implies "a process of transformation, of metamorphosis, and more particularly a change from *potential* form into *actual and spatial* form" (*HGH* 74). To understand it in this original sense, before it took "the unmistakable stamp of Darwinism" (*HEW* 185), requires the same development of imagination that true self-consciousness demands. If self-consciousness is the mind's experience of itself as subject-object in the act of thinking-perceiving, it does so as a metamorphosis within, and of, time. It is to experience one's biography not as a causal push-pull or a staccato succession of unrelated moments, but as an "unfolding" in the present of the polar tension of past and future. In fact, the notion of "polarity" became central for Barfield because it encompasses the generation of the temporal tension that is the fleeting "present" out of the interpenetration of past and future. This is similar not only to the "silent voice" of poetry, but also to the interpenetration of speaker's and lexical meaning that yields a word's meaning in any given moment, the polarity of thinking and perceiving within consciousness, and the fusion of oneself as the "inner" curve of the cosmos with its circumambient "outer" rim.

As is no doubt obvious by now, we have long since crossed over into metaphysics. Barfield was well aware of the need for a metaphysic, as we have seen—those who say they have done away with it are "lying" because "their metaphysics are implicit in what they say about the world" (*HGH* 9). It should be evident that the "evolution of consciousness" cannot be both dualistic and successful, in fact that "polarity" is an attempt to rehabilitate "duality." Barfield's metaphysics is the subject of the next chapter, but it is worth noting as we close this one that he is as wary of idealism as he is of materialism. "One of the disadvantages of being an out-and-out materialist," he says,

> is that you can no longer use the word "nature" with any consistency, because in your system it includes everything; just as one of the disadvantages of being an

out-and-out idealist is that you can no longer use the word "spirit" meaningfully, because in your system it includes everything. (*HGH* 2)

Barfield saw the same pitfalls that Collingwood noticed, and repurposed Collingwood's attempt to define metaphysics as a science of "absolute presuppositions" as his notion of "collective habits." Barfield's claims for polarity, temporality, the self, thinking, and so on, still require a metaphysical ground because they are, indeed, implicit in everything he says about the world.

3

The Antecedent Unity

Metaphysics

The introduction that Barfield wrote for *The Rediscovery of Meaning* justifies the existence of a diverse collection of essays on a diverse range of subjects with the comment that there is "an effective unity of content underlying the apparent fragmentation" (*RM* 3). This mirrors Barfield's belief that his books and essays as a whole are "always really saying the same thing over and over again" (*RM* 3), and that "in my case the 'same thing' that is always being reaffirmed is the importance of penetrating to the antecedent unity underlying apparent or actual fragmentation" (*RM* 3). In other words, beneath the wide range of his subjects Barfield would like us to keep in mind the metaphysical principle at the back of all of them. Even if one denies that penetrating to the antecedent unity is what Barfield said over and over again, there is no question that it is part of the core of his mature philosophy, and that it was his view that this principle is at the back of everything he has to say, retrospectively applying even to the early development of his poetics.

And yet, Barfield often seems to distance himself from metaphysics. We saw at the end of the last chapter that Barfield disavows the labels "idealist" and "materialist" and says of his most famous book, *Saving the Appearances*, "this is not a book about metaphysics" (*SA* 17); this, of a book built on a distinction between "representations" and the "unrepresented." One is reminded of Donald Verene's comment that Ernst Cassirer was "metaphysics shy" (Verene 94). Though this is not as true for Barfield as it is for Cassirer, he does think that metaphysical inquiry has its limits. Barfield was impatient with those people who "say they have no metaphysics" (*HGH* 9), but he declines to develop or embrace a complete (that is to say, fully deduced) metaphysical system, even as he expresses the longing for one. In this respect, he follows not only Coleridge but also the mainstream of post-Kantian German idealism, especially such Romantics as Goethe and Novalis, who "embraced . . . scepticism about first principles and systems, and made that scepticism an integral part of their own *Weltanschauung*" (Beiser 2002, 9). As we saw in exploring his poetics, Barfield worried as early as 1923 that "we can never enter into the mind of anyone who lived more than a few years ago" because "the very words they used to express themselves do not mean the same now as they did then, for human consciousness evolves" (Barfield 1923c, 525). This important early claim recalls the development of Barfield's poetics and his theory of the evolution of consciousness, but it also contains metaphysical assumptions, including that language creates hermeneutical horizons that are historical, if not individual. This in turn recalls, at the very least, the phenomenological hermeneutics of Dilthey, Heidegger, Merleau-Ponty, Ricoeur, and Gadamer; Barfield knew about, and took interest in, the work of Heidegger, Merleau-Ponty, and Ricoeur, though he found Heidegger's style off-putting. In a 1988 letter, Barfield says:

> It is not true that I "reject" Heidegger, of whom I have read quite a bit. It is just that I find him rather irritating. Determined to be "impressive." Paradox, oxymoron and aphorism are all useful, even essential in this kind of context. But Heidegger *surfeits* you with them; with the result that their impact is deadened and they no longer perform their function of enabling intuitive penetration in the otherwise inexpressible.

In fact, Barfield would never lose the cautionary impulse he shared with Heidegger. He thought that literal translation was impossible due to "the very nature of language" (Barfield 1961b, 73), that inquiries into the origin of language were doomed efforts to grasp "the origin of origin" (*SA* 123), and that "people living in other periods, or even at the same period but in a totally different community, do not inhabit the same world about which they have different ideas, they inhabit different worlds altogether" (*WA* 172).

Barfield's emphasis in such moments on what Nelson Goodman called the "world-making" power of language, with the limitations that impose on the inhabitants of any particular linguistic universe, parallels the limits of philosophical understanding.[1] Barfield says in the notes he wrote for the Bollingen edition of Coleridge's lectures on the history of philosophy that for Coleridge "the business of *modern* philosophy is not the discovery of fresh truths but the refutation—not of false philosophy; that had already been done by the ancients themselves—but of the 'effects' of false philosophy on the general mind" (Barfield 2000, 874). Barfield's comments about modern philosophy in *propria voce* show that here too, as in so many things, he agrees with Coleridge. Barfield's emphasis on personal transformation as the ultimate human good is one indication of this agreement. Though the idea of the fully deduced metaphysical system had a lifelong appeal for Barfield, as it did for Coleridge, he is more consistent than Coleridge in seeing metaphysics, first, as a useful corrective to flawed metaphysical systems that do cultural damage, like logical positivism or Sartre's version of Existentialism; and, second, as a foundation for the "leap of faith" into the "intuitive penetration" that thorough personal transformation finally requires.

The reference to Coleridge points to one of the major philosophical influences on Barfield. The other is Rudolf Steiner.[2] Barfield braided them together in articulating his own metaphysic, while weaving in discussion of such fellow travelers as Cassirer, Erich Auerbach, and Gabriel Marcel, each of whom Barfield encountered too late for them to have a formative influence on him and whom he referred to in the 1973 afterword to *Poetic Diction* as "friends" (*PD* 214).[3]

1. Steiner and Phenomenology

Barfield's earliest references to metaphysics present Steiner as a central figure. It may be, as he thought in 1926, that "Romanticism, at any rate as a metaphysic, is a failure" because "its potentialities seem to have been left hanging in the air, its numerous loose threads ungathered" (Barfield 1926, 118). Even so, "Dr. Rudolf Steiner" was able to build "on the foundations laid by that prince of Romantics, Wilhelm Goethe, a new and solid edifice of metaphysic" (Barfield 1926, 118). Barfield did not specify in this or his other early articles what stones Steiner used to build the "solid edifice of metaphysic." Though Barfield did not yet attempt to articulate Steiner's epistemology or metaphysics, he was impressed that "anthroposophy included and transcended not only my own stammering theory of poetry as knowledge, but the whole Romantic philosophy" (*RCA* 8).

The books by Steiner that formed the foundation of Barfield's education in this new "Romantic philosophy" were *Goethe's Theory of Knowledge* (1886), *Truth and Science* (1891), and *The Philosophy of Freedom* (1894). Steiner's main focus in them is on epistemology, with implications for metaphysics that he only fully delivers in the cosmology of Anthroposophy: "we seek," he says, "by looking at the process of knowledge, to arrive at a view about reality" (Steiner 1993, 58). Steiner, like Barfield, suggests that the point of philosophical labor is personal transformation: "the process of knowledge, according to our argument, is the process of developing toward inner freedom" (Steiner 1993, 60). Barfield also agrees with Steiner in seeing philosophy as fundamentally antagonistic to metaphysical error. Whereas

Barfield battled positivism from *Poetic Diction* until the end of his life, Steiner saw overturning the neo-Kantian schools located in Marburg and Baden as central to his philosophical project. The positive project of "lay[ing] the foundation for a truly satisfying view of the world and of life" requires that "we place ourselves in decisive opposition to this thinker," Kant, from whom "present-day philosophy suffers ... an unhealthy belief" (Steiner 1993, i). The:

> now predominant Kantian view ... limits our knowledge of the world to our mental pictures—not because it is convinced that things cannot exist beyond these mental pictures, but because it believes us to be so organized that we can experience only the changes of our own selves but not the things-in-themselves that cause these changes. (Steiner 1964, 50)

Steiner saw a fundamental danger to human freedom and the scope of inquiry in this philosophical school, which busied itself with defining the nature, scope, and limits of scientific and philosophical thought. Philosophers like Johannes Volkelt base this conclusion (which they take to be an unassailable premise) on the understanding that "our phenomenal world is physiologically subjective" (Steiner 2008, 23). Steiner argues, though, that the determination that sensory experience is the product of physiology is itself an act of judgment—that is, the product of thinking—and that one must first account for the act of thinking itself, free of such assumptions.

As part of presenting "a truly satisfying view of the world and of life," Steiner turned to the idealist tradition of Fichte (the subject of his doctoral dissertation), Goethe, Hegel, and the phenomenological explorations of his teacher, Franz Brentano.[4] Though Steiner wrote more about the idealists than he did about Brentano, perhaps the latter had a greater influence on his philosophical methods. Steiner said of him what he said of no other philosopher—including those like Schelling, Hegel, and Fichte, who might come more easily to mind—that although "no one can accuse Brentano's way of picturing things of having even the slightest tendency in an anthroposophical direction," nevertheless "from my anthroposophical viewpoint, I am in a position to approach the philosophy of Franz Brentano with unconditional reverence" (Steiner 1996b, 63). Steiner follows Brentano in establishing "epistemology as a science that is totally free of presuppositions" and extends this effort by "bringing Fichte's attempt to create an absolutely certain foundation for the sciences into closer connection with our task" (Steiner 1993, 4).

Steiner begins his phenomenological account of knowledge with the "unmediated given," which he frees of all predicates or assumptions:

> Such a start can only be made, however, from the *directly "given" world picture*, i.e., from that world picture which lies before the human being prior to his subjecting it in any way to the process of knowledge; that means, before he has said even the least thing about it, before he has undertaken even the least conceptual characterization with regard to it. What there passes by before us and before which we pass, this world picture, which is incoherent and yet also not separated into individual details, in which nothing is differentiated from anything else, nothing related to anything else, and nothing appears to be determined by anything else: this is the directly "given." At this stage of existence—if I may use this term—no object, no happening is more important, more significant than any other. (Steiner 1993, 23-4)

Steiner's notion of the "given," articulated in 1891, anticipates that of another student of Brentano, Edmund Husserl, who later argued for the "suspension of the natural attitude" and that "in genuine phenomenological viewing we are not permitted *any* scientific or philosophical hypotheses. We should attend only to the phenomena in the manner of their being given to us, in their *modes of givenness*" (Moran 2000, 11).[5] Steiner posits "the given"—which, as Barfield notes, he uses in "two different ways" (*RCA* 318)—as a way to get to the other side of the premises of "naïve realism" and "critical idealism" that restrict supposedly "fundamental" inquiries into the most basic "stage of existence."[6]

"The given" in Steiner's first sense—the "net given"—shares obvious affinities with Heidegger's "Being" that is the ground of beings and with Barfield's "antecedent unity."[7] Since it is "incoherent" and prior to "the least conceptual characterization," it resists all but apophatic description. Thus, Steiner contends that:

> if we are to have a name for the first way that we observe reality, we really believe that the most adequate term in this case is "appearance to the senses." We understand by the term sense not only the outer senses as mediators of the external world, but also all bodily and mental organs that serve our awareness of the immediate facts. (Steiner 2008, 27)

This "appearance to the senses" is "prior to all conceptual determinations whatsoever" and "never actually experienced" but rather is arrived at "not empirically, but by analysis" (*RCA* 321).

The second "given," by contrast, is "full of conceptual determination" (*RCA* 32). Our awareness of ourselves as thinkers, as attuned the world in sensitive ways, and as possessed of inviolable personal identity, manifests out of "the given" along two routes: through the senses as "percepts" and through thinking as "concepts." Knowledge consists of uniting concepts, which are wholly general, with percepts, which are wholly particular. By arguing that concept and percept are equally important, Steiner avoids both the Kantian position that concepts are an epiphenomenal overlay on the "manifold of sensibility" and Hegel's equation of the real with the rational (Steiner 2008, 34–5), which in the popular mind at least reduces the real to the conceptual. That is, Steiner endorses another of Hegel's positions, that the true is the whole:

> In every scientific approach to reality, this is the process: We encounter a concrete percept, which confronts us as a question. An impulse arises within us to investigate its true nature, which the percept itself does not convey. That impulse is simply the upward activity of a concept from the darkness of our consciousness. We then hold this concept firmly as the sense percept goes along in parallel with the thought process. The mute percept suddenly speaks an intelligible language, and we realize that the percept is seeking the concept we have grasped. Thus, a judgment has occurred, which is different from the form of judgment that unites two concepts without reference to percepts. (Steiner 2008, 46)

Steiner rejects the positivist position that concepts, if they are well-formed, correspond to preexisting percepts, and that truthful statements accurately represent what the senses deliver. Steiner also rejects the neo-Kantian position that individual subjectivity systematizes and categorizes the unformed or not directly knowable "manifold of sensibility" in ways that may or may not accurately represent "things in themselves."

For Steiner, there is no realm of things in themselves beyond the infinite richness of the "given" as it manifests in concepts and percepts, though as we shall see in the next chapter, his whole poetic cosmology lies within the "given." Percepts light up as "mute" phenomena for which concepts are the voice, and concepts—which require the activity of thinking in order to manifest—form the kind of "infinite closed sphere" that Einstein thought characterized space itself:

> the moment one's mind conceives two corresponding thoughts, it notices immediately that they actually flow into one another to make a unity. It finds, everywhere in its thought-realm, what is interrelated; one concept is connected with another, while a third illuminates or supports a fourth, and so on. (Steiner 2008, 39)

Percepts, one pole of the knowing activity, retain the complete particularity granted by their conceptual identification and categorization; concepts, the other pole, necessarily exist in relation to each other: a concept that stands outside the cohesive web of concepts is a contradiction in terms. The evolution of consciousness, at one level, is the slow-motion revelation of the wider universe of concepts that in practical terms remains infinite and that reveals more and more of the forest of percepts that surrounds us.

One can easily understand why Barfield, reading Steiner in the 1920s as he worked on *History in English Words* and *Poetic Diction*, felt that Steiner articulated the metaphysic implicit in his theory of meaning. The "antecedent unity" of which mythological thinking is an already late echo, the evolution of consciousness out of the unity that mythological thinking points toward, the phenomenology that underpins the "felt change of consciousness" that is crucial to the experience of metaphor, and the explanation for why imagination and metaphor increase knowledge are all here. At the same time, Steiner's early philosophical writings do not provide a metaphysic, at least in the traditional sense. For Steiner, who had a deep affinity for Nietzsche, philosophy is an art form devoted, like all art forms, to the transformation of its audience. "All real philosophers have been *artists in the realm of concepts*" (Steiner 1964, xxx) because they are not essentially concerned with building metaphysical systems. They seek to awaken an aesthetic experience in their audience that mobilizes and enlivens the soul: "knowledge has value only in so far as it contributes to the *all-round* development of the *whole* nature of man" (Steiner 1964, xxx), which reveals itself in the "whole" person when one becomes an artist of thinking, creating in that act works of art that become the foundation for one's action in the world. Thinking itself becomes a form of initiation and the initiate a speaker of truths that are not "the ideal reflection of some real thing or other, but rather a free creation of the human spirit that would not exist anywhere at all if we ourselves did not bring it forth" (Steiner 1993, iii). This is a Nietzschean "joyful science" of the utmost seriousness:

> the task of knowledge is not to *repeat* in conceptual form something already present somewhere else, but rather to *create* a completely new realm which, along with the world given to the senses, first constitutes full reality. With this, the highest activity of man, his spiritual creativity, is incorporated organically into the general working of the world. (Steiner 1993, iii)

Barfield was convinced that Steiner practiced this kind of artistic thinking in the many books and lectures he wrote and delivered over the next thirty years, until his death in 1925. Steiner's artistic thinker is Barfield's poet; it is no wonder that for Barfield, Steiner's writing had the force of poetry (*RCA* 17). His settled opinion would remain that:

> only Steiner, as far as I know, has clearly apprehended this [imaginative] activity as part, and but the first part, of a long, sober process of cognition that may end in man's actually overcoming the dichotomy [between perceiving subject and perceived object]—sober, but involving a plus of self-consciousness amounting to a mutation, since it presupposes no less than a crossing of the stark threshold between knowing and being. (RCA 25)

This picture of the thinker as artist, and of cognitive transformation as the purpose of philosophical work, implies a phenomenological project. Barfield acknowledges that Steiner's "own epistemological method and his own outlook were developed absolutely organically and uninterruptedly out of Goethe's" (RCA 47). He summarizes his early understanding of Goethe's and Steiner's phenomenological method, and implicit metaphysic, in a way that will be important for understanding his later philosophical writing. Speaking of Steiner's early book *Goethe's Theory of Knowledge*, Barfield claims that:

> in it Steiner exemplifies and defines more closely these *Urphänomene*—the "prime phenomena," such as the blue of the sky—behind which it is really meaningless to try to penetrate. These are the true "laws of Nature." They are apodeictic. And to seek either for objective "causes" or for subjective formal principles of apprehension which compel us to "accept" these laws is to depart from nature and knowledge into the realm of fancy. . . . The point is that these *Urphänomene* are *neither objective nor subjective*. They come into existence *as* types, or *as* laws, only as they are intuited by human beings. And until they have so come into being, the object itself is incomplete. Knowledge in fact, so far from being a mental copy of events and processes outside the human being, inserts the human being right *into* these processes, of whose development it is itself the last stage. (RCA 48)

"Prime phenomena" like the sky's blueness are "apodeictic" because they form a limit to metaphysical speculation—there is neither need nor capacity to get "behind" them—and are neither subjective nor objective. They cannot be resolved into pure percept or pure concept but come into existence as "intuitions" of the human being. It is metaphysically fruitless to analyze blueness into light wave spectra to which the physiology of the eye is adapted; knowledge is not a "mental copy" of a precedent reality but the completion of a process. As Hegel and Cassirer might put it, truth is not correspondence but wholeness. This is all the more important because the fruits of imagination are no less self-justifying than the sky's blueness: "the truth of imagination is apodeictic, not empirical, and [Steiner] makes accordingly no less a claim for the results of his spiritual investigation. For imagination is not a *reasoning about*, it is a *Schauung*, a seeing, and indeed a *being*, the object. Systematic imagination is, in fact, clairvoyance" (*RCA* 49).

Between the two passages quoted earlier, Barfield comments that "the Goethe-Steiner system" is consistent with "Aristotle's conception of the reality (ειδοσ) which only exists potentially (δθναμει) until it is known, and when it is known has its full existence actually (ενεργεια)" (*RCA* 48). This suggests what may already be obvious, that for Barfield the "Goethe-Steiner system" implies a metaphysic that neither Goethe nor the early Steiner supplies. In the same year that he wrote "An Introduction to Anthroposophy," Barfield found a more recent and compelling support than Aristotle: the metaphysical system of Samuel Taylor Coleridge.

2. Coleridge and Objective Idealism

Only in his maturity did Barfield realize his full alignment with "the fundamental simplicity of Coleridge's objective idealism" (Barfield 1970c, 78). His awareness of Coleridge's importance to him begins, fittingly, with a phenomenological experience, that an "early manifested innate *imaginative* experience of the unreality of the 'subjective-objective' illusion had predisposed him" to seek its solution in a theory of imagination. Barfield's use of Coleridge throughout the 1920s in developing his poetics grows out of his recognition of this affinity. Shortly after Barfield published *History in English Words* and *Poetic Diction*, two events awakened him to Coleridge's true philosophical depth and importance: Alice Snyder edited a collection of Coleridge's hitherto unpublished writings on language and logic, *Coleridge on Logic and Learning* (1929), and J. H. Muirhead's study *Coleridge as Philosopher* (1930) appeared. Snyder's collection was particularly meaningful for him because Barfield believed that Coleridge made explicit in these hitherto unpublished writings the metaphysical foundations of the theory of meaning in *Poetic Diction*, the historical phenomenology of its unfolding in *History in English Words*, and the metaphysical foundations of "the Goethe-Steiner system."

Barfield's review of Muirhead's *Coleridge as Philosopher* presupposes the cultural importance of metaphysical convictions. Barfield affirms that Muirhead has written "an extremely important book" (*RCA* 191) but critiques him for defining Coleridge's primary significance as "the historical anticipation ... [of] modern idealism" (*RCA* 197). By "modern idealism" Barfield has in mind the neo-Hegelian British idealism of Bradley and Bosanquet, which Muirhead views as an improved and modernized Platonism. For Barfield, this school's philosophy is not only fundamentally different from Coleridge's but also "lacks the courage of its convictions" because it "proves to us that thought is not merely subjective—and then, boggling at the consequence of its own doctrine, goes on to talk of it as if it were a process taking place inside the head" (RCA 198). Considered as cosmology, the subjective idealism that Muirhead valorized "underlies the whole Newtonian philosophy" that renders the mind a "lazy Looker-on on an external world" (RCA 199). This matters because if "you *really* regard the mind as an active participant in and not 'a lazy Looker-on' to Nature, the ground is automatically knocked away beneath the whole of Newtonian science" (RCA 199).

What stood out for Barfield was Muirhead's discussion of hitherto unfamiliar texts like *Logic*, the *Essay on Faith*, and *Theory of Life*, which Barfield now realized are "unmistakably behind" popular writings like the lectures on Shakespeare. Barfield finds within Coleridge's scattered writings a "system of thought [that] is incoherent in its outer form alone" because "we recognize the same clear principles working their way to the surface from beneath whatever he wrote" (RCA 192). These clear principles include the "central intuition of 'polarity', which is ... the immovable axis about which the cosmos of Coleridge's thought perpetually revolves" (RCA 195). Synecdoche, which Coleridge called "tautegory," becomes his core concern: "The question for him became rather, granted that the individual 'is' ultimately the Whole, to explain how more than one individual can 'be' the same Whole, yet without ceasing to be separate individuals" (RCA 196). The "universal law of polarity" is the metaphysical idea that explains the crystallization of percept and concept out of the "given," even as Coleridge's tautegory is the logical concept that can elaborate both the active imagination and the experience of the part as the whole, oneself as another, microcosm as macrocosm. At the end of his review, Barfield brings Coleridge into connection with Goethe's work in botany. Goethe's *Urpflanze* is closer to Coleridge's "Idea" than the British philosophers whom Muirhead believed Coleridge to have prophesied, and Coleridge is more important than those he precedes. Barfield criticizes Muirhead for being unaware "of the existence of a Goethean science, whose method actually *assumes* from the start this participation of the mind in the production of phenomena" (RCA 200). This is as much as to say that a truly contemporary reading of Coleridge should align him not with Oxford Hegelianism but with Steiner's Anthroposophy.

In the following year, Barfield again linked Coleridge and Goethe, this time in a lecture at the Goetheanum in Dornach, Switzerland, the global center of

Steiner's movement. It reflects his quickly deepening immersion in Coleridge's philosophy, spurred by his direct reading of Coleridge's recently published writings on language and logic in Alice Snyder's collection. It offers a light sketch but articulates themes that he will more fully develop decades later in *What Coleridge Thought*. First, the "ancient semantic unity" central to his earlier books earns a metaphysical foundation as "the world of grammar [that] subsists between the two poles of verb and noun" arising from, and unified by, the "I am" that alone is "both verb and noun at the same time" (*RCA* 211–12). This grammatical bifurcation also reflects a felt experience of the division of self and other. Just as "I am" is the microcosmic "unity in multeity" that later splits into noun and verb, so too the Logos is the unified origin of what we come to experience macrocosmically as subject and object.

Each of these pairs is held together by *"the universal law of Polarity"* (*RCA* 211), as is the larger polarity of language and the self. Indeed, one finds polarity at work in all dynamic, living systems and between such systems when they come into contact or create progeny. Here too, Coleridge is of larger cultural and philosophical significance in combating "the so-called 'philosophy' which was fashionable in his time and which . . . is still fashionable in our own—the Atomic Philosophy" (*RCA* 213). The chief exponent of Atomism in Barfield's day was Bertrand Russell, a frequent target for Barfield's polemical invective as advocate for "a 'mechanic system' [that] insists that . . . knowledge is limited to distance and nearness, in short, to '*the relations of unproductive particles to each other*'. This . . . is the *philosophy of Death*" (*RCA* 213). Coleridge, as Barfield sees him in this essay, is again prophetic of Steiner's Anthroposophy. Coleridge's breakthroughs in educing "the law of polarity as the process which underlies all life," in discovering this law in "the act of self-consciousness" (*RCA* 213), and in discovering in the homology of logic and metaphysics a philosophy of the Logos make him a forerunner of Steiner's philosophical work. Immediate personal experience of the polar relation of mind to world, and of mind to itself, "is the rock on which the whole of [*The Philosophy of Freedom*], and indeed the whole of Spiritual Science, is built" (*RCA* 208). Here, then, is the "solid edifice of metaphysic" that completes and perfects the "Goethe-Steiner system."

These first two serious engagements with Coleridge's philosophical writings plant the seed that Barfield would develop forty years later in *What Coleridge Thought*, as well as fertilizing his own engagement with Anthroposophy in the intervening years. As we have seen, he had already been convinced by Steiner's philosophical writings that the fundamental problem of modernity that needs overcoming is the alienation of the individual from the world that lurks within our every experience:

> the task of knowledge is not to *repeat* in conceptual form something already present somewhere else, but rather to *create* a completely new realm which, along with the world given to the senses, first constitutes full reality. With this, the highest activity of man, his spiritual activity, is incorporated organically into the general working of the world. (Steiner 1993, iii)

Thus, while "the universe appears to us in two opposite parts, '*I* and *World*,'" we "never cease to feel that in spite of all, we belong to the world, that there is a connecting link between it and us, and that we are beings within, and not *without*, the universe." Because of this intuition, we "strive to bridge over this antithesis, and in this bridging lies ultimately the whole spiritual striving of mankind. The history of our spiritual life is a continuing search for the unity between ourselves and the world. Religion, art and science follow, one and all, this aim" (Steiner 1964, 14). At this first threshold in his philosophical development, Barfield shared Steiner's aims and his epistemology, now underwritten by Coleridge's "universal law of polarity" as a metaphysics of the Logos that is polarized as a noun-verb structure in both self and nature, which also stand in polar tension as they emerge from the antecedent unity of "the given."

3. Scientism, Sartre, and Cassirer

Barfield developed his synthesis of Steiner and Coleridge in a number of essays following the Second World War. These reflect his deep engagement with contemporary developments in logical positivism, linguistic analysis, existentialism, and phenomenology. By this time, Barfield's philosophical views were mature—he does not appear to have been moved by his wide reading to alter his views but rather to challenge critics and find affinity with fellow travelers. For example, "The Time-Philosophy of Rudolf Steiner" (1955), ostensibly written for an Anthroposophical audience, reflects Barfield's absorption of "the things that have been happening in the realm of philosophical enquiry in our own century and especially in the second quarter of it" (*RCA* 253). Barfield's original audience must have found it to be a remarkable synoptic account, including not only the movements listed earlier but also neo-Thomism, scientism, psychoanalysis, metamaterialism, and so on.

The essay performs the twofold task that Barfield saw philosophy as having: purging the harmful errors of the day and opening the way for the leap from "knowing" to "being." It begins by endorsing Etienne Gilson's neo-Thomist definition of truth as "conformity to the being of the thing" in *The Spirit of Medieval Philosophy* but only in order to illustrate our distance from the medieval experience that "truth was nature re-forming herself in the mind of man"; for modern humanity, thinking is exiled from "the bosom of the word" (RCA 246). The essay ends with a return to this theme, though not with philosophy or the Middle Ages. Barfield closes it with quotations from Steiner's highly compressed, Christological *Leading Thoughts* that claim that "only through Michael's activity and the Christ-Impulse, can man achieve the leap across the gulf of Non-Being in relation to the cosmos" (RCA 269). Barfield does not complete the deduction of the identity of truth and being but urges his audience to take up the work of cognitive transformation that makes possible one's personal experience of their identity by stepping into Steiner's cosmology.

The bulk of the essay focuses on the many contemporary exilic paths through non-Being situated between these pictures of alienation from, and the promise of renewed participation in, "the word." Indeed, the evolution of consciousness, as it is revealed in the history of philosophy, has a trajectory of increasing alienation from Being:

> If the Greeks produced philosophies of Being, and the Middle Ages philosophies of the Word, the "classical" philosophies . . . may properly be called philosophies of the Mind. The history of European philosophy, from Descartes onward, might indeed be loosely described as a steady progress, or transition, from Philosophy to Psychology. (*RCA* 248)

This picture will be familiar to readers of Heidegger, whom Barfield mentions as "grappling once more, like any Socrates, with the old problem of Being and Non-being" (*RCA* 259). Like Heidegger, Husserl, and the other phenomenologists, Barfield was concerned that there is now "a sort of Iron Curtain between nature and the human mind" (*RCA* 249), and like Heidegger he detected the key role of technology—for example, "the telescope and the microscope"—in hastening their division.[8] "These instruments," he writes, "have the effect of cutting off, as it were, the microcosm from the macrocosm" (*RCA* 248). Of course, though Barfield shares Heidegger's view of the destructive effects of technology, the importance to him of the recovery of a productively polarized and tautegorical relation of mind to the world separates him from Heidegger's anti-idealist image of the radical finitude of Dasein.

Barfield also sketches the spectrum of contemporary philosophical views in a way that is reminiscent of Heidegger. He suggests that "the kernel of Anthroposophy is *the concept of man's self-consciousness as a process in time*" (*RCA* 252), that "Rudolf Steiner 'reached a different level of time-consciousness' from the ordinary man's" (*RCA* 251), and that this implies a "concept of *process*, which as yet found no acceptance, no real acceptance, anywhere outside the Anthroposophical Movement" (*RCA* 252). Though Heidegger was antipathetic toward the idealist overtones of "self-consciousness," this is obviously related to the *Lebensphilosophie* as a whole, and specifically to Heidegger's interest in the metaphysics of time and his research into the "history of Being" as the history of its concealment, in part under the cloak of our modern, mechanized, instrumental, and alienating experience of temporality.

A panoply of contemporary schools of philosophy, including Heideggerian ontology, share in common the impulse to go beyond:

> the picture of nature as consisting of a more or less unreal tapestry of sense-perceptions hung in front of, and concealing, a reality of a quite different order. . . . Previous philosophies have sought in one way or another to resolve and explain this contrast. They have wrestled each in its own way with the problem which F. H. Bradley took as the title of his book, the problem of *Appearance and Reality*. Whereas today it is being said that there is no such problem to wrestle with. That is the difference; that is the break. (*RCA* 254)

As Barfield was undoubtedly well aware, Russell and Moore launched their own movement of Logical Atomism as an attack on Bradley and the other British Hegelians.[9] By 1955, it had evolved into "metamaterialism" or "scientism," which does away with Locke's substratum, Descartes's object, Kant's Ding-an-Sich, or any other analogue to the "reality" beneath "appearances," by declaring that "all philosophy, or at all events, all metaphysics, is meaningless" (*RCA* 255) because it "abolishes the classical contrast between appearance and reality by affirming that words used in this way simply have no meaning" (*RCA* 256). Barfield argued at length and in many places against this view, echoing the common objection that the reduction of meaningful claims to verification through the senses "cannot itself have originated as a sense-impression" (*PD* 25).

One unintended consequence of scientism's vigorous reductionism is that it seems to logically entail one of the central features of Sartre's Existentialism:

> It was quite true that mechanical causality had reduced man himself, man the spirit, to a kind of zero. But by the very fact of doing so it had made him free. He might call himself nothing, but that nothing was free. Indeed it was free

because—so far at least as nature was concerned—it was nothing. Or you could put it this way: if man exists *at all*, then he is free. (*RCA* 250)

In its very rigor, scientism evokes the specter of Sartrean freedom. Barfield was rather amazed that "Sartre, by a kind of audacious philosophical *coup*, actually *equates* human consciousness with Not-being" (*RCA* 259). This emptiness of the self leads Sartre to conclude that "Man is a useless passion" (*RCA* 267) who is "*condemned* to freedom" (*RCA* 260) by virtue of this nullity. In this respect, Barfield seems to see Sartrean Existentialism as the "inner" aspect of the "outer" reduction performed by proponents of scientism:

> Between the very moment of consciousness and all else whatsoever, including any number of remembered or empirical selves, there exists for Sartre, "an irreducible gulf of Non-being." Man does exist, then, and he is free. But this fact of his existence gives him no content, no inside. Man's existence is not anything which can be effectively analysed or discussed. It can only be *lived*. It is behaviour that counts. For "man is only what he is doing." (*RCA* 259)

Barfield was fond of quoting Coleridge's dictum "extremes meet," for which he seems to have found surprising confirmation in scientism and Sartrean Existentialism. They see only their mutual opposition but share an impulse to overcome "the classical 'model' of a detached mind observing a pre-established world" (*RCA* 259). This form of Existentialism swerves away from Husserl's intention in proposing the phenomenological reduction, however, by reintroducing the very dualism it is supposed to deny, this time as a functional dualism of the "in-itself" and the "for-itself."[10]

Barfield further suggests that scientism and Sartre arrive at the same dead end because they are not interested in "the history of meaning" and consequently do not see where "the time-process of self-consciousness [is] most intimately displayed. For the history of meaning is the inner surface of the history of thought" (*RCA* 262). Thus, they miss, for example, not just that Aquinas had a different understanding of the relation of truth to being but also that he had a different felt experience both of the question "what is the relation of being to truth?" and of the relation itself. The evolution of consciousness is an essential aspect of the purportedly timeless inquiry into such questions. This brings to mind Ernst Cassirer, the philosopher with whom Barfield had the greatest affinity in the postwar years.[11]

We have already seen that Barfield lists Cassirer prominently among his "friends" in the afterword to *Poetic Diction*. We should note that in discussing "a weakness common to pretty well all the 'friends' to whom I have referred" (*PD* 222), Barfield mentions that:

> the truth is, it is not possible to speak convincingly of the active role of the individual human spirit in the world, while you continue to feel in your bones, whatever your intellect may be saying to you, that the individual human spirit is something that is encased in an individual human body. It was when this encapsulation began to be the general experience of humanity that the stream of Platonism, though it did not cease, became, as Neo-Platonism, an underground stream, and philosophically not quite respectable. (PD 223)

Barfield singles out Jung as particularly prone to this "residue of unresolved positivism" and notes the same elsewhere of Suzanne Langer, Cassirer's disciple. As we saw in the last chapter, Lovejoy, Lewis, Berlin, and Collingwood fail in the same way. However, Barfield never says the same of Cassirer; in fact, despite the difficult questions that continue to preoccupy Cassirer specialists and historians of philosophy—whether Cassirer is primarily a neo-Kantian, Hegelian, or a representative of some other school; whether he has a metaphysics at all or disavowed the subject as a whole; and so on—it is clear that Barfield thought Cassirer had a metaphysic, and that it had the same fundamental shape as his own, though with one crucial difference. "In my own field of study," he says in *Speaker's Meaning*:

> everything points to an evolution of consciousness, which, up to as recently as three or four centuries ago, has mainly taken the form of a contraction of meaning and therefore of consciousness—an evolution from wide and vague to narrow and precise, and from what was peripherally based to what is centrally based. . . . If history has been par excellence the period of developing thought, prehistory was par excellence the period of developing language . . . the period therefore during which man was slowly and painfully extracting his subjectivity from language; that is, as Cassirer, for one, has so convincingly demonstrated, from the inside of nature through the medium of language. (SM 110–11)

Compact within this comment are the main themes Barfield draws from Cassirer: the antecedent unity from which consciousness and nature crystallize, the role of the symbol in facilitating that process by mediating between the two, and the record of that process in the history of language itself. Barfield seems not to have troubled himself with whether Cassirer's late statements about language and reality in *An Essay on Man* are fully consistent with the fuller and more detailed accounts in the three volumes of *The Philosophy of Symbolic Forms*, whether Cassirer's functionalism has unwelcome metaphysical implications, or whether neo-Kantianism taints Cassirer's philosophy as a whole. Barfield refers primarily to *The Philosophy of Symbolic Forms*, notes with apparent approval

Language and Myth and *The Platonic Renaissance in England*, and says that he has read "many" works by Cassirer (including, presumably, *The Individual and the Cosmos in Renaissance Philosophy*).[12]

The section on metaphysics that Cassirer wrote in 1929 while composing volume three of *The Philosophy of Symbolic Forms*, which he intended to form its conclusion, was published for the first time in 1995. Barfield obviously cannot have known about that work, though he may have known something of Cassirer's metaphysics from the essay "Spirit and Life" that was published in the "Library of Living Philosophers" volume devoted to Cassirer. However, Barfield seems to have intuited some of its basic features. For Cassirer, metaphysics takes up "the dynamics of the giving of meaning" (Cassirer 1995, 4), not simply the formal structure, domains, and limits of knowledge as outlined in Kant's critical project. Cassirer is clear that his project "cannot stop" (Cassirer 1995, 4) at the boundaries imposed by Kant, though he does retain and often employ Kant's method of the transcendental deduction. At the same time, Cassirer rejects as useless Schelling's version of Absolute idealism. Cassirer begins volume two of *The Philosophy of Symbolic Forms* with a discussion and critique of Schelling's groundbreaking work on the philosophy of myth. Schelling finds within it a dialectic or "twofold direction, toward the subject and the object, in regard to the self-consciousness and the absolute" (Cassirer 1955, 5). Cassirer offers a patient analysis of Schelling's view that "the mythological process is a theogonic process: one in which God himself *becomes*, by creating himself step by step as the true god" (Cassirer 1955, 6).[13] The progress of the Absolute toward self-knowledge from its origins in mythic consciousness reveals:

> the characteristic merit and limitations of Schelling's idealism.... It is the concept of the unity of the absolute which truly and definitively guarantees the absolute unity of the human consciousness by deriving every particular achievement and trend of spiritual activity from a common ultimate origin. The danger of this concept of unity is however that it will ultimately absorb all concrete, particular differentiations and make them unrecognizable. (Cassirer 1955, 9)

This criticism of Schelling's Absolute Idealism is essentially the same as Hegel's claim that it is "the night in which all cows are black." Cassirer does not offer an opinion on the "theogonic" perspective on myth, except to say that it is a philosophical dead end. Neither does he endorse Hegel's Absolute. Cassirer instead retains the emphasis on dialectic common to the post-Kantian idealists (Fichte, Schelling, Hegel) and both Hegel's critique of Schelling and his definition of the true as the whole:

we start from the concept of the whole: the whole is the true (Hegel). But the truth of the whole can always only be grasped in a particular "aspect." This is "knowledge" in the *broadest* sense—"seeing" the whole "in" an aspect, through the medium of this aspect. With this, the problem of representation becomes the central problem of knowledge. Knowledge is "organic" insofar as every part is conditioned by the whole and can be made "understandable" only by reference to the whole. It cannot be composed of pieces, of elements, except to the extent that each part already carries in itself the "form" of the whole. The concept of "form" ειδος, μορπη was already grasped in this way in Greek philosophy and goes through the whole history of Western philosophy. (Cassirer 1995, 193)

Hegel's "concrete universal" is visible in the background behind the notion of "form," as is the holistic or tautegorical presence of the whole in the part that Barfield also emphasizes, though detached from Hegel's metaphysics of the Absolute. Likewise, the whole is the true, but Cassirer omits Hegel's picture of the necessary teleological progress, out of logical necessity, of the Absolute's journey toward completely self-aware self-transparency.

Cassirer's metaphysics does not have a single unifying principle like Heidegger's "Being" or Schelling's "Absolute." For Cassirer, it is a polarity of "life" and "spirit," organic in the sense he gives in the passage quoted here. The cultural productions of "spirit" reflect in their particularity the "undifferentiated unity" of "life" (Cassirer 1995, 5). As if extending an olive branch to Heidegger, but also invoking Plato's *Timaeus* and Hegel's *Logic*, Cassirer defines life as "nothing other than a pure kind of internal being; in fact its basic character appears to be defined by this very Being-in-itself and Remaining-in-itself" (Cassirer 1995, 9). Indeed, Cassirer's distinction of "life" from simple "being" seems surprisingly to bring him closer to Heidegger: "the concept of Life is distinguished from the concept of Being in the older metaphysics and from its 'ontology' by virtue of this one basic feature: it recognizes no substantiality other than that which consists of pure actuality alone" (Cassirer 1995, 9). Yet, in addition to "eternally flowing abundance" or "flux without pause" (Cassirer 1995, 9), life is an "intellectual oxymoron" (Cassirer 1995, 9) because it is also "individualized, and therefore always a bounded form which continually jumps its bounds" (Cassirer 1995, 9). Thus, Cassirer endorses Simmel's paradoxical statement that "the essence of concrete life as it takes place is (not something that is added onto its being, but that of which its being consists), 'that *transcendence is immanent in life*'" (Cassirer 1995, 9).

"Spirit" crystallizes out of "life" and must be defined in relation to it. Whereas animals belong to the "circle of action" characteristic of life, human beings, because they discover by means of concepts the "objective characteristics and objective contexts" that order the organic realm, attain the "circle of vision" (Cassirer 1995, 76). Human beings belong to the circle of action, and to the subjectivity and sheer becoming of the pole of "life," but in their crystallization of concepts achieve timeless objectivity. Spiritual activity is cultural activity through the medium of symbolic forms. In the context of symbolically ordered cultural norms and activities, human beings become conscious of themselves and the world around them, ultimately finding "a new means for distinguishing and critically setting the limits between 'nature' and 'geist,' between 'life' and 'consciousness,' a delimitation which nevertheless remains strictly within the world of thought and utilizes only its own, immanent means" (Cassirer 1995, 55). These immanent means are the symbols that constitute myth. Language in particular is instrumental in lifting the human being out of unselfconscious life into the reflective thinking that is "spirit." Cassirer earned Barfield's deep and enduring admiration for his meticulous, painstaking unfolding through his analysis of language, myth, and phenomenology (used by Cassirer in Hegel's, not Husserl's, sense) of the history of "spirit" as it emerges from, gives form to, and continually returns to "life."[14]

Even so, Cassirer's equivocation on "life" as both "eternally flowing abundance" and discrete living things and processes is obviously vulnerable to critique. Heidegger, if his critical review of the second volume of *The Philosophy of Symbolic Forms* is any indication, would no doubt notice and condemn that Cassirer effectively equates "Being" with "beings." Barfield would surely notice that whereas Coleridge has a "logos philosophy" in which the antecedent unity of the Logos polarizes into "life" and "spirit," respectively, Cassirer has deprived himself of this resource:

> This insight into the determining and discriminating function, which myth as well as language performs in the mental construction of our world of "things," seems to be all that a "philosophy of symbolic forms" can teach us. Philosophy as such can go no further; it cannot presume to present to us, *in concreto*, the great process of emergence, and to distinguish its phases for us. (Cassirer 1946, 15)

Cassirer's metaphysical shyness, induced by or reflected in his equivocation on "life," returns him to the crux of post-Kantian idealism: the essence of the antecedent unity. Furthermore, he leaves himself no good way to determine whether, say, living things that have not been subject to "spirit" are the "same" as those that have. For Barfield, even Cassirer ultimately must join the philosophers who stub their toes on "the concept of man's self-consciousness as a process in time" (*RCA* 252).

4. *What Coleridge Thought*

What Coleridge Thought, which Barfield worked on throughout the 1960s, is his major effort to address the questions raised by his reading of modern philosophy. A few years after its publication, Barfield noted that he and Coleridge advocated "objective idealism," and that the objective variant differed from both Platonic and Berkeleyan idealisms.[15] The definition of "objective idealism" as opposed to a "subjective" variant was a prominent part of the debates among the post-Kantians, as Beiser notes:

> There was first of all the "subjective" or "formal" idealism of Kant and Fichte, according to which the transcendental subject is the source of the form but not the matter of experience. Contrary to it, there was the "objective" or "absolute" idealism of the romantics (Hölderlin, Novalis, Schlegel, Schelling, and the young Hegel), according to which the forms of experience are self-subsistent and transcend both the subject and the object. The basic difference between these forms is simple and straightforward. While subjective idealism *attaches* the forms of experience to the transcendental subject, which is their source and precondition, objective idealism *detaches* them from that subject, making them hold for the realm of pure being as such. (Beiser 2002, 11)

In Barfield's understanding, Platonism is sterile because it posits for Ideas "a kind of independent separate existence of their own" (Sugarman 18). This is due, as he put it in *What Coleridge Thought*, to the fact that "that polarity between subject and object, which is at the base of Coleridge's system, is nowhere to be found in Plato. It is only in Coleridge therefore that we find such a concept as that of an 'initiative idea,' on which method depends" (*WCT* 125). Subjective idealists, meanwhile, "treat ideas as a subjective process in individual human minds but nevertheless, in the development of this philosophy, it presents them as being more real than the objective world" (Sugarman 18).

Barfield's "objective" idealism denies the division:

> Objective idealism contends that that disjunction is itself an unreal one, and that reality, individual being, however you think of it, consists of the polarity between the subjectivity of the individual mind and the objective world which it perceives. They are not two things, but they are one and the same thing and

what you call the objective world is merely one pole of what is a unitary process and what we call subjective experience is the other pole, but they are not really divided from each other. (Sugarman 18)

Here are Cassirer's two poles of "life" and "spirit" recast along the lines of an Absolute Idealism that avows the indifference of subject and object or, as Hegel famously defined it, the identity of identity and nonidentity. *What Coleridge Thought* is Barfield's attempt to justify, through Coleridge's philosophy, what he puts forward here as his own commitment to objective idealism.[16] Moreover, beyond attempting to bring Coleridge's fragmentary expression into a single coherent presentation, Barfield also argues for "the relevance of Coleridge's thought to our time" in his "radical critique of . . . [the] major presuppositions, upon which the immediate thinking, and as a result the whole cultural and social structure of this 'epoch of the understanding and the senses' (including supposedly radical revolts against it) is so firmly . . . established" (*WCT* 11). These major presuppositions are the post-Cartesian underpinnings of our fundamental, preconscious experiences of the self, the world, and the relation (or lack thereof) between them. It encompasses, for Barfield, not merely the "ghost in the machine" generated by Descartes and Berkeley but also positivist efforts by the likes of Gilbert Ryle to rid ourselves of it. It is also, we recall, one of the "collective habits" that prevents our easily grasping the evolution of consciousness.

The sequence of the chapters in Barfield's book is not so much an overview of Coleridge's philosophy as the elaboration of an argument. The first two chapters present the polar phenomenology of consciousness: the first chapter focuses on the "active" or "inner" pole, Cassirer's "spirit," through the question "what is thinking?" and demonstrates, among much else, that it is not self-evidently a "subjective" or private possession. The second chapter takes up the "passive" or "outer" pole, Cassirer's "life," with the question "what is a phenomenon?" (*WCT* 23) and again calls into question the "externality" of the objects of our experience. The third and fourth chapters recapitulate the first and second but from a higher perspective: the third chapter again takes up the pole of "activity," this time by beginning to sketch a theory of polarity as the basis of a metaphysic that will replace those founded on the "unquestioned grounds" of "matter and motion" (*WCT* 23). The fourth chapter alternates to the passive "outer" pole again and raises the "phenomenon" to a higher level by examining Coleridge's answer to the question "what is life?" The fifth chapter brings the first section of the book to a close. It joins the poles explored in the first four chapters by deducing from an initial unity the separation of inner activity from outer manifestation, a process Coleridge describes as the establishment of "outness." It defends the thesis both that "interior is anterior" and that the "exterior," though subordinate, is a structural component of consciousness. The middle third of the book, chapters six through nine, focus on the structure of consciousness through an analysis of imagination, fancy, reason, and understanding. These do not constitute a quasi-Kantian faculty psychology but rather are "powers [that] themselves interpenetrate one another" (*WCT* 93). The final third of the book focuses again on the "outer" or phenomenal world, our being-in-the-world, in the form of a philosophy of science and Coleridge's social and historical vision.

Like many of Barfield's books, *What Coleridge Thought* deserves a longer study of its own. I can instead only focus on a few of the themes in the book: first, the deduction and description of polarity; second, the distinction of reason from understanding, and the forms of thought appropriate to each; and finally, arising directly from these themes, the transformation of metaphysics into cosmology that occurs at the limit of philosophical thinking.

In the chapter on "Life," Barfield says about Coleridge what he could just as easily have said about himself: that his "whole system of thought . . . was rooted in, and must stand or fall with, his critique of the Cartesian dualism" (*WCT* 49). The refutation of dualism is also the underpinning of the positive argument for polarity, which Barfield carries out by a kind of transcendental deduction.[17] The account of "thinking" and "phenomena" in the first two chapters goes some way toward this refutation. The chapter on "thinking" seeks to establish, contra the Empiricists, that in the act of thinking the *res cogitans* is inseparable from the percepts that are its objects: "This refusal to *distinguish* between thinking and perceiving, and thus between the mind and the senses, was . . . based on the fact . . . that the two are in practice found to be inseparable" (*WCT* 18). So too, in defining "life" the "materialists ostracised any reference to a teleological principle in living organisms as an impermissible 'argument from design'" and the rationalists insist on "the direct intervention of God in an otherwise admittedly clockwise universe" (*WCT* 49). Because both attempts fail to offer an adequate account of "life," we must have recourse to the only means of supplying an account of its undeniable existence and uniqueness. Like Kant in the *Critique of Judgment*, we are driven by the inadequacy of rationalist and empiricist metaphysics to find something else that will save the appearances. For Barfield and Coleridge, this "something" is polarity, without which an explanation is impossible.

Polarity is a difficult concept to grasp because it affronts the laws of noncontradiction and the excluded middle. While "a logical contradiction is mere negation . . . the essence of polarity is a *dynamic* conflict between coinciding opposites" (*WCT* 187). This dynamic conflict invites a logical description: whereas "logical opposites are contradictory, polar opposites are generative of each other—and together generative of a new product" (*WCT* 36). A "metaphysic based on the universal law of polarity" opposes "the metaphysic of abstractions developed by exclusive reliance on the understanding and the senses" (*WCT* 181) by, in part, substituting a paradox for a contradiction. The need for such a substitution results both from the failure of the many forms of the post-Cartesian "metaphysic of abstractions" and from the pragmatic benefits of assuming the existence of "two forces of one power." Barfield himself questions whether, in making such claims, he has only succeeded in offering "definitions of the undefinable" (*WCT* 36). We arrive in this way at the limit of philosophy as traditionally understood: "the apprehension of polarity is itself *the basic act of imagination*" and "only imagination will do" (*WCT* 36) in grasping it.

"Outness" is the basic phenomenological experience that compels us to take up "polarity" as the fundamental law of the nature of the world, the mind, and the interactions of them both. Its examination also compels us to see thought and perception as grounded in an underlying unity. We have seen that for Barfield and Coleridge there are:

> in every human mind . . . two absolute convictions, or certainties, neither of which requires demonstrating, and both of which are in fact indemonstrable, because they are the twin constituents of human consciousness itself. Perhaps we may call them "awarenesses." The first is the awareness "that things exist without us," in other words, naïve realism, not as a doctrine but as common experience and common sense. The second is that I am perceiving things. (*WCT* 63)

These indispensable "awarenesses" are deeply and irremovably rooted in our experience. We take them so unquestionably for granted that "the certainty *is* the outness" at the bedrock of experience as such. They are dogmas that form the axiomatic starting place, the absolute presuppositions, of our failed metaphysic—Cartesians take one pole and make it axiomatic of the other, physicalists take the other pole and do the same. For Coleridge and Barfield, though, the surprising conclusion is not that they exist but that on close observation the "outness" that their polar tension produces "is not only coherent but identical, and one and the same thing, with our own immediate self consciousness" (*WCT* 64). This insight—that self-consciousness and outness are correlative and simultaneous phenomena—compels the conclusion that subject and object are the two fundamental forces of an implicit anterior power, from which both derive. This "one power" is most fully explored not as a metaphysical entity but by way of Coleridge's distinction between reason and understanding.

It is easy to forget the indivisible irreducibility of thinking and phenomenon when turning to Barfield's account of Coleridge's philosophy of mind. This difficulty, and the inability of post-Cartesian worldviews to overcome it, is itself a by-product of "understanding." The understanding is a twofold power, having a "lower" form that we share with animals and that grows out of instinct. Its "higher" form, which is an abstracting, rule-forming power that makes language possible:

> it entails the power not merely to behave by rules, but also to formulate them—to know, in fact what the word *rule* means. For what renders understanding human is precisely this ability to identify by naming. It is this that gives the possibility of the distinctively human acquirement of speech. No abstraction, no language. (*WCT* 99)

We are reminded of the "rational principle" in Barfield's poetics. Though necessary to language, this gift of abstraction is double-edged. On the one hand, because "it is concerned *only* with names" it gives rise to nominalism and its Cartesian and Kantian descendants; ironically, its gift of accuracy is also the sharpest tool to refute such systems. It tends to forget it is "important as a means, not as an end in itself; and the ends towards which it should be employed are imagination and the ideas of reason" (*WCT* 100). Consequently, it invents idols that "we have been tempted into revering as ends" (*WCT* 100). Chief among these false ends is the gift of alienation:

> Understanding, alone, gives "outness," accuracy and the experience of unity; but this unity is not unity in multeity; it is unity by the exclusion of multeity. Understanding, alone, assures us that we exist as separate and distinct points; but only *as* points, only as the nothings of Sartre-type existentialism. (*WCT* 101)

In the sphere of language, then, "understanding" generates and is limited to naming; in psychology, it defines the self as a fixed null point that can only be discerned through negation; as a mode of thought, it operates through logic. Its negating thrust limits valid thinking to the "principle of contradiction," which "tells us nothing of what nature, or anything else, *is*. It tells us only what it is *not*; and, in doing so, clenches our absurd detachment from it—which we perhaps choose to call our 'analytical unity'" (*WCT* 110).

Logic, like the "outer," fixed phenomenon itself, is necessary to consciousness but itself requires an explanation—it is a product no less than *natura naturata*. Should we attempt to leap from nature as fixed and dead to its "living" quality, we immediately run up against the boundary of understanding: "beginning, change, motion itself, development, evolution, life—anything whatever that is *naturans* as well as *naturata*—eludes the rigorous *either: or* of understanding plus the senses" (*WCT* 110). Reason, for Coleridge and Barfield, allows us to grasp the generative phenomena that exceed understanding. Indeed, reason generates understanding itself: "the immediate product of reason in the understanding is the principle of contradiction. But only that which itself transcends two contradictories can have produced them. Thus, if we do not remain wilfully blind, our attention is drawn, by the truth of contradiction itself, to 'the truths of reason'" (*WCT* 111). This is so because reason both furnishes forth the law of contradiction and is "producent of products in contradiction with one another" (*WCT* 111). Seen in this light, reason is the source of the laws of logic that constitute understanding; contradiction itself, then, is a frozen polarity: "the first step towards apprehending reason, as active, is thus the apprehension of polarity; it is to apprehend reason as 'productive unity,' as 'separative projection,' as 'the tendency at once to individuate and to connect, to detach, but so as either to retain or to reproduce attachment'" (*WCT* 111).

The "tendency to individuate," which understanding calcifies into the "onlooker" approach to nature that forty years earlier Barfield called a "philosophy of Death," finds its vibrant fulfilment in the light of reason. Like the understanding, it has a negative and a positive aspect:

> As negative, it brings about the total detachment which individuality presupposes. As positive reason, it is the being of the individual so detached. . . . The light of reason is thus both the origin and the abiding basis of individuality. Without the positive presence of reason to the understanding, there is no individuality, only the detachment which individual being presupposes. Reason, in both its positive and negative aspect, is the individualizer. (*WCT* 106)

And yet, as both ground and surface of the self, "its whole characteristic is to *be* superindividual. It individualises because it is, and by being, superindividual; by being *totus in omni parte*—'entire in each and one in all'" (*WCT* 106). Reason is Being itself. It generates the powers (like the fancy, understanding, and imagination) by which we distinguish ourselves from "outer" phenomena and is what constitutes the uniqueness of the individual.

At this point, a "difficulty appears for most people" (*WCT* 106) because reason, like "polarity," requires the bracketing of logic by the "fundamental act" of the imagination. Barfield does not try to force through a deduction of reason as a kind of Absolute. At the pivotal moment, he asserts that "each true self is (*totus in omni parte*) a distinctive unity of that multeity. Another name for it is Reason. But Reason is Being" (*WCT* 176). The individual is not a fragment of a larger whole, or an alienated island, but *is* the whole: the logic of reason is based in synecdoche and metaphor. Here, Barfield again confronts us with the paradox of selfhood as Being, or Being as selfhood, and suggests that the "noetic hierarchy" it entails:

> is not only actual but also, in theory, knowable—but only by a knowing which is at the same time a being. Coleridge seems further committed to the view that such qualitative knowledge could be *communicable*, not it is true directly, in terms of an understanding working only with quantities, but by that "symbolic use of the understanding" which is the function of imagination. (*WCT* 176)

This view of the self as both part and whole, as most whole when most individual, implies the figurative logic of synecdoche. If understanding is limited to naming, to logic, to quantities—all of which are provided by reason itself; reason's fundamental gesture is the qualitative figure. To experience the self *as* Being is "to experience likeness as a *polarity* of sameness and difference" (*WCT* 112). That is to say, it is "to experience metaphor as metaphor" (*WCT* 112). Perhaps surprisingly, Barfield does not deeply explore Coleridge's theory of the symbol in *What Coleridge Thought*. He is content to lead us to the limit of deductive reasoning and to invite us to make the leap into the figurative thinking required by the experience of "likeness as a *polarity* of sameness and difference" (*WCT* 112).

It may seem that deep exploration of Coleridge's Objective Idealism has taken Barfield far from his phenomenological roots. Two essays written in the years immediately after the publication of *What Coleridge Thought*, "Matter, Imagination, and Spirit" (1974) and "Language and Discovery" (1973), show him bringing the two apparently antithetical positions together in a productive polarity while opening the way yet again to the Anthroposophical project of personal transformation, through the articulation of, and participation in, a poetic cosmology. Barfield wrote "Matter, Imagination, and Spirit" for an audience of religious scholars. It begins by defining "matter" and "spirit" by how we use them and appears to parody the methods of the positivists of whom he was sharply critical but perhaps actually reflects some influence of the Scottish "common sense" school about which Barfield expressed appreciation at the time.

In any case, while Barfield endorses Leibniz's definition of matter as "coagulum spiritus" he is content to say that in our contemporary common-sense "matter" means that which is practically or theoretically available to the senses. As for matter's opposite pole, "by 'spirit' we must mean 'that which is not matter,' and by 'that which is not matter' we mean that part of the totality which is not perceptible to the senses" (*RM* 146). One discerns here once again both Barfield's affinity for Cassirer and the subtle distinction between them. Matter and spirit correspond to Cassirer's poles of life and spirit, but whereas for Cassirer "life" is both the antecedent unity and one of the poles from which it emerges, Barfield recognizes that maintaining simultaneously that matter is coagulated spirit and that spirit is "that which is not matter" entails that "we should have no good name left for all that is *not* . . . perceptible" (*RM* 146) and therefore a "rather meaningless meaning" for spirit.

Barfield therefore retains the polarity of matter and spirit rooted in our common usage of the terms, abandons his facetious deduction of their "ancient semantic unity," and raises instead the intentionally vague, but practical, question "how do we get at spirit?" (*RM* 146). Clearly, given the common-sense definitions of matter and spirit, we cannot say that we can get at spirit by means of perception. Rather, we do so through what phenomenologists call "intentionality" and post-Kantian idealists like Fichte and Schelling (and the young Hegel) term "intellectual intuition":

> there is *one* thing we *never* suppose we have perceived, one thing of which we are perhaps aware during most of our waking lives, and of which we are perhaps aware most of all in the act of perceiving other things. I mean of course ourselves, who are doing the perceiving. We come back to the definition of matter. Just as we cannot really think of spirit, *as* spirit, unless we are also able to think of matter, so we cannot think of matter, *as* matter, unless we are also able to think of spirit. Matter is always that *of which* I am conscious; but correlative to it, and at the opposite pole, is the "I" who am conscious. (*RM* 215)

Here we have a kind of deduction of the polarity of perceiver and perceived, life and spirit, from common sense itself, though Barfield is aware that in our post-Cartesian, post-Kantian age we experience the polarity as a contradiction. Precisely because "matter is . . . the *occasion* of the spirit's awareness of itself as spirit" (*RM* 148) one feels oneself to be like "a small helpless creature caught in a trap between the two" (*RM* 150). Thus, we are like Sartre's poor creatures condemned to freedom as we struggle to "live in that abrupt gap between matter and spirit" (*RM* 150).

Barfield's answer to Sartre is that "a strengthening and deepening of the faculty of imagination—or better say the activity of imagination—is really the only way in which we can have to do with the spirit" (*RM* 149–50). The gap itself is, as Sartre maintains, the reason "we exist . . . as autonomous, self-conscious individual spirits, as free beings" (*RM* 150). The gap is also the necessary condition for imaginative activity, but "in this case not as a small helpless creature caught in a trap between the two, but rather as a rainbow spanning the two precipices and linking them harmoniously together" (*RM* 150). Thus, Barfield's practical suggestion, and his answer to Sartre, is that "it seems better to realize the gap and live in it not as a creature caught in a trap, but as the rainbow that spans it" (*RM* 150). Barfield points in particular to Goethe, Hegel, and Steiner as figures who have blazed this path methodologically (*RM* 151, 153). Barfield was no doubt aware that the role he ascribes to "imagination" in this essay parallels the role played by "symbolic form" and language in Cassirer's and his own metaphysics. The essay, then, offers a phenomenological account of the polarity of matter and spirit, along with imagination, as the activity that spans the divide, while using the techniques of the "common sense" school to respond to the reductionism of positivism and Sartrean existentialism. At the same time, Barfield invites his readers to take up the practical work of training the imagination so that they might, for example, "experience another in the same mode as we experience ourselves, when we experience him not across the gap between matter and spirit, but as being on the same side of the gap as *we are*" (*RM* 222).

5. Metaphysics as Revelation

Two late essays, "The Concept of Revelation" (1980) and "Meaning, Revelation and Tradition" (1982), help to illustrate the continued importance of Coleridge specifically, and metaphysics in general, to Barfield, as well as retroactively justifying the equivalence that Barfield posits in his early Anthroposophical essays of "imagination" and "clairvoyance" (as we will explore in the following chapter). The essays may even be considered a diptych, connected by Barfield's interest in "revelation" and Coleridge's help in unpacking it. The first essay attempts to carve out a new critical-philosophical use for the concept of revelation: "Revelation is related to criticism as discovery is to observation and judgment. It may be an unfamiliar term in the vocabulary of literary criticism, but it is not an entirely new thing in literature" (Barfield 1980, 119). By the end of the essay, this has expanded to include literature and theology because "a healthy future for both literature and religion depends on what I would call the idea of literature coalescing, as it were, with the idea of religion in an evolutionary concept of revelation" (Barfield 1980, 125).

"The Concept of Revelation" takes for granted conclusions Barfield believed he had secured in *What Coleridge Thought*. Most importantly, with regard to the concept of revelation he minimizes the importance of the seemingly ubiquitous distinction between "within" and "without" because it assumes that "within" is synonymous with "the cuticle of a human organism" (Barfield 1980, 120). This of course is also one benefit of shifting the subject/object distinction to one between "spirit" and "matter." Barfield, true to his phenomenological commitments and his conviction that consciousness does not end at the surface of the skin, favors a distinction "between what is or could be an object of the senses and what is not and could not be so" (Barfield 1980, 120–1). This is necessary to "forming a satisfactory concept of revelation in *any* sense" (Barfield 1980, 121). Also important, and consonant with Coleridge's historiography, is Barfield's "bald synopsis" that:

> The element of attention and intention in contemporary sense perceptions makes hay of any hypothesis, for example, of natural selection as the only, or even the predominant, agent of evolutionary process in its early stages. Further, in its later stages (namely pre-history and history of humanity), there is ample evidence, for instance in the history of language, of a continuing evolution of perception itself away from a pre-intentional towards an increasingly intentional experience and activity. (Barfield 1980, 122)

On the basis of these premises, Barfield sketches an evolution of the experience of revelation. He begins with ancient cultures in which, because "the whole relation between sensation, intention, and thought, which is embodied in language, was very differently adjusted" (Barfield 1980 122), they experienced revelation as coming "from without, that is, through the phenomenal medium" (Barfield 1980 123). It is characteristic of the modern experience, however, that revelation comes from within—that is to say, not from objects of the senses but from acts of imagination. Or, as Barfield summarizes his point:

> Either we accept the real presence of a divine or supernatural agency, or we do not . . . . If we do accept such agency, and further the possibility of that agency disclosing any knowledge of itself, then there appear to be two conceivable kinds of disclosure. The one from *without*, that is through the senses, and the other from *within*. My suggestion, with support from Coleridge, is that this second kind, not less than the first, may properly be called "revelation," whether it is found in sacred or profane literature. (Barfield 1980, 120)

This argument is a continuation of *What Coleridge Thought*. Barfield takes for granted that the phenomenology of the sacred is homologous with poetic language, that the subject is not limited to the "cuticle" of the body, and that perception itself is woven through the conceptual, in the form of intentions, preconscious identifications and distinctions, and so on. Barfield applies Coleridge's thoughts to the evolution of consciousness as a way to make available in the modern age the concept of "revelation," from which we are so distant that it is either wholly unimaginable or desiccated by "source hunting" academic research.

"Meaning, Revelation and Tradition in Language and Religion," Barfield's last major essay, was published when he was eighty-four years old. It too takes up the theme of "revelation," this time as part of a meditation on the opening of The Gospel of John, which, Barfield notes, has been at the heart of "practically all I have ever written on the subject of language and other matters connected with it" (Barfield 1982, 117). The essay turns on the nature of the symbol. Previously, Barfield took Coleridge to task for what he called "the Coleridge-Lewis doctrine" (*RM* 93), and in *What Coleridge Thought* he gave Coleridge's theory of the symbol scant attention. In this essay, Coleridge's famous claim in the *Statesman's Manual* that the symbol "is also *part* of what it symbolizes" (Barfield 1982, 118) returns like a motif, with deepening meaning, throughout the essay. Indeed, Coleridge's definition of the symbol as a close relative of synecdoche, if not a species of it, helps to explain the structure of Barfield's essay. At its center is the prologue to the Gospel of John and in concentric circles around it: the definition of the symbol, of words as the "primary symbols of consciousness," of phenomena as symbols, and finally of divine-phenomenal human beings as "primary symbols" that resemble words as "the likeness between the generated and the generant, the kind of likeness which allows us to call the manifest an 'image' of the unmanifest" (Barfield 1982, 127).

Immediately after endorsing Coleridge's definition of the symbol, Barfield's notes that words are our primary symbols, and that "if words are symbols, they are symbols not of *things* but of *meanings*—not of something physical but essentially of something mental" (Barfield 1982, 118). A word has "a remarkable, even paradoxical, quality—namely that it both goes out and remains where it was to start with" (Barfield 1982, 117). It "remains where it was" insofar as it is "the ink marks on the paper or the sound in the air" but it also "has a second element, inasmuch as it expresses or symbolizes, or what you will, something that is *not* perceptible to the senses, the something that is called its meaning" (Barfield 1982, 117–18). The paradoxical nature of the word, then, itself symbolizes the fundamental problem of the symbol that nests within the problem of meaning.

It is therefore unsurprising that the simply "literary approach to the symbol" is "unsatisfactory" because it "hardly reaches down to the problem of meaning itself, of meaning as such" (Barfield 1982, 119). This failure is understandable, though, since words are *"primary symbols*—symbols you can't get behind.... they are what Paul Ricoeur has called 'fundamental symbols of consciousness'" (Barfield 1982, 119). In this respect, as the site of the disclosure of concepts and percepts, the paradox of the word is the paradox of the phenomenon. Barfield endorses Henri Corbin's Heideggerian definition of "the word 'phenomenon': 'The phenomenon is that which shows itself, that which is apparent and which in its appearance shows forth something which can reveal itself therein only by remaining concealed beneath the appearance'" (Barfield 1982, 119).[18] The phenomenon is, as it were, a secondary symbol, disclosed by the "primary symbol" of the word, exhibiting the word's paradoxical structure of revelation and concealment.

In these difficult circumstances, it is no wonder that contemporary attempts:

> to explain in words how words come to *be* symbols, or just what symbolizing means in that case, is merely using what are already symbols to explain symbols. It is therefore not *explanation*, but merely *substitution*. In fact, the objection to this process is very similar to Coleridge's objection to the philosophy of science as it prevailed in his day—and still does in our own. That philosophy, he said, is based on the false assumption that phenomena (that is, everything perceptible to the senses) can be explained by other phenomena.... It is, with another hat on, the same old problem you started out to explain—the problem of how the world came into existence. Claiming to investigate origin, all you have really done is to discern rearrangements. (Barfield 1982, 119)

Ricoeur, Auerbach, and Cassirer make valuable attempts to explore the threshold where primary and secondary symbols meet, but because we still have "the bandage of Cartesian and Kantian dogma drawn across [our] eyes," and so have an "undue obsession with the physical brain," we lack "a convincing psychology of fundamental symbolism" (Barfield 1982, 120). Psychology for us remains "physiology in disguise" (Barfield 1982, 121), with the danger that "if we forget that all words are primary symbols of consciousness, then in the end we simply fail to apprehend it as meaning" (Barfield 1982, 124).

The beginning of the way out is, once again, Coleridge. His dictum that "there is one principle which produces the object of perception and the same principle at the other pole produces the contemplation of that object" (Barfield 1982, 121) is already implicit in the dual nature of the word. For Ricoeur, the symbol gives rise to thought; for Auerbach, it is a sign that is also a fulfilment; for Barfield, it is a going out that is also a remaining still. In this sense, it is "what can equally well be called 'revelation'" (Barfield 1982, 122) insofar as it concerns "the primary mystery of the unmanifest becoming manifest." This "is the only profitable frame of mind in which to approach this problem of words as *primary* symbols" (Barfield 1982, 122) because:

> such an approach mitigates our tendency to over-emphasize the factor of likeness in building our concept of symbol—of likeness between one created thing and another. . . . We should strive rather to conceive the kind of likeness that may subsist between the generated and the generant, to conceive of the manifest being in some manner the "image" of the unmanifest. (Barfield 1982, 122)

To strive for this polar understanding and experience of "likeness" is to "re-acquire the pristine energy, so to speak, of revelation" (Barfield 1982, 125), which in its "primary" form helps us in "transcending our limited understanding of . . . the essentially symbolic nature of the word" (Barfield 1982, 124). Because human speech begins with the "inner word" that for medieval philosophers precedes articulated speech, it "is always something at the same time proceeding from the intellect and remaining within the intellect" (Barfield 1982, 124). It requires for its creation "the Divine Word [that] is self-generating" (Barfield 1982, 124).

Such a definition, of course, recalls the distinction between understanding and reason. It reminds us of the insight Barfield gained on his first encounters with Steiner and Coleridge: that imagination must first be experienced before it can become the subject of philosophy, and that the importance of philosophy is to clear away the errors that obscure it and then to awaken us to its significance. It also recalls that if the human being is the nexus where primary symbol and primary mystery meet, as it grounds, discovers, and speaks itself into being, then the human being is also a mystery to itself. It is the convergence of idea and phenomenon, speech and silence, the speaking of oneself into existence in an act of self-positing that is also a self-recollection; as we will see in Chapter 5, it is the equitable encounter with the other that is also, and for the first time, an introduction to oneself. And, as Barfield makes sure to note with regard to the unresolved positivism that gets in the way of such an affirmation, "it is one thing to overcome it as theory and another to overcome it as experience. . . . To overcome it as ordinary daily experience would mean you would have to become a different kind of human being" (Sugarman 15). The method and practice of becoming a "different kind of human being," and the poetic cosmology in which the human being as "primary symbol" can be fully articulated, are the gifts, for Barfield, of Anthroposophy, to which we now turn.

4

The Door to Eternity

Anthroposophy

The fruit of Barfield's metaphysics is the transcendental deduction of the imagination and the principle of polarity (which entail one another) as well as the demonstration of the antecedent unity and figurative identity of subject and object, spirit and matter, imagination and revelation, and the "primary symbols" of the word and the word-bearing human being. For Barfield, this was the distant shore of metaphysical deliberation, after which one must make the leap into the direct experience and practice of imagination-revelation itself—the thinker, we recall, must become an artist of thought. For, as we also saw last chapter, Barfield was convinced by Steiner that "the truth of imagination is apodeictic, not empirical ... [f]or imagination is not a *reasoning about*, it is a *Schauung*, a seeing, and indeed a *being*, the object. Systematic imagination is, in fact, clairvoyance" (*RCA* 49). The Goethean practice of "systematic imagination" through the careful cultivation of figurative thinking—in particular, deliberately fostering metaphor and synecdoche as modes of relation—is one means to address our personal and social ills. Barfield, as we know, shared Heidegger's diagnosis of the calamitous effects of dualism and positivism and appreciated Heidegger's insight that "paradox, oxymoron, and aphorism" were necessary tools for "enabling intuitive penetration in the otherwise inexpressible." What cannot be expressed, of course, is a fully deduced metaphysic; one must take the elliptical path of figuration—paradox, oxymoron, and aphorism are among the stones that pave it—if one is to uncover the necessarily intuitive point of penetration. However, where Heidegger's step beyond metaphysics entails, for Barfield, becoming irritatingly vatic and repetitive, and Yeats's "stylistic arrangements of experience" (Yeats 14, 19) were for Barfield too capriciously eclectic, he embraced the poetic cosmology of Steiner's Anthroposophical movement, which combined for him philosophical credibility, the force of poetry, and an ethical imperative to personal transformation.

This chapter follows Barfield's gradual, increasingly detailed, immersion in Steiner's poetic cosmology as a systematic, practical exercise of imagination that was for him identical with clairvoyance and revelation, by tracing the progress of his writings about Anthroposophy in Anthroposophical journals, from those of his first tentative exploration of the movement in the 1920s through the essays of the 1950s that cluster around and culminate in *Saving the Appearances*. The latter was his first published book to bridge both general and Anthroposophical audiences, and he considered it to be his best and most important work.[1] One reason he gave it this high-water mark was that it brought together the different themes and audiences that occupied his attention over those decades. Of course, we have already seen that Barfield's immersion in and commitment to Anthroposophy is not limited to these essays, and it does not end with *Saving the Appearances*. We will see it again in the subsequent chapters of this book. It is present in other ways as well—his work as a solicitor on behalf of the English branch of the society, translations of Steiner, introductions to translations by others, and so on.

Steiner, whose collected works number over 300 volumes, was near his death when Barfield encountered him in person for the only time, in 1924. Steiner launched his movement in 1900, by which time he had found success as a philosopher and editor (of Goethe, Jean Paul, and Schopenhauer, declining Elisabeth Förster-Nietzsche's offer to oversee the Nietzsche Archives). Despite his misgivings, Steiner allied himself with the Theosophical Movement: "I immersed myself in the mystical element in which I had swum in Vienna for some time, to an almost frightening degree.... One might welcome this phenomenon (i.e. Theosophy at the ducal court) as it probably is the last stage before the final demise" (quoted in Lissau 12). In the coming decades, Steiner revised and expanded the Theosophical picture of the nature and history of humanity, as presented in the writings of Madame Blavatsky and others. This included such exotic (for the time) notions as karma and reincarnation, communion with the dead, hierarchies of spiritual beings, the underlying unity of diverse spiritual traditions, and the spiritual origin and evolution of the material world. Barfield encountered Steiner's movement at the crest of what G. R. S. Mead, one of the more respectable Theosophists, called "the rising psychic tide" (Mead 226), within which one could find swimming at different depths such notable writers and artists as Rilke, Pessoa, Hilma af Klint, Charles Williams, Pound, Yeats, Kandinsky, Klee, Kafka, D. H. Lawrence, and many others.[2]

In 1940, seventeen years after his first acquaintance with Anthroposophy, Barfield reflected on some of the complex ways in which it changed him over the years:

> I find it much more difficult to write on matters connected with Anthroposophy than I used to several years ago, and I think I have discovered one reason for this. . . . [A]s it becomes more and more a part of ourselves, it grows more alive, and this *should* enable us to write or speak of it more fruitfully than we could do when it was merely a system of novel and interesting thoughts and imaginations. But on the other hand, it becomes by the same token more and more entangled with our personal idiosyncrasies and the accidents of our personal history. For our memory, our feeling and will are inevitably more personal to ourselves than our thoughts, and so a particular grouping or connection or imagination which is useful and important for us may turn out to be of little significance to others. This makes one diffident as to the propriety of communicating it. Yet, if there *is* anything universal in them, it is just these thoughts and imaginations which have become part of ourselves, and on which we rely for support in the practical difficulties of life, that we ought most of all to try and express. (Barfield 1940b, 1)

Barfield notes a number of things here: his relation to the movement changed from the early years when it was for him "merely a system of novel and interesting thoughts and imaginations" to the subtler way in which it became inextricable from his memories, feelings, and volitions. He also discerns a paradox: our early, superficial tinkering with intriguing new ideas should have more universal appeal than "the accidents of our personal history," yet these new ideas become universal only when we become existentially implicated in them. This is one highly personal expression of a core Anthroposophical tenet, which Barfield will refer to often as his own view: a human being, the primary symbol, is most universal when most individual, and most individual when most fully an epitome of what he refers to in *History in English Words* as the "cosmos."

Northrop Frye reminded us long ago of Paul Valery's aphorism that "cosmology is a literary art" (Frye 14, 6). Frye went on to distinguish "two kinds of cosmology, the kind designed to understand the world as it is, and the kind designed to transform it into the form of human desire. Platonists and occultists deal with the former kind" (Frye 14, 6). By contrast, "Blake's cosmology . . . is a revolutionary vision of the universe transformed by the creative imagination into a human shape" (Frye 14, 6). Frye's distinction, implicit in Valery's account, is an example of what Blake himself would call a negation. If Frye had continued his quotation beyond "cosmogony is one of the most ancient literary forms," we would find that Valery adds:

> the problem of the totality of things, and of the origin of this whole, arises from a very simple state of mind. We want to know what came before light; or perhaps we try to find whether one particular combination of ideas might not

take precedence over all others and engender the system which is their source, meaning the world, and their author, who is ourselves. (Valery 170–1)

For Barfield, this is yet another example of animism, one of those "endeavours to explain the mind of early or of primitive man ... in front of phenomena identical to our own, but with his mind *tabula rasa*, and suppos[ing] the origin of human consciousness to lie in his first efforts to speculate about those phenomena" (*SA* 66). Valery sees the origins of poetry and science as crude efforts to answer basic questions about phenomena much like our own. Frye's choice between a cosmology modeled on "a human shape" and one that seeks to capture "the world as it is" assumes the same "primitive man."

Barfield transforms the implicit literalism of Frye's proposed dichotomy into a productive polarity. He proposes, via Anthroposophy, that a true poetic cosmology (including Blake's), is both "occultist" and imaginative insofar as the imagination envisions "the world as it is" as a human shape from the beginning because the metaphorical and synecdochical identity of part and whole, human being and the cosmos, is the primary relation from which our literalism devolves: the primary symbol is present all the way down. Barfield is led to this esoteric, poetic cosmology by a threefold irreducibility we discovered in the previous chapter: of imagination to the canons of logic, of spirit and matter to each other, and of words to a purely denotative function. These compel us to conceive the language-bearing human being as a "primary symbol," just as we cannot, in metaphysics, meaningfully reduce "pure phenomena" to some more basic physical substratum.

Barfield considered Anthroposophy to be a poetic cosmology that "saves the appearances," consistent with Steiner's own definition of Anthroposophy as "a path of knowledge, to guide the Spiritual in the human being to the Spiritual in the universe" (Steiner 1973, 13), whereby the "path of knowledge" is in part the transformation of thinking itself, such that an individual experiences her relation to the cosmos as one in which she is simultaneously a part of the whole and the whole itself by virtue of being a part of it. Its success as a poetic cosmology is more important for Barfield than its other exoteric accomplishments because those results depend on its essentially imaginative character. "Many of the statements and ideas which I found there," Barfield reports, "produced an effect very similar to the combinations of words to which I have already alluded. ... [T]his effect was independent of belief" (*RCA* 21). The effect Barfield indicates is the "sudden and rapid increase in the intensity with which I experienced lyric poetry" (*RCA* 17). For this reason, Barfield describes Steiner as the epitome, indeed the only modern example, of "the Western poet-philosopher" (*RCA* 52). Barfield thought of Steiner "with reverence as *il maestro di color che sanno*" (*RCA* 11) because of his apparent mastery of every field in which Barfield considered himself to be competent, but the knowledge he imparted came poetically, as metaphors that "enhanced meanings [that] may reveal hitherto unapprehended parts of reality" (*RCA* 3). Barfield fancies himself not as Dante but as a humble pilgrim, for whom Steiner is an Aristotle-Dante hybrid whose system is simultaneously an all-encompassing philosophical-scientific edifice and a vast poetic cosmology extending from the center of the earth to the periphery of the cosmos.

Barfield makes this understanding clear throughout his career. For example, he opens his essay "The Light of the World" (1954), which we will look at in more detail later, with a comparison of the mechanistic thinking prevalent in postwar Europe and Steiner's organicist alternative:

> When man, in the exercise of his mechanical function, puts together a structure, he does it by adding one part to another, so that they lie side-by-side in space, and the whole is made up of all the parts added together. But when nature constructs, she follows a different principle—one which man also, when he is functioning not as mechanic but as artist or poet, must strive to follow. In an *organic* structure it will be found that the parts interpenetrate and, as it were, express each other in a characteristic way, and that often a single part will seem at the same time to be the whole, or to be potentially the whole. And this is the structural principle which at all levels from the highest to the lowest, Anthroposophy reveals to us as present in the universe itself. (Barfield 1954a, 1)

Anthroposophy speaks to and for the "artist or poet" for whom the organic world, at least, consists of metaphorical and synecdochical relations—that is to say, relations in which discrete phenomena "interpenetrate" and "express each other" and in which the "single part" may be "the whole." Indeed, this form of relation extends beyond the organic realm to "the universe itself," the sum of phenomena "at all levels." For Barfield, "The Case for Anthroposophy," as he titled a selection of translations from Steiner's *Von Seelenrätseln*, is that Steiner advances beyond philosophy by working as a poet-philosopher developing a cosmology. He makes substantive contributions to existing fields of knowledge that at present deny the need for any such poetic cosmology while maintaining his system's internal coherence, including, in the aforementioned selection, "a genuinely psychosomatic physiology" (Barfield 1970b, 22). Barfield lauds Steiner for his contributions to semiotics and the evolution of consciousness and for the rigorous logic of his philosophical works but castigates Yeats, a similarly ambitious poet-philosopher, because he "declined or was unable to look below the fitness of an idea for the special kind of lyric he was determined to write" (*RCA* 20–1). Barfield may be unfair to Yeats once again here, but he pits Yeats against Anthroposophy because the latter provides fit ideas that are more than mere "metaphors for poetry" whose truth value is irrelevant (Yeats 14, 7). In the language of Barfield's poetics, ideas should be products of concrete thinking that satisfy the poetic and rational principles alike.

Barfield makes a similar point in an introduction to a collection of Steiner's lectures. Steiner's project is "to endeavour to be esoteric in an exoteric way" because "that was what he believes the crisis of the twentieth century demands" (Barfield 1960, 12). Steiner's method for achieving exoteric esotericism is to avoid literalism, even in the disguised form of simile. Steiner's descriptions of things like "soul world . . . [and] aura . . . are taken as reproductions of the reality that underlies them instead of as similes. . . . No one who studies the teachings of Rudolf Steiner seriously remains in any real danger of succumbing to this sort of literalness" (Barfield 1960, 8). Barfield sees Anthroposophy as navigating the Scylla of "linguistic philosophers [who] . . . flatly decline to look" at the possibility of expanding the boundaries of natural science or ordinary experience and the Charybdis of capricious system-building done by mystagogues like Graves or Yeats. An example personal to Barfield of Steiner's impressive exoteric reach is that "anthroposophy included and transcended not only my own poor stammering theory of poetry as knowledge, but the whole Romantic philosophy" (*RCA* 23), because "so far as concerned the particular subject in which I was immersed at the time, that is the histories of verbal meanings and their bearing on the evolution of human consciousness, Steiner had obviously forgotten volumes more than I had ever dreamed" (*RCA* 22). Steiner supplemented Barfield's investigations of poetics and the evolution of consciousness with what Barfield considered to be a vast knowledge of both subjects, and he made philosophical arguments that stand as sound on their own. He meets the exoteric needs and goals of the wider literalist public by advancing knowledge in such spheres as agriculture, medicine, and pedagogy—fields that Barfield points to elsewhere— and meets the mystic's esoteric goal of poetically expanding knowledge through metaphor without relying, like such other poet-prophets as Yeats and Graves, on automatic writing or "proleptic thought" (Graves 1966, 343).

Before proceeding to a closer reading of Barfield's Anthroposophical writings, it may be useful to have a brief overview of the movement's picture of the human being and the evolution of consciousness, without becoming enmeshed in the minutia of Steiner's cosmology, which uses a dauntingly large and specialized nomenclature. The appeal for Barfield was the experiential and imaginative grounding of his metaphysics:

> my *experience* of polarity I owed to Steiner largely, because everything he writes is in terms of polarity—he doesn't philosophize about polarity in his philosophical books, but in his nonphilosophical, scientific, or spiritual-scientific writings everything is presented in terms of polarity. It's taken for granted so to speak. What you get there is the imaginative experience of it, as a matter of course. (Sugarman 17)

A careful reading of Barfield bears out the accuracy of his observation. For example, Steiner, like Barfield, rejects Cartesian and Kantian dualisms in favor of a tripartite picture of the human being as consisting of "body," "soul," and "spirit," in which the potential dualism of matter and spirit engenders a productive polarity in the soulful rainbow bridge between them. "Body" Steiner defines as "that by which things in the environment of a man reveal themselves to him" (Steiner 1910, 13). "Soul" is "that by which he links the things to his own being," and "spirit" is "that which becomes manifest in him when, as Goethe expressed it, he looks at things as 'a so-to-speak diving being'" (Steiner 1910, 13). In addition, each of the three members has a polarized, threefold structure: the polarity of spirit and body produces soul as a mediating third principle. Moreover, each of these three principles is itself a threefold polarity. For example, the human body is a trinity that Steiner terms the physical, etheric, and astral. The physical body is Descartes's "res extensa." The "etheric" and "astral" bodies are irreducible to the physical body. The "etheric" or "life" body is similar to Goethe's "Urphanomen." Steiner defines it as the "inner determining forces innate in all that is living" (Steiner 1910, 25). It is the "species-forming force" that in each individual living creature is the "life-force" (Steiner 1910, 25). The "astral" body is the carrier of the "inner life" (Steiner 1910, 29), synonymous with consciousness as the fundamental awareness of a world at all. According to Steiner, all earthly beings, from the mineral to the human, have physical bodies; plants, animals, and human beings have "life" bodies, and animals and human beings have "astral" bodies. Only human beings, who possess the fourth body or "ego," are capable of saying "I" to themselves, though this latter is also the human spirit.[3] So too, and without going into detail at this point, the soul and spirit have a threefold, polarized constitution so that in total the human being may be considered a ninefold entity.

The microcosm is a polarity cubed; in Steiner's account, the macrocosm is the same. Thus, Steiner (like Barfield) endorses Leibnitz's definition of matter as coagulated spirit and describes the ninefold human being as reflecting the nine hierarchies of spiritual beings the names of which Steiner adopts from Pseudo-Dionysius (though he says other names, such as those derived from Hinduism, could be used instead of the conventional Christian ones). The ninefold microcosm reflects and emerges out of the "antecedent unity" of the ninefold spiritual cosmos, and the evolution of consciousness, in its broadest arc, is from an oblivious immersion in the spiritual into and through our current exilic estrangement from our origin, to the possibility of our freely chosen reintegration as microcosm in the macrocosm.[4]

1. Early Essays

Barfield's first four Anthroposophical essays—dating from the 1920s, while he wrote his early poetry and developed his poetics—intersect with the topics he discussed in his other essays and books of the time. In particular, they involve the relation of Anthroposophy to Romanticism, the relation of language to thought, and the relation of the history of ideas to the evolution of consciousness. These Anthroposophical essays help us to see the ways in which he considered his independent research in poetics and semiotics to be corroborated and expanded by Steiner and by other Anthroposophists, including Carl Unger and Hermann Beckh.

"Romanticism and Anthroposophy," which Barfield chose not to republish after its initial appearance in the Easter, 1926 volume of *Anthroposophy Quarterly*, is the first of these four early essays. It makes clear that for Barfield, Steiner offered key guidance in navigating Romanticism as a historical movement and as a vitally relevant aspect of Barfield's response to the challenges of the modern age. The essay continues the work of his mentor Logan Pearsall Smith's *tour de force* "Four Romantic Words" (Smith 1925, 66–134), published the previous year, by inquiring into "the modern meanings of those two popular words *romance* and *romantic*" (Barfield 1926, 111). Barfield sees the main current of the Romantic movement as developing two branches, the first of which applies "on the one hand ... to tales which were alive with medieval colour and witchery and to human imaginations which had fed on such tales; on the other, to Nature herself, as she could be perceived in the light of such an imagination" (Barfield 1926, 113). The second branch is the attempt by Coleridge, Schelling, and others to develop a metaphysics of the imagination, but this yielded only "failure" and "the obscure and self-contradictory mazes of German transcendental philosophy" (Barfield 1926, 118). These seeds bore unpleasant fruit in the "orchid-like perfection" of the "minute and dilettante reminiscences of one's earliest childhood" by "the late M. Marcel Proust" (Barfield 1926, 118n). Barfield seems here to endorse parts of the Hulme-Eliot critique of Romanticism as spilt religion. Its philosophy is a failure, and its bathetic contemporary adherents "pour themselves without fear of check, and without the risk of soaking away through banks too weak to hold them—leaving nothing behind but a few puddles of promiscuous sentimentality" (Barfield 1926, 118–19).

Where Proust and other high Modernists failed to satisfactorily combine transcendental philosophy and imaginative tales, Rudolf Steiner had the answer: he systematically developed imaginative activity itself. Barfield outlines "the two first stages of the 'supersensible cognition'" (Barfield 1926, 119), imagination and inspiration, that Steiner describes in his writings. Barfield notes that "to-day, Imaginative Cognition can be recovered—with the added element of full self-consciousness—partly by definite exercises in concentration and partly by letting the imagination dwell on these myths and on the historical events of the spirit which underlie them" (Barfield 1926, 119). Anticipating Jung's practice of "active imagination" and paralleling Yeats's ritual practices as a member of the Golden Dawn, Steiner retains the wonder of the imagination's workings while making possible its systematic development through the complementary use of "exercises of concentration" and historical imagination. "Inspiration," meanwhile, develops in a similarly systematic way as the sympathetic participation in nature pioneered by Wordsworth. In inspiration, one:

> begins to experience the spiritual reality underlying the world of Nature, to perceive and feel the manner of its working in flower and animal, in earth and water and sky. It is not that nobody else receives intuitions of a lofty and spiritual nature from the living beauty of this Earth; but that in Inspiration, as it is defined and inculcated by Rudolf Steiner, one lives with the Spirit of the Earth in a specially vivid and secure way—one has relations with Nature which differ from the ordinary ones as a great poet such as Wordsworth differed from the ordinary man. (Barfield 1926, 120)

Barfield sees a way out of the wasteland in Steiner's program for the imagination's practical, methodical development. The Romantic poets intuited both the problem and the solution of modern life, but Steiner made it repeatable and practical by developing a nomenclature and method of "spiritual cognition" by which the twofold imagination—its fantastic productivity and its communion with nature—could be systematically developed.

The second essay in the sequence, "Thinking and Thought," was published in Easter of the following year. It is significantly more sophisticated than "Romanticism and Anthroposophy." Where the former brings in Steiner as an ally in the Romantic/Classic debate, the latter makes use of the new phrase "evolution of consciousness." The concept "evolution" requires reference to "the real life force, the true creative Logos" that would raise it from "merely a theory" to "an actual experience ... which is the evolution of *consciousness*" (*RCA* 76). The distinction between thought and thinking is the same as that between the merely theoretical concept "evolution" and the "creative Logos" that Barfield gives a Johannine resonance. "The following," he says at the beginning of his essay, "is intended to be a kind of digest of notes for a possible history of thinking—not of thought, but of thinking—as it has developed in the Western world from the beginning of Greek civilization down to our own day" (*RCA* 60). The history of thought contents itself with studying the use of fixed concepts like "law"—the example Barfield employs in his essay—while practitioners of the history of thinking:

> have to be much more conscientious; and, once having perceived that such a concept as "law" in its application to nature only entered into human consciousness at a certain period, we must try for all previous periods, as it were, to *unthink* that concept together with all its intellectual and psychological implications and consequences. This requires a very real effort of the imagination, besides a fairly intimate acquaintance with the customary process of our own intellects. (*RCA* 64)

This is Barfield's first account of the method of studying the evolution of consciousness. Focusing on Bacon's novel use of "law" leads back through the Latin *lex* and the related word *forma*, to the Greek understanding of form.

This in turn leads Barfield to "the famous puzzles of Greek philosophy, the puzzles about the One and the Many, and so forth" (*RCA* 70), but as with all questions of metaphysics, Barfield is not interested in their complete solution. He instead explores the way that the eruption of philosophical thinking reveals how ancient Greek consciousness differs from our own. Sounding like an Oxford-educated Heidegger, he claims that:

> as a thinker or knower, the Greek tended to be at home, as it were, in the coming-into-being, or becoming; whereas our own thought, built as it is on the secure but rigid framework of *logic* (which the Greeks did not succeed in evolving for us until Aristotle's day), can only deal with the "become", the finished product—except, of course, where it is willing to bring in the aid of poesy and metaphor. (*RCA* 65)

A close consideration of the prelogical Greek understanding of, or wrestling with, the concept of "form" reveals a thinking that is "living" insofar as its essential element is habitual, preconscious awareness of "becoming." We witness in the eruption of Greek philosophy that it is "occupied with a problem which we are now able to *name* as that of 'coming into being' or 'becoming', [but] they themselves could have no such name for it, for being conscious *in* it, they could not get outside it and be conscious *of* it" (RCA 71). Preoccupied as they were with "how matter, at certain times and seasons imitates or takes the 'form' of spirit . . . it is no wonder that the Greeks were a nation of artists" (RCA 72).

By contrast, "dead" thinking pervades the industrial West. In Barfield's paradigmatic example, Bacon succeeded in replacing Greek "forms" with "his own abstract 'laws'" (RCA 72). Modern thought—post-Baconian, essentially bound up with "law" and other fixed entities—is comparatively dead, because "natural law is observable in its effects only" (RCA 74). Barfield laments that "the modern civilisation which has arisen along with this static thought and the machinery which it has produced" consists of institutions that are "the bodies or husks of concrete thinking in the past" (RCA 74). As Barfield puts it in a remarkable passage, the result is the devastating loss of:

> the memory, so far as it had been retained by European thought since Plato's and Aristotle's day, of those elements, as it were of νους ("nous")—of the mind—or spiritual world, which the best Greek thinking could still apprehend in its time as living Beings. They were a faint shadowy recollection of those Thought Beings, neither objective nor subjective, which Greek thinking could actually enshrine within itself—Beings, by whom the part of Nature which is perceptible to our senses is continually brought into being and again withdrawn, in the rhythm of the seasons and of life and death. (RCA 72)

The leap from metaphysics to cosmology in this passage mirrors in microcosm the larger leap that Barfield makes at the culmination of his metaphysics. The withering in the West of the consciousness of "becoming" is not merely a shift from one state of consciousness into another and does not merely make it difficult to grasp the concept of evolution. The activity that underlies becoming is a surging tide of spiritual "Thought Beings" that are the macrocosmic correlate of the "concrete thinking" that Barfield posits in *Poetic Diction* in that they too are "neither subjective nor objective." The "evolution of consciousness" records a changing relation to a "spiritual world" in which we participate to the extent that we engage in concrete thinking. Indeed, the West's self-destruction can only be averted if it begins to do so:

> the period which culminated in the Industrial Revolution and the Great War has altered the world out of all recognition. Is it not painfully obvious on all sides that, if the continuity of Western civilisation is to be preserved, we need fresh creative thinking, the power to create fresh forms out of life itself, that is to say, out of the part of Nature which is still coming into being, the Spiritual World? (*RCA* 74–5)

The "fresh creative thinking" needed to stave off destruction, which Barfield aligns more conventionally elsewhere with the imagination, involves purposeful participation in the "coming into being" of "the Spiritual World."

Barfield again turns to Steiner as having offering the most fruitful response to our dilemma: "Rudolf Steiner's comprehensive work is . . . more than enough to enable any really unprejudiced, unobsessed mind to realise that this great world of formative thinking is still there, awaiting us, if we have but the will to reach it" (*RCA* 77). Steiner convinces Barfield that "science must itself *become* an art, and art a science; either they must mingle, or Western civilisation, as we know it, must perish" (*RCA* 81). Those who take up Steiner's writings and methods "have felt out of the depths of their being the fearful need of this living, creative thinking" (*RCA* 82). To make a polarity of science and art, to embrace the "fearful need" of "creative thinking," is to make England, too, a nation of artists.

Barfield published the third essay in this sequence, "Speech, Reason, and the Consciousness Soul,"[5] in the Christmas 1927 issue of *Anthroposophical Quarterly*. If the first essay brought Steiner in relation to Romanticism and the second essay distinguished the history of ideas from the evolution of consciousness, this essay takes up the themes of *Poetic Diction*. It asks "a kind of connected series of questions: (i) are words dependent on sense-perception for their meaning? (ii) if so, is Reason dependent on Speech? (iii). If so, is there any intellectual activity which is *not* dependent on 'Reason'?" (*RCA* 84). These questions arise for Barfield out of his conviction, discussed at length in *Poetic Diction*, that almost any word can be traced back to "a time when it, or some older word from which it is derived, had reference to either a material object or a bodily action" (*RCA* 83). Rather than follow Kant and the post-Kantians into the metaphysics and epistemology of pure reason, though, Barfield proposes to "begin by approaching the matter historically" (*RCA* 85), situating the question within the evolution of consciousness: what can we say about the relation of speech to reason in different epochs?

Barfield had published *History in English Words* the year before but builds his discussion here with explicit reference to Steiner because "Steiner's perpetual theme . . . [was] that human consciousness is perpetually evolving" (*RCA* 89). Pursuing the three questions around which his essay pivots, Barfield compares medieval and modern experiences of the relation of speech to sense and reason, following Steiner in calling the epoch from classical Greece through the Middle Ages the "Intellectual Soul" age and that from the Scientific Revolution through and beyond our own time the age of the "Consciousness Soul."[6] Neither term can be defined a priori or in the abstract—"Steiner was never content with general statements" (*RCA* 98)—but Barfield amasses detailed descriptions of each stage. The "Intellectual Soul" era, for example, "worshipped Logic, in which—through the concept of the 'term'—the word and the thought are kept as close together as possible" (*RCA* 85). Indeed, this is the root of medieval intolerance: "identifying the thought with the words, they felt that truth could be wholly embodied in creed and dogma and identifying the self with the thought, they were—quite rightly—intolerant" (*RCA* 86).

Barfield contrasts this sharply with his own time. "Today," he notes, "everybody is tolerant. We are really extraordinarily polite to each other nowadays" (*RCA* 86) because "we have *ceased to identify ourselves with our thoughts*—at any rate, with such thoughts as can be expressed in words. We are for 'the spirit and not the letter' today. We distinguish between thinking and believing" (*RCA* 87). Thus, we can say of the Intellectual Soul that "though clearly discerning itself from perceptible objects over against it in space, the Ego still feels its words and thoughts to be part of itself" (*RCA* 89). By contrast, "the Consciousness Soul indicates the maximum point of *self*-consciousness, the point at which the individual feels himself to be entirely cut off from the surrounding cosmos and is *for that reason* fully conscious of himself as an individual" (*RCA* 89). Hence the pervasive Eliot-inspired "reason why irony—not irony over some particular matter but just irony in general—is expected of the poet or artist who claims to be 'contemporary'" (*RCA* 88). Because the Consciousness Soul experiences everything as "not-I," it cannot experience any statement as wholly true—it is alienated from itself and from the world at a level that precedes articulation. Well-known expressions of modern estrangement and disenchantment can be understood as the Ego's increasingly intimate, often painful, experience of everything and everyone, including itself, as "not-I."

This is another moment in which Barfield considered Steiner to be helpful. Steiner "spoke from the Consciousness Soul to the Consciousness Soul" in that "he trusted his hearers *not* to believe" (*RCA* 94). Rather, Steiner encourages the "concrete thinking" of the undivided Ego that precedes synthesis and analysis:

> to become an anthroposophist is not to believe, it is to decide to use the words of Rudolf Steiner (and any others which may become available) for the purpose of raising oneself, if possible, to a kind of thinking which is itself beyond words, which *precedes* them, in the sense that ideas, words, sentences, propositions, are only subsequently *drawn out of it*. This is that concrete thinking which is the *source* of all such ideas and propositions, the source of all meaning whatsoever. (*RCA* 95)

Concrete thinking, the core of Barfield's poetics, is also the heart of Anthroposophy. Like Coleridge's Imagination, it cannot be fully deduced because "experience alone can prove it" (*RCA* 96). As in "Thinking and Thought," Barfield describes concrete thinking as "living thinking" that has "a very close connection" with "all that is metaphorical and figurative" (*RCA* 96). Concrete thinking is the first sign of the future era of the Imaginative Soul, for which "the mystery of Poetry" is identical with "the whole great mystery of Meaning" that is "the marriage of spirit and sense." It is the only way out of the wasteland for the Consciousness Soul: "the arid subtleties of a logistic intellectualism, which no longer has any life, though it once had" must give way to "uniting itself with the Spirit of the Earth, with the Word. . . . It differs from the seed only in this, that the choice lies with itself" (*RCA* 97).

The final and most ambitious essay in the sequence of Barfield's early Anthroposophical essays, "Of the Consciousness Soul," was published in two parts in the Christmas 1928 and Easter 1929 issues of *Anthroposophy Quarterly*, at the same time that Barfield published *Poetic Diction* and put the finishing touches on *English People*.[7] It gathers the threads from the three essays that precede it and shows a greater mastery of the details of Steiner's system. For example, it adds to the two eras of the last essay—Intellectual Soul and Consciousness Soul—seven other stages in the evolution of consciousness through which humanity passes in the course of its history so that for each "member" of the human being there is a corresponding epoch. For Barfield, this evolution describes "that metaphysical conception of the human being, which sees him as a 'microcosm' evolving from a 'macrocosm' and finally returning, in a sense, to the great whole from which he took his birth" (*RCA* 103). When the Consciousness Soul undergoes its Sartrean encounter with "this paradoxical zero-point, where self-consciousness and nonentity coincide" (*RCA* 106) it absorbs the painful realization "that this severance, or birth, of the human microcosm from the macrocosm has just been completed. The consciousness soul, we might say, *is* 'the having been cut off'" (*RCA* 104).

Barfield follows Steiner's lead in his account of the evolution of consciousness and his assessment of the crisis posed by the modern world. He also agrees with

Steiner that "the isolated Ego . . . [has] two alternatives open to it: untimely death or nonentity on the one hand, and on the other the first step towards an expansion again to the macrocosm—an expansion of such a nature that the centre and source of life is henceforward within instead of without" (RCA 118). Barfield argues in this essay that Anthroposophy, which he defines here as "the science of meaning" (RCA 121), is best able to provide a meaningful answer when "we are brought up against the whole question of the relation between 'inner' and 'outer' in human experience, between the 'objective' and the subjective'" (RCA 121). It does so by seeing such basic spatial relations as themselves metaphors: "inner" as opposed to what? "Outer" in relation to whom? The path forward is to reconfigure our phenomenological experience of inner and outer, to have a felt experience of consciousness as a microcosm by recognizing that "in genuine creative imagination . . . you are already taking the first step towards reunion with the macrocosm; for it is not man alone who creates in Imagination, but Nature herself" (RCA 122). In other words, in "genuine creative imagination" nature imagines through us, even as we participate in macrocosmic nature in the act of imagining it.

Barfield also hints toward the Christological focus his later essays will have, and that I will discuss more fully later: "the incarnation of Christ in a human body, and subsequently in the 'aura' of the Earth, was the solution in fact of that divorce between a subjective and an objective world which had only recently arisen in human experience" (RCA 123). This puts a special point to "the question whether . . . the whole Earth . . . should henceforth have any meaning" (RCA 123). Anthroposophy answers the question to the extent that it takes up:

> the problem of establishing a living umbilical connection between macrocosm and microcosm, in order that life might pass from one to the other. It is easy to see how this problem, when we recapitulate it in consciousness, must be the problem of "subjective" and "objective." In what way does the macrocosm, the world which presents itself as "outside" me, live in me, so that it is indeed I, so that its tremendous forces are some day to become forces of my will? *In what way* is Imagination true? (RCA 152)

The central symbol of the weaving together of macrocosm and microcosm is the resurrection, which must be "recapitulated as an event in consciousness" (RCA 151), and achieves its fullest realization as a symbol in "the resurrection of the body; for that is the full re-union with the macrocosm" (RCA 159).

2. Anthroposophy at Mid-Century

Barfield's Anthroposophical essays of the 1920s reveal the ways in which his insights into semiotics and the evolution of consciousness were deepened and fructified by his encounter with Steiner's "novel and interesting thoughts." Barfield accepted and adopted the whole of its poetic cosmology, from its phenomenology, anthropology, and socioeconomic prescriptions to its explanation of the evolution of consciousness as movement from Sentient Soul through Consciousness Soul epochs, the middle or Intellectual Soul age including the "turning point in time" of Christ's death and resurrection. Though he produced relatively little as a specifically Anthroposophical writer during the 1930s and 1940s, Anthroposophical ideas began to interweave with his whole personality, as is evident when he again began publishing major essays for Anthroposophical journals at the beginning of the 1950s. These include important essays on Steiner's philosophy and essays that more directly anticipate *Saving the Appearances*, such as "The Art of Eurhythmy" (1954), "The Light of the World" (1954), and "Israel and the Michael Impulse" (1956).

"The Art of Eurhythmy" describes the art form that Steiner invented, akin to dance and accompanied by music or poetry.[8] Barfield notes that Steiner considered it "one of the most important contributions made by Anthroposophy to the civilization of our time" (Barfield 1954b, 53) and Barfield doubtless agreed. Barfield's poem "The Eurhythmist," published two years earlier, imagines the modern self as a nonentity that takes on substance to the extent that it becomes an artist of gesture. The observer of the performance wonders: "Has Emptiness aplomb and stance? / Can Nothing journey here or there, / Because she lifts it in her hands / And carries it about with care?" (Barfield 1952, 8) but recognizes that the impression of emptiness due to his "vain idea" merely contains "sophisticated negatives" (Barfield 1952, 8); the artist herself "is animated to become / The countenance of an Étude" (Barfield 1952, 8) as she develops herself through disciplined creative activity to rise from the Consciousness Soul to the Imaginative Soul.[9] Barfield's essay makes clear how eurythmy achieves this aesthetic effect. Barfield notes that eurythmy is similar to ballet but differs because each of the artist's myriad gestures is a "visible speech" that evokes specific vowels and consonants. In seeking to appreciate eurythmy:

> this notion of "talking with the body" would be a good first step. It was so that Rudolf Steiner himself referred to it as "a metamorphosis of dancing," or as a sort of attempt to restore "temple-dancing"; which was itself, he said, an attempt to

reflect the movements of the stars and planets, whose creative forces streamed into and fashioned man.... [B]ut Steiner also pointed out that Eurhythmy is not dancing but "visible speech" and "visible song." (Barfield 1954b, 55)

Following Steiner, Barfield understands eurythmy as a contemporary metamorphosis of the ancient sensibility that uses "temple-dancing" to express the shaping of the microcosm by the heavenly macrocosm. Eurythmy is the art in which the microcosm speaks back to the "creative forces" of the cosmos. Barfield contends that "what is interesting about it ... is that by approaching the subject with a warmth of enthusiasm but in a strictly empirical way ... [one] does, nevertheless, arrive at a conception of speech as being originally and essentially—gesture" (Barfield 1954b, 55). He reminds us of the point he made decades earlier, in "Thinking and Thought," that "the Greek word which has been translated 'was made' is the ordinary one for 'becoming' or being born" (Barfield 1954b, 55-6) in order to conclude that "a Word which produced not only the audible but also the visible or tangible world which we see around us, must have been gestural as well as phonetic" (Barfield 1954b, 56)—not merely this but also that:

> the human being ... as he stands before us, is the product of the eurhythmic movements which correspond to the sounds of the alphabet.... [Eurhythmy] is trying to "restore the primordial movement" and in so doing to make us aware of the relation between speech and the genesis of man, and therefore between cosmic being and human being. (Barfield 1954b, 56).

It is implicit in this formulation that human beings are themselves words: our bodies are gestures that gesture; the movements of the new art form are words moved by words, logoi shaped by the Logos, echoing the sounds of the cosmos in that "it is the Zodiac which corresponds with consonants, and the planets with vowels" (Barfield 1954b, 56). The new art attempts to capture "the delicate reciprocity of giving and receiving" (Barfield 1954b, 61) so that "we find it opening the door to eternity" and discover therein "the Christ impulse" (Barfield 1954b, 61). No wonder Barfield could write that he "had the greatest difficulty in understanding the French 'Symbolist' movement in poetry, for the simple reason that he could not conceive of any other kind of poetry" (*RCA* 115), as Baudelaire's doctrine of correspondences seems tame by comparison with this audacious aesthetic.

"The Light of the World," the other Anthroposophical essay Barfield published in 1954, may be his most explicitly esoteric. It begins, as we have seen, with the statement of Anthroposophy's synecdochical cosmology, in which "a single part will seem at the same time to be the whole" (Barfield 1954a, 1). It goes beyond this, though, into detail about "the vast number of spiritual beings and the relations between them" that constitute "the substance even of the physical world" and "of the inner world of consciousness" (Barfield 1954a, 1). Nor do these angelic beings that make up matter and consciousness stand alone or apart from one another, for "already, at this exalted level, we find that peculiar relation between whole and part, to which I have referred" (Barfield 1954a, 1). The ninefold spiritual world corresponds to and constitutes the ninefold human being, within each of which "we also find Father, Son and Spirit manifest *within* each Hierarchy" (Barfield 1954a, 1).

The concrete thinking required to grasp the relation of the spiritual world to the mundane world extends to relations within the mundane world itself. It is worth reading a longer passage to experience the density of Barfield's cosmological vision, which itself is a reflection of Steiner's:

> If we now descend, from this brief glimpse at the structure of the Spiritual World itself, to man as he lives on earth, we find the like hierarchical, or organic, relation between the four principles of which he is composed—and one which needs the like mobility of thought or imagination for its comprehension. We speak of man as consisting of the four principles, Physical, Etheric, Astral and Ego. And here, too, we find that we not only have these four principles, as it were, primarily and in their own right; but also, if we confine our attention to only one of them, we shall find all four in a secondary way manifested, reflected, aspected—how you will—in that one. In the physical body, for instance, we find the Ego principle represented—where? In the blood. And in the same way we detect the astral, the etheric and the physical as present in a special way in the nerves and senses, in the glandular system, and in the bones.
>
> And so it is with the Etheric. Here I say "Etheric" rather than "Etheric Body," because, although man certainly has an etheric body, yet this body is not insulated from the rest of the etheric—and elemental—world in the same way that the physical body is from the physical world around it. In the Four Ethers of which Rudolf Steiner has said so much, we find again the four principles of which man is composed. We find physical, etheric, astral and ego in the Warmth Ether, the Light Ether, the Chemical or Sound Ether and the Life Ether respectively. (Barfield 1954a, 2)

It is beyond the scope of this chapter to spell out in detail all of the other complex aspects of this mutually infolding cosmology. The most important point for our purposes is that in order to think such concepts as "etheric body" at all requires a fundamentally different way of thinking that is, once again, grounded in imagination-infused experience rather than inference or deduction:

> It is indeed very different for minds—trained, as ours have mostly been, to assume that there is nothing between a physical force, at one extreme, and an abstract idea at the other—to learn to imagine, or to realise in experience, something which is a force, and yet not a physical force; something whose influence is inward from the periphery, not outward from the centre; and yet which works upon that centre expansively and not contractingly.... One begins to perceive, or rather to *feel*, that the light itself—this light from the sun that comes to us through the senses—is etheric and that the etheric is a kind of light. (Barfield 1954a, 2–3)

This experience of the "etheric" as a paradoxical polarity of action from the periphery that expands from the center, and that seems identical with the experience of light itself, is the objective pole of a larger polarity. At the subjective pole, one experiences that this "very deeply moving experience" is "much deeper than mere observation" because it "goes to the roots of one's being" (Barfield 1954a, 3). Indeed, one "will begin to feel that the light is not only outside in space, but also within oneself" and that "one is aware, not only of seeing or feeling the light, but also of breathing it" (Barfield 1954a, 3). The feeling that accompanies this experience is "the sort of joy that we see made manifest in the sunlight dancing on the water. Deep draughts of pure joy, which obliterate, while they last, all anxiety, all sorrow, all considerations of karma, and even all memory of such things" (Barfield 1954a, 3).

This ecstatic experience of "a world of joyous light," which deepens into "the realm where the Divine Word is not only seen, but also *heard*" (Barfield 1954a, 5), requires that one travel "the way of initiation" (Barfield 1954a, 5)—that to say, the transition from imaginative to inspired cognition. We have seen initiation as a theme in previous chapters and will see it again in the Burgeon trilogy. Barfield describes it here as "the great leap in the dark" and as requiring one "to cross the Threshold" (Barfield 1954a, 5) between ordinary and higher experiences. The first step, which we have seen in Barfield's earlier Anthroposophical essays and at the heart of both his poetics and his metaphysics, is to overcome the ever-present "subjective-objective duality" (Barfield 1954a, 5). Conventional philosophical discourse has noticed that:

> there is, on the outer side, that *of* which I am conscious, and, on the inner side, that in me which *is* conscious. I can never at any moment be conscious of that innermost in me which is actually "doing the business of being conscious." If I

say I am conscious of it, I am deceiving myself—for I necessarily presuppose a yet more inner innermost, namely the "I" which is saying so. We get, in fact, what the philosophers call "an infinite regress." (Barfield 1954a, 5)[10]

We have seen how Barfield discusses this impasse in his writings on the metaphysics of the self. Here he uses Anthroposophical terms to offer a different solution:

> But where the philosophers speak of an infinite regress, we speak of astral and ego; of the divine Hierarchies; and of the Father in us. For we assume that, besides the ordinary experience of human beings today, a different kind of experience is possible. We think that the part of us which *is* conscious—as distinct from the parts *of* which we are conscious—is not just a sort of phantom subject of the grammatical sentence "I am conscious of . . .", but a Being in a world of Beings. And it is that world which we call the astral world, and, at a further stage, the spiritual world. Thus, the difficulty still remains; but it has ceased to be merely logical and has become—awful. For it follows from what I have said, that to penetrate into the astral is to turn what by its very nature is an *inner*—what for ordinary experience is indeed inwardness itself—into an *outer*, into something like an environment. It involves—to use a very crude and perhaps rather offensive expression—a sort of turning inside out. (Barfield 1954a, 5)

Once again, the solution to a philosophical paradox is an imaginative experience. In this case, it involves holding up one's thoughts, feelings, and volitions as objects for one's meditative consideration, thereby making one's inner world a kind of "outer" environment. The self-transformation, the "sort of turning inside out," that this involves when pursued rigorously leads in the end, as the first step on the "way of initiation," to an encounter with the "Divine Word."

"Israel and the Michael Impulse" (1956), which Barfield published the year before *Saving the Appearances*, is almost a précis of the book. Like the book, it contends that "the way in which men think about the outer world determines, in the long run, the way in which they *perceive* it also" and that "the world which men perceive to-day, as the result of the age of materialism, is a world which consists, essentially, of a multitudinous collection of detached objects" (Barfield 1956a, 1). It contends that what distinguishes our own age is that it has lost the "instinctive, effortless participation [that] was still present vestigially at least, in the experience of ordinary men right down to the close of the Middle Ages" (Barfield 1956a, 2). The precipitating cause of our present alienation was the Scientific Revolution, though "the elimination of the old, participating consciousness, which was finally accomplished by the Scientific Revolution, had by no means begun with it" (Barfield 1956a, 2). In the background were two powerful forces—the development by Greek culture of analytical speculation and the rigorous iconoclasm developed by the Jewish people.

As we will see later, this is a highly compressed form of the argument that Barfield makes at greater length in *Saving the Appearances*. The real focus of the essay is on the iconoclastic impulse in Jewish culture, a theme that is also important in Barfield's book. This is true in many small details that reveal Steiner's hidden influence. For example, when Barfield refers in *Saving the Appearances* to the biblical story of "Phinehas in Shittim, seizing a javelin in his right hand and staying the general relapse into idolatry by transfixing his compatriot in the very arms of the Midianitish woman" (*SA* 109), he echoes a reference made by Steiner to the story of Phinehas (Barfield 1956a, 4). More importantly, though, Barfield gives his whole treatment a specifically Anthroposophical focus. He notes, for example, that his larger theme about earlier "participation" in phenomena that over time is lost to the West comes from Steiner. What a reader of only *Saving the Appearances* would miss is that for Barfield, again following Steiner, the culmination of materialistic thinking at the end of the nineteenth century coincides esoterically with the assumption by the archangel Michael of "rulership" over the present era of the evolution of consciousness. Indeed, the recognition that these two events coincide is "the distinguishing feature of Anthroposophy, compared with other traditions of occultism" (Barfield 1956a 1).[11] For Barfield, the argument of *Saving the Appearances* is ancillary to "Rudolf Steiner's teaching of the mission of Michael" (Barfield 1956a, 1). Likewise, Barfield ends his book with the statement that "the other name for original participation, in all its long-hidden, in all its diluted forms, in science, in art and in religion, is, after all—paganism" (*SA* 186). Barfield's more attentive readers will recall that in this article he carefully notes that:

> It might perhaps be maintained that there is room in Anthroposophy as a whole for a different approach, but (if I have understood Rudolf Steiner rightly) the Being whom he names *Michael* is not interested in any kind of pantheism; in any pagan veneration of, or participation in, nature; in any incontinent going forth into nature; in any direct astral or etheric participation in a nature, whose life and being are conceived as existing independently of man; in any participation of which the Ego is not total master.

The participation which Michael wills for man, is an ultimate participation in the phenomena of nature as, and because, the Ego itself participates in the Divine Hierarchies who are the substance of nature. (Barfield 1956a, 8)

We will see in a moment what Barfield means by "participation," as he develops the concept in *Saving the Appearances*. For now, it is simply worth noting that he sees his argument as involving "the higher knowledge which begins with Initiation" (Barfield 1956a, 8). It is in this light that we must understand his references to "the Cosmic Intelligence which creates and informs nature" (Barfield 1956a, 1–2) and to "Michael's hope that the Cosmic Intelligence shall gradually become embodied in the human personal intelligence—giving man an intellectual soul at once detached and not detached from its cosmic origin" (Barfield 1956a, 2). This is the esoteric aspect of Barfield's argument about the transition from Original Participation to Final Participation by way of the hard path of nonparticipation, which makes up the bulk of *Saving the Appearances*, to which we now turn.

3. *Saving the Appearances*

As in our discussion of *What Coleridge Thought* in the last chapter, we can only emphasize certain aspects of a book as rich and complex as *Saving the Appearances*. Barfield is explicit that:

> [T]he object with which this book was originally conceived was none other than to try and remove one of the principal obstacles to contemporary appreciation of precisely [Rudolf Steiner's] teaching—the study and use of which I believe to be crucial for the future of mankind. (*SA* 141)

Even so, it is one measure of the extent to which Barfield disguised its underlying esotericism that T. S. Eliot, who was very leery of "self-induced trance states, calculated symbolism, mediums, theosophy, crystal-gazing, folklore and hobgoblins" (Eliot 2021 4, 679), praised it in a 1962 letter to Barfield as "one of those books which makes me proud to be a director who publishes them."[12] And yet, the esotericism is there. Even the opening image of the rainbow, and the use Barfield puts it to in his discussion of how we constitute phenomena in the act of perception, appears to be inspired by Steiner. Here is the way that Barfield begins his book:

> Look at a rainbow. While it lasts, it is, or appears to be, a great arc of many colours occupying a position out there in space. It touches the horizon between that chimney and that tree; a line drawn from the sun behind you and passing through your head would pierce the centre of the circle of which it is a part. And now, before it fades, recollect all you have ever been told about the rainbow and its causes, and ask yourself the question *Is it really there?* (*SA* 15)

Compare that with this passage from Steiner:

> Think of a rainbow. If a rainbow is to appear, there must be a particular combination of sunlight, rainclouds and so on. The rainbow cannot be absent if this combination between sunlight and rainclouds exists. The rainbow is therefore a consequence, a phenomenon brought into being from without. The physical body too is, in a way, a pure phenomenon. You must look in the whole surrounding universe for the forces which hold the physical body together. (Steiner 2000, 13)

We will soon see that Steiner's passage is an esoteric answer to the question with which Barfield's opening paragraph concludes, and that Barfield's own answer is an exoteric paraphrase of Steiner. For example, we have already seen that in "The Light of the World" Barfield says that "the substance even of the physical world consists primarily . . . of a vast number of spiritual beings and the relations between them" (Barfield 1954a, 1), and in "Israel and the Michael Impulse" he again refers to "the Divine Hierarchies who are the substance of nature" (Barfield 1956a, 8). He is more reserved in *Saving the Appearances*, preferring to stay within the limits of his phenomenological metaphysics. He uses the rainbow as a symbol for the unity of subject and object and is content to show that the physical world cannot be made of unparticipated matter, which he refers to not with the Aristotelian term "substance" but instead calls "particles" or "the unrepresented." So, for Barfield, while "physical science postulates an unrepresented, as a something which is independent of our consciousness in a way, or to an extent, to which the phenomena are not" it is equally clear that "all attempts to conceive the unrepresented in terms of idol-matter in idol-space and idol-time break down" (*SA* 153). We will return in a moment to idolatry and the spatiotemporal conditions of experience. For now, it is enough to note that the unrepresented "particles," which of course are not literal particles because we cannot represent them spatiotemporally, are the "background of our perceptions, the *familiar* world which we see and know around us" (*SA* 18).

In keeping with the phenomenological practice we looked at in the last chapter, Barfield brackets the unrepresented in *Saving the Appearances*. He even brings back the "blue sky with white clouds in it" (*SA* 18) that he used over twenty-five years earlier in "An Introduction to Anthroposophy" as an example of a "prime phenomenon" (*RCA* 48). Every epistemology with the exception of Berkeley's (Barfield could add Hume but does not) includes an "unrepresented" of some kind, and modern physics demands it. The unrepresented itself, though, obviously cannot be part of a system of representations, and it is enough for

Barfield if he demonstrates that all phenomena are representations and that "the practical difference between a dream or hallucination of a rainbow and an actual rainbow is that, although each is a representation or appearance (that is, something which I perceive to be there), the second is a *shared* or collective representation" (SA 16). This distinction is among those with which he aims to "clear away certain misconceptions" (SA 16), and it is enough for his purposes to show that because "super-naïve realism" (SA 38) is untenable, our phenomena are representations that are at least in part the product of our own mental activity:

> Let me repeat it. On the assumption that the world whose existence is independent of our sensation and perception consists solely of "particles," two operations are necessary (and whether they are successive or simultaneous is of no consequence), in order to produce the familiar world we know. First, the sense-organs must be related to the particles in such a way as to give rise to sensations; and secondly, those mere sensations must be combined and constructed by the percipient mind into the recognizable and nameable objects we call "things." It is this work of construction which will here be called *figuration*. (SA 24)

We have already seen that for Barfield the "particles" are spiritual beings and are fitted to our sense organs because those powers constitute the "outer" world and our consciousness alike. Here he works from the other end, making no assumptions about the unrepresented but positing that ordinary perception involves figuration, a two-step process of reception and shaping.

In turn, figuration and "alpha thinking," the thinking about representations that extends from conscious identification to scientific speculation, can easily slide into one another such that "we must conclude that figuration, whether or no it is a kind of thinking, is something which easily and imperceptibly passes over into thinking, and into which thinking easily and imperceptibly passes over" (SA 27). This is so because even the simplest act of recognition or naming involves a thought about the phenomenon in question. Every phenomenon—that is to say, every discernible object of conscious attention, whether "inner" or "outer"—is a representation insofar as it is at least in part shaped by our own activity. In this sense, every representation is figurative, exceeding itself as a thing in the same way that words are things that exceed themselves as things; once again, the boundaries of speech, reason, and perception are permeable—distinguishable but indivisible. Even the unrepresented has a figurative nature, insofar as the efforts of physical science to plumb the depths of matter, from "atoms, protons and electrons" to even smaller subatomic particles, "are now perhaps generally regarded, not as particles, but as notional models or symbols of an unknown supersensible or subsensible base" (*SA* 17).

Saving the Appearances, then, grows out of the premises of Barfield's phenomenological metaphysics, aligns with his Romantic poetics, and expresses exoterically what he describes esoterically for specifically Anthroposophical audiences. It also includes one of his most sustained and incisive discussions of the evolution of consciousness and its distinction from the history of ideas. The former focuses on the relation of figuration to alpha-thinking, while the latter is a history of alpha-thinking alone or of the interaction of alpha-thinking and beta-thinking (i.e., thinking about thinking). In fact, to study the evolution of consciousness is to study the evolution of phenomena because it requires only:

> the bare acknowledgement in beta-thinking that phenomena are collective representations—in order to see that the actual evolution of the earth we know must have been at the same time an evolution of consciousness. For consciousness is correlative to phenomenon. Any other picture we may form of evolution amounts to no more than a symbolical way of depicting changes in the unrepresented. (*SA* 65)

The phenomena that surround us, and that are the domain of study for, say, geologists and botanists, are forests of symbols inextricably bound up with our participatory figuration, just as figuration is inseparable from language.

Participation is "an awareness . . . of an extra-sensory link between the percipient and the representations" (*SA* 34). It "begins by being an activity, and essentially a communal or social activity" that in ancient and indigenous cultures "takes place in rites and initiation ceremonies" (*SA* 32). Since it is "the extra-sensory relation between man and phenomena" it is similar to figuration, the nexus at which active consciousness, language, and essence coincide: "in the measure that man participates his phenomena, in that measure the name *is* the form, and the form is the name" (*SA* 105). Investigation reveals that if we explore the histories of words "they point us back, not to metaphor, but to participation" including those that "without being traceably connected with any particular system of thought, in one way or another . . . stem from a time before [the] exclusive disjunction between outer and inner" (*SA* 118–19).

The evolution of consciousness is the same as the evolution of participation. Barfield's picture maps onto the stages that Steiner identified, from "prehistory" through the profound ancient Sumerian, Indian, and Persian cultures, Greek and Jewish cultures, the Middle Ages, post-Renaissance scientism, and contemporary nascent spiritualism. The stages correspond to epochs identified by Steiner, with history proper beginning with the "Sentient Soul" era that corresponds to ancient or "primitive" cultures, and so on. These oldest cultures are marked by original participation, the essence of which is that "there stands behind the phenomena, *and on the other side of them from me*, a represented which is of the same nature as me" (*SA* 42). Relative to us, ancient Sumerians were more alive to "'mana' or 'waken' (which *we* can only translate by abstract terms like 'totemic principle', 'life principle' or—since it is present also in inanimate objects—'being')" (*SA* 32). This experience is "not only pre-logical, but also pre-mythical" and involves an "extra-sensory participation of the percipient in the representation . . . [and] a similar link between the representations themselves, and of course between one percipient and another" (*SA* 32). This is the experience of the "living" or "antecedent unity" Barfield describes elsewhere. It is marked by a symbiosis in which "the individual feels he *is* the totem" (*SA* 32), and as a consequence "the represented . . . is conceived as outside, so that there is no question of conscious figuration" (*SA* 41). Put in the language of "Israel and the Michael Impulse," the earliest cultures take for granted the supersaturation of "cosmic intelligence" in the phenomena that constitute nature and culture but show little of the "Michael impulse" that encourages the conscious participation of the Ego in the act of figuration.

As in "Israel and the Michael Impulse," Barfield isolates two primary contributors to the uprooting of original participation—Greek speculative thinking and Jewish iconoclasm. The former is responsible for the notion of "saving the appearances" at all. Plato's three levels of knowledge correspond to "three different levels of astronomy" (and, implicitly, to Barfield's three ways of working with collective representations (*SA* 23)). To save the appearances, for ancient astronomers, was to explain "the apparent movements of the heavenly bodies, and particularly of sun, moon and planets, which were the most difficult to account for, by devising hypothetical patterns of movement, which would account for the appearances without infringing the fundamental principles" (*SA* 47). It strikes a balance between making bare observations "without attempting to account for them or reduce them to any system" (*SA* 46) and "the only true knowledge . . . which is an unobscured participation in the divine Mind, or Word, itself . . . [that] manifests itself only to him who participates in however slight a degree in the pure and divine intelligence" (*SA* 47). To propose geometrical patterns that exhibit divine intelligence as a means of rescuing phenomena from chaos was to invent hypotheses:

> they were arrangements—devices—for saving the appearances; and the Greek and medieval astronomers were not at all disturbed by the fact that the same

appearances could be saved by two or more quite different hypotheses. . . . All that mattered was, which was the simplest and the most convenient for practical purposes; for neither of them had any essential part in truth or knowledge. (*SA* 49)

It is clear on reflection, though Barfield does not say so explicitly, that the truth status of hypotheses was irrelevant for Greek astronomers because the phenomena were still participated, that is to say, figurative. The transition to the modern, Consciousness Soul, era began when "men began to take the models, whether geometrical or mechanical, literally" (*SA* 51), which they did because phenomena themselves became literal. The interaction of literalizing alpha-thinking and literal (i.e., unparticipated) phenomena marked the loss of "the divine Mind, or Word" and instead "produced the mechanomorphic collective representations which constitute the Western world to-day" (*SA* 52).

We will see in a moment how Barfield redeploys "saving the appearances" to fit modern needs. First we must understand Barfield's subtitle by seeing how Jewish culture helped to excise participation with its focus on "idolatry." For Barfield's purposes, an idol is "a representation, which is collectively mistaken for an ultimate" (*SA* 62). Today "phenomena *themselves* are idols, when they are imagined as enjoying that independence of human perception which can in fact only pertain to the unrepresented" (*SA* 62). This modern idolatry is the partial product of the Jewish effort to exclude participation, as "the heathen idols which the Jews reprobated *were* experienced as [representations]" (*SA* 110). Thus, their goal was to "destroy, not merely that which participation may become, but participation itself" (*SA* 111). Judaism limited the divine, and so participation, to the radically other and interior divinity. Because the divine name is "I AM," and "no being who speaks through his throat can call a wholly other and outer Being 'I'" (*SA* 114), phenomena become unparticipated but this "might with equal truth be described as a concentration or centripetal *deepening* of participation" (*SA* 114) because "a waxing experience of the *inwardness* of the Divine Name was the proper counter-pole to their loss of original participation" (*SA* 157).

Another way to put it is that whereas Greek thinking was concerned with spatial relations, Jewish culture focused on "the apprehension of form in time—that is, of events themselves, as images, whether of the past or future, or of a state of mind" (*SA* 150). Judaism recognizes what Barfield indicates as Steiner's insight in his eurythmy essay, that language is essentially gestural:

the Semitic languages seem to point us back to the old unity of man and nature, through the shapes of their sounds. We feel those shapes not only as sounds, but also, in a manner, as *gestures* of speech-organs—and it is not so difficult to realize that these gestures were once gestures made with the whole body—once—when the body itself was not detached from the rest of nature, after the solid manner of to-day, but when the body itself was spoken even while it was speaking. (*SA* 124–5)

The Jewish God rejected representations as idols and turned His worshippers instead toward "the creative Word" (*SA* 125) that issues from His self-positing name, in which we all share in the act of positing ourselves as egos.

Through this circuitous route we reach Barfield's prescription: the need to work toward what in his Anthroposophical essays he calls Imaginative Soul and here calls final participation. For, as Barfield puts it:

> the progressive loss of original participation necessarily involves one of two alternatives, *either* an ever-increasing experience of the inwardness of the Divine Name and the Divine Presence—which is the religious aspect of what I have called "final participation"—*or* an ever increasing idolatry, in religion as elsewhere. (*SA* 158)

Final participation is the means by which to save the appearances by smashing the contemporary idols of materialism and literalism. As with imagination and "intuitive penetration," its existence can nearly but not completely be deduced. The crucial thing is to actually work toward developing it:

> let us call the man-centered participation with which the opening chapters of this book were concerned *final participation*. Beta-thinking, then, can convince itself of the *fact* of final participation. It can convince itself that we participate the phenomena with the unconscious part of ourselves. But that has no epistemological significance. It can only have that to the extent that final participation is consciously experienced. Perhaps . . . we may say that final participation must itself be raised from potentiality to act. (*SA* 137)

Final participation is closely related to, but not identical with, imagination. It is "to be won today by special exertion; . . . it is a matter, not of theorizing, but of imagination in the genial or creative sense. A systematic approach towards final participation may therefore be expected to be an attempt to use imagination systematically" (*SA* 137). Figuration stands to imagination as the primary imagination does to the secondary imagination. The latter "participates the creative activity" of the former such that "it has itself been dimly felt to be, and described as, 'creative'" (*SA* 160). Final participation is "the proper goal of imagination" (*SA* 147) and the means by which appearances will be saved from the literalness that constitutes modern idolatry (*SA* 144). It is to be conscious of figuration in the act of figuring, with the ultimate goal to "gradually eliminate the unrepresented by rendering it phenomenal" (*SA* 153).

It is perhaps unsurprising that Steiner is the pioneer of the "systematic approach towards final participation." Barfield closes his discussion of final participation by once again comparing Steiner to Dante:

> to say that he advocated, and practised, "the systematic use of imagination" is to place so much emphasis on the mere beginning of what he taught and did, that it is rather like saying that Dante wrote a poem about a greyhound. Steiner showed that imagination, and the final participation it leads to, involve, unlike hypothetical thinking, the whole man—thought, feeling, will, and character—and his own revelations were clearly drawn from those further stages of participation—Inspiration and Intuition—to which the systematic use of imagination may lead. (*SA* 141)

Barfield refers here to the three stages of "higher knowledge"—imagination, inspiration, and intuition—that describe an increasing identification of knowledge with Being, culminating in intuition, which is "that kind of knowledge that leads into the 'innermost nature' of beings" (Steiner 1967, 57). The transition out of "hypothetical thinking" is not into dogma but into poetic cosmology:

> whether it is more practical and straightforward, and whether the human mind is likelier to get somewhere, by thinking of man as surrounded by a cosmos or sphere of wisdom; or by thinking that space is spherical and the universe of finite size, although unbounded and getting bigger, are questions everyone will decide for himself. It is . . . the former conception . . . upon which the whole argument of this book converges; and from now on I shall assume its validity. (*SA* 154)

Barfield does not insist on the "truth" of the hypothesis that we participate appearances, though that saves them. He chooses it as "more practical and straightforward" and makes the leap into the synecdochical thinking that his choice entails.

For us, "the life of the image is to be none other than the life of imagination"; that in turn requires that "it must be, not indeed self-created, but certainly self-willed, or else—it is not imagination at all; and is therefore incapable of iconoclasm" (*SA* 179), which recall involves for Barfield smashing the idols of materialism and literalism. More than this, "iconoclasm is made possible by the seed of the Word stirring within us, as imagination. From him that hath not this seed—of final participation—there shall be taken away, even that residue—or original participation—that he hath" (*SA* 179). This Christological reference—Imagination as Logos—is not accidental, for "in final participation—since the death and resurrection—the heart is fired from within by the Christ; and it is for the heart to enliven the images" (*SA* 172). Of course, this identity of Christ with imagination is a hallmark of William Blake's prophetic books *Milton* and *Jerusalem*:

> a certain humble, tender *receptiveness* of heart which is nourished by a deep and deepening imagination and by the self-knowledge which that inevitably involves. Perhaps this is what Blake had in mind, when he called Imagination "the Divine Body of the Lord Jesus, blessed for ever." (*SA* 163)

So too for Barfield, in Christ "the inwardness of the Divine Name had been fully realized; the final participation, whereby man's Creator speaks from within man himself, had been accomplished. The Word had been made flesh" (*SA* 170). The Eucharist is a "tender shoot of final participation" because it nurtures the participant's identity with realized final participation that is the goal of imaginative activity.

The separate threads of Barfield's work on the evolution of consciousness, metaphysics, and Anthroposophy braid together where final participation, Christology, and imagination meet, as a kind of revival in full self-consciousness of the medieval sensibility. Systematic practice of the imagination, beyond saving humanity from the danger that it will "eliminate all meaning and all coherence from the cosmos" (*SA* 144)—that is, beyond "saving the appearances from chaos and inanity" (*SA* 146)—is a consciously realized revival of medieval consciousness, for which "the universe was a kind of theophany, in which he participated at different levels, in being, in thinking, in speaking or naming, and in knowing" (*SA* 92). Because for Barfield "Anthroposophy is, in one sense, the intellectual soul speaking to the consciousness soul" (*RCA* 121)—that is to say, the scholastic sensibility speaking to modern humanity—we are unsurprised by Barfield's assertion about the Middle Ages that "the whole purpose of [*Saving the Appearances*] is to show that its spiritual wealth can be, and indeed, if incalculable disaster is to be avoided, *must* be regained" (*SA* 85).[13] Among these treasures are the "background picture ... of man as a microcosm within the macrocosm" (*SA* 78), the felt perception of "extra-sensory links between ourselves and the phenomena" (*SA* 77), the experience of the close "connection between words and things" (*SA* 84), the irreducibility of the figurative to the literal (*SA* 87), and the felt experience that "all creatures [are] in a greater or lesser degree images or representations, or 'names' of God" (*SA* 90). These are all aspects of Steiner's Anthroposophical vision; they are not theories for Barfield but participated phenomena—and "participation is a *way* of experiencing the world in immediacy, and not a system of ideas about experience, or about the world" (*SA* 75).

5

A Coinherence of Selves
Ethics and Politics

1. Moral Imagination

While Barfield's poetic philosophy expanded into a cosmology, it also expanded into a practical philosophy; indeed, Barfield would maintain that they too form a polarity. We saw in Chapter 1 that Barfield castigated those like Eliot and Arnold who rejected Shelley's moral and political philosophy. In Chapter 3 we saw that in response to the ethics implicit in Sartre's metaphysics, Barfield proposes that we should "experience another in the same mode as we experience ourselves, when we experience him not across the gap between matter and spirit, but as being on the same side of the gap as *we are*" (*RM* 222). This anticipates neatly the way that poetics and ethics converge for Barfield. His research into the evolution of consciousness brought to a point the question of the historical present: whither, and from whence, are we evolving? This entailed for Barfield the further, pressing question of the metaphysics of the self. Anthroposophy offered an answer to that question and was not seen by him as an impractical, otherworldly movement—Steiner had a number of diagnoses and remedies for contemporary social ills. In his moral philosophy, in particular, Barfield brought to bear his epistemological conviction that the imagination is a faculty for acquiring knowledge.[1] Barfield's alertness to ethical and political issues is apparent as early as "Seven Letters" (1922), "The Spiritual Basis of Fascism" (1924), and "Danger, Ugliness, and Waste" (ca. 1924) and extends to his final long work, *Eager Spring* (1985).

It is also no wonder, to take one example among many, that Barfield responded warmly when his friend Charles Davy published *Towards a Third Culture* in 1961. Davy's book supplements Barfield's equal admiration for Lewis's *The Abolition of Man*—which he was rereading at the same time—and its critical analysis of "the belief that we can invent 'ideologies' at pleasure, and the consequent treatment of mankind as mere . . . specimens, preparations, begins to affect our very language" (Lewis 1944, 74). Davy's attempt to elicit a counterculture *avant la lettre* balanced Lewis's caution that one cannot simply invent or redefine truth and knowledge willy-nilly. Davy's book was a response to Sir Charles Snow's influential "two cultures" lecture of 1959. Snow's concern was with how to bridge the apparent incommensurability of the discourses of the humanities and the sciences; Davy sought to address this "well publicized and unresolved conflict" (Barfield 1962, 17), which was also important to Barfield as another symptom of the strain on modern civilization as it labored under the "tremendous weight and power of materialism" (Barfield 1962, 18) that imposed itself on "many different spheres—education, biology, psychology, soil erosion, and a dozen others" (Barfield 1962, 17). Perhaps inspired by Davy's book and the Snow controversy, Barfield also took up the theme of cultural dissociation as a modern allegory of the cave in *Worlds Apart* (1963): "spiritually we are *all* hermits sitting in our caves, reading *The Times Literary Supplement*, the Sunday papers and so forth—peering through the printed word one watertight compartment after another—and never seeing a single sluice opened" (*WA* 11).

Of course, this was not a new or unique concern. T. S. Eliot, for example, showed a similar "growing anxiety [about] the career of this word *culture*" due to the "unparalleled destructiveness" of the war years (Eliot 2021 7, 196). This inquiry followed upon Eliot's Coleridgean concern with the question "what—if any—is the 'idea' of the society in which we live? To what end is it arranged?" (Eliot 2021 5, 685). For Eliot, as for Davy and Barfield, these were questions of immediate existential import, as they were for contemporary continental thinkers as diverse as Albert Camus, Hans Blumenberg, and Martin Heidegger, and the more recent work of Alasdair MacIntyre, Charles Taylor, Louis Dupré, and Thomas Pfau suggests that such questions continue to nag.[2] It is not difficult to find a family relation between these modern Catholic intellectuals, the Anglo-Catholicism of Eliot, the Anglicanism of C. S. Lewis, and the heterodox and mystical Christianity of Davy and Barfield. Though these thinkers arrive at different destinations, they are equally interested in rescuing a sense of the self that is anchored in a concept of cultural cohesion that also informs a vision of moral and social health.

Davy's "third culture" is not simply a reference to the *rapprochement* sought by Snow but also points to Steiner's claim that society already does implicitly and should explicitly consist of three spheres: the cultural, the legislative, and the economic. It is perhaps a happy accident that three of Barfield's earliest writings with direct ethical and political import correspond to these three spheres: "Seven Letters" takes up the "cultural" sphere in both form and content, "The

Spiritual Basis of Fascism" concerns the "rights" or political/legislative sphere, and "Danger, Ugliness, and Waste" focuses on the economic calamity suffered in rural Wales. Barfield pointed directly to Steiner's "threefold sociology" as foundational to his own thoughts, as early as "The Problem of Financing Consumption" (1929) and as late as his introduction to the Lindisfarne Press edition of Vladimir Solovyov's *The Meaning of Love* (1985). In the latter, he notes that:

> it is tragic to reflect how few are aware that, as long as sixty years ago, a social structure incarnating the idea of organic solidarity was adumbrated, even into political and economic detail, by Rudolf Steiner in *The Threefold Social Order*, *World Economy* and other books and lectures. (Barfield 1985, 15)

For much of that sixty years, Barfield did his best to "incarnate" the same "idea of organic solidarity." This underscores Barfield's comment of 1972 that Steiner's social program is "the best place to go for good advice" on how to create a "threefold sociology" that is "nervous and flexible enough to reconcile the principle of political equality with economic and spiritual diversity" (*RM* 213).

Steiner defines the "cultural" sphere—Barfield's "spiritual diversity"—as everything that involves "the free life of the mind and spirit" (Steiner 1999, 10). This includes such wide-ranging activities as education, the sciences, the arts, and the humanities. Most important among these for present purposes is the domain of moral judgment. Barfield adopts the term "moral imagination" from Steiner and defines it as an act whereby "we experience another's spiritual activity in speech, in gesture, in the mobility of his countenance, and so on, in the same mode as our own—and thus as if it were our own" (*RM* 151). This is nearly a paraphrase of Shelley's argument for the essentially imaginative nature of moral judgment:

> The great secret of morals is Love; or a going out of our own nature, and an identification of ourselves with the beautiful which exists in thought, action or person, not our own. A man, to be greatly good, must imagine intensely and comprehensively; he must put himself in the place of another and of many others; the pains and pleasure of his species must become his own. The great instrument of moral good is the imagination; and poetry administers to the effect by acting upon the cause. (Shelley 659)

This is not to suggest, for Barfield or for Shelley, that the imagination is inherently virtuous. It is value-neutral insofar as "imagination is not, as some poets have thought, simply synonymous with good. It may be either good or evil" (*SA* 145). After all, it was the power of the imagination that exploded over Hiroshima and

Nagasaki (*PD* 36). Even so, "we may divine in this age a very close and special relation between . . . imagination and goodness" (*SA* 161) because only by means of the former can we develop the empathy that is necessary for the latter. Likewise, "there *is* a valid connection, at some level however deep, between what I have called 'literalness' and a certain hardness of heart. . . . Here I think is a deep-down moral gesture" (*SA* 162–3).

Barfield points to William Blake, "the very St. George of Iconoclasm" (*SA* 161), as a pioneer of this relation. As we saw in the previous chapter, Blake evokes:

> on the positive side, a certain humble, tender *receptiveness* of heart which is nourished by a deep and deepening imagination and by the self-knowledge which that inevitably involves. Perhaps this is what Blake had in mind, when he called Imagination "the Divine Body of the Lord Jesus, blessed for ever." (*SA* 163)

The line by Blake that Barfield quotes here appears in *Milton* and *Jerusalem*, both poems that have moral imagination as a central concern. Blake brings out another aspect of "moral imagination" that Barfield does not emphasize but that is implicit in his account. In *Milton*, the eponymous hero experiences moral imagination at a pivotal moment:

> Say first! what mov'd Milton, who walkd about in Eternity
> One hundred years, pondring the intricate mazes of Providence,
> Unhappy tho in heav'n, he obey'd, he murmur'd not. he was silent
> Viewing his Sixfold Emanation scatter'd thro' the deep
> In torment! To go into the deep her to redeem & himself perish?
> What cause at length mov'd Milton to this unexampled deed[?]
> A Bard's prophetic Song! (Blake 96)

Blake's Milton is inspired to self-sacrifice not by moral examples or laws—examples of the "literalness" that Barfield maintains is the "besetting sin" of our age (*SA* 161)—but by the imaginative act, driven by empathy, of the "unexampled deed." How is it, Blake's poem asks of us, that Milton is able to form the concept of the unexampled, and so truly moral, deed at all, except insofar as his imagination is attuned to the "Bard's prophetic song?"

Steiner also emphasizes the "unexampled" nature of "moral imagination," or genuinely free moral intuition. For the "unfree spirit" the "link between concept and percept . . . is given from the outset. Motives are present in his consciousness from the outset in the form of mental pictures" (Steiner 1964, 162). For such a person, "whenever there is something he wants to carry out, he does it as he has seen it done, or as he has been told to do it in the particular case" (Steiner 1964, 162–3). The unfree person is happiest having a clear picture of the rules in a given situation and acting accordingly:

> conceptual form belongs to laws for inhibiting actions: Thou shalt *not* steal! Thou shalt *not* commit adultery! These laws, too, influence the unfree spirit only by means of a concrete mental picture, for example, that of the appropriate secular punishment, or the pangs of conscience, or eternal damnation, and so on. (Steiner 1964, 163)

The unfree spirit, then, is bound to past experience and the weight of cultural expectation. She begins with a predetermined concept—say, the "moral law" that compels one to obey—and, faced with a given percept (a situation or a feeling, for example), forms the proper mental picture and undertakes the prescribed action. Such unfree moral thinking, bound by Urizen's "moral law" or Kant's "categorical imperative," faces the notorious difficulty of applying universal norms in the diverse circumstances we actually face as well as condemning us to the permanent childhood of obedience to authority.

Unlike such unfree spirits "who merely preach morality" (Steiner 1964, 164), what "the free spirit needs in order to realize his ideas, in order to be effective, is *moral imagination*" (Steiner 1964, 163). Free spirits are not bound by the predetermined concepts that render the rest of us unfree. Rather, they—one is tempted to say, the *Übermenschen*— tell themselves "moral laws . . . are first created by us" (Steiner 1964, 165) in that they begin with "a definite sphere of percepts" (in other words, a given situation) and proceed to "evolve productively, out of their imagination, the not-yet-existing actions of the future" (Steiner 1964, 163). The test of this freedom is the determination of our own motives for action:

> I am free only when *I myself* produce these mental pictures, not when I am merely *able* to carry out the motives which another being has implanted in me. A free being is one who can *want* what he himself considers right. Whoever does anything other than what he wants must be impelled by motives that do not lie within him. Such a man is unfree in his action. (Steiner 1964, 171)

Thus, moral imagination has a twofold nature, "*firstly*, through the intuitive element, the activity that is necessary for the human organism is checked and repressed, and *then* replaced by the spiritual activity of the idea-filled will" (Steiner 1964, 173). The first step involves the bracketing of the biases, prejudices, assumptions, impulses, sympathies and antipathies, and so on that are "necessary for the human organism." This allows one to move to the second step, which is "to realize in his acts of will the same mood of soul that lives in him when he becomes aware of the forming of purely ideal (spiritual) intuitions" (Steiner 1964, 174). In Blake's poem, Milton needs to free himself from the web of moral laws created by Urizen so that he can be as creative in his actions as he is in his poetry; in Steiner's moral epistemology, we must free ourselves from the pervasive moral conventions in which we are immured so that we can intuit moral ideas with similar artistry.

2. Love, Death, and the Self

The resonance of "moral imagination" in Barfield's thought is perhaps nowhere more clear than in an article he wrote for a general audience at a pivotal moment in British history. On July 24, 1940—two weeks after the Nazis began attacking cargo ships in the English Channel and one day before the RAF scrambled its planes for the first time—Barfield published "Effective Approach to Social Change" in *The Christian News-Letter*. Barfield had long been critical of Chamberlain's policy of appeasement,[3] but the "bottomless abyss" opened by Chamberlain merely revealed, and was made possible by, a wider cultural debility. Barfield was now "compelled to doubt the effectiveness of *any* appeal to reason in this present age. Something has happened either to the minds of men or to the thoughts that fill them. These have grown somehow *thinner*" (Barfield 1940a). Whether due to "too much newsprint . . . or systematic propaganda . . . the average man of to-day does not arrive at his convictions dialectically. He has lost faith in ideas" (Barfield 1940a).

The deeper reason for reason's self-apostasy, though, is "the peculiarity of our age . . . that it is possessed with a desire to become more conscious of the nature of such fundamental . . . impulses [as] the impulse to individualism" (Barfield 1940a). The vast majority do not have a conscious grasp of "what an 'entelechy' is . . . [but] dimly feel its reality in their own spiritual background" (Barfield, 1940a). The impulses arising from the unconscious mind overwhelm and exhaust our mental energies, sap our ability to think rigorously, and breed a distrust of our thoughts as merely superficial symptoms of underlying pathologies or dark urges. In the case of the Anglo-American world, the impulse to manifest the "principle of individualism—of freedom," to make conscious its "deep, deep roots" (Barfield 1940a), has been "stunned" by the "collectivism" that has "run mad" under Hitler and Stalin and has been distorted by an equation of freedom with wealth. Barfield echoes a conviction of Steiner that "we should see that the economic life of a community is *not* the part of its life in which individualism can find expression" (Barfield 1940a). Rather:

> the true vehicle for the impulse to individualism is men's spiritual life. That part cannot *fail* to express individualism and remain human. We should see that man must be free, not because he is a trader, but because he is a spirit; he must be an individual because God speaks to and through the individual, and for no other reason. (Barfield 1940a)

The realization of the full potential of the individual spirit in free spiritual life belongs not just to "moral well-being" but is also "necessary for the growth and development of society" (Barfield 1940a). This is so because society is the product of each individual spirit's "creative thought and moral imagination, and these are functions of the individual human spirit in its sacramental relation to the Holy Spirit" (Barfield 1940a). Much is compact in these final sentences, in which Barfield brings "moral imagination" directly to bear. Against the backdrop of the collective habit of defining the human being through her economic role, as a "trader," and the "bottomless abyss" of contemporary cultural and political incoherence—Eliot's panorama of anarchic futility—Barfield combines Steiner's notion of the "moral imagination" with Coleridge's deduction of "conscience" from the "I-Thou" relation to the divine. In aligning "moral well-being" with the health of society as a whole, Barfield simultaneously reflects a core principle of Aristotle's ethics and Steiner's threefold social organism. "Moral imagination" correlates with "creative thought," and each is not only inspired by spiritual experience but also embedded in, and transformative of, a network of social relations.

Barfield's essays "Death" (1930),[4] "Destroyer and Preserver" (1932), and "Style" (1933) offer similar examples of his way of dealing with ethical questions during the rise of fascism on the continent. They coincide with Barfield's development of a metaphysic and begin to redress his regret in "The Philosophy of Samuel Taylor Coleridge" (1932) that "I should have liked to show from Coleridge's other writings how his morality, too, was derived from the two fundamental conceptions of Reason as productive unity and of polarity" (*RCA* 222). "Death" in particular, with its lyrical expression and highly compact, associative logic, presents Barfield's considered views in germinal form, utilizing an existential phenomenological analysis of death to educe the "productive unity and . . . polarity" of Reason and the idealist metaphysical justification of the primacy of the self.

Barfield suggests that death casts a pall due to the rarity of "any honest attempt to represent the everyday phenomenon of death as a necessary and harmonious step in the progress of a human being" (Barfield 2008, 48). Like Tolstoy's Ivan Ilych, a story Barfield would evoke in his trilogy of plays *Angels at Bay*, most of us have "an uneasy feeling that most of our private and social planning, our daily lives, even in the midst of danger, if not our very deaths themselves, are carried on under a polite conspiracy of silence which cannot hold out much longer" (Barfield 2008, 48). If we are followers of Ryle or Ayer, we bring to the problem of death "the exact methods of physical science" and find we must follow Wittgenstein's famous adumbration that "what we cannot speak about we must pass over in silence" (Wittgenstein 89); if, like Yeats, we fruitlessly follow the "table-rapping Spiritualist," we "apply [the] senses to the investigation of ... the 'other' world" (Barfield 2008, 48).

We are flummoxed by death "only because the death of a human being is not merely a physical but also a spiritual phenomenon" (Barfield 2008, 49). However, "its strangeness begins to disappear" when we recognize that we are troubled not by the dissolution of the body but by the dispersal of "a spiritual activity which we designate as consciousness, soul, personality" (Barfield 2008, 49). With the realization that personality is distinct from the body, we discover that for the former every change involves a kind of death, and that that is a good thing; indeed, "just in so far as death is a spiritual phenomenon, we can, if we choose, will it ourselves. For we can will to change our personalities. Moreover, in every unsupported activity of will, we *are* willing to change our personality" (Barfield 2008, 50).

Thus, Barfield not only rejects the common avoidance of the question of death, religious dogmatism about it, positivism's declaration that it is meaningless, and spiritualist reductionism, he also draws from a phenomenological encounter with it a diametrically opposed conclusion to that of Heidegger, who at this time carried out his own more famous analysis. Heidegger, like Barfield, is critical of our common "*fleeing in the face of death*" (Heidegger 298). As such, "our everyday falling evasion *in the face of* death is an *inauthentic* Being-towards-death" (Heidegger 303). Like Barfield, Heidegger is sensitive that the problem of death is fundamental because it involves "the utter loss of Being-in-the-world" (Heidegger 280). However, Heidegger rejects the idealist lexicon of the self, spirit, personality, and so on, in favor of "Dasein" because he considers the former to be tied to a fatally flawed essentialist metaphysic. An authentic relation to death, for Heidegger, must avoid the metaphysics of the "spirit." Instead, Heidegger sees death as "constitutive for Dasein's totality" (Heidegger 284) insofar as it marks the absolute limit of its relation to itself and the world: death is not an event but the non-Being that marks the end of events.

Barfield draws a different conclusion from his own phenomenological analysis: "to will to die is one with highest life" (Barfield 2008, 52) because in affirming one's self-transformation one also affirms that one's death is a self-transcendence. There is no limit to self-transcendence. The dichotomy of body and personality resolves in the "continuous subtle interplay between the bodily and the spiritual self" in which "we are free to substitute progressively the solidity of a constant will for the transient solidity of the flesh. The body is solid will. It is frozen will, and we have to thaw it again. We have to make it *our* will" (Barfield 2008, 52). This follows from Barfield's metaphysics: "man includes all nature, because nature is but a name for the sum-total of his experience through the senses" (Barfield 2008, 50). To fully take up the project of self-transformation is to will one's death, even to its final mystical limit in the transformation of the physical body. Approached from one side, then, death presents a paradox: as the extinction of the personality, it becomes the perpetual life of self-transformation, even at the horizon where one transforms physical death through the transformation of the body.

One finds a similar paradox if one approaches from a different starting point. "To will to die," besides being "highest life," is also "the open secret; the omphalos of the moral earth; the mystery at the heart of all the mysteries" (Barfield 2008, 52). It is the mystery of mysteries because "my immortality begins from that moment at which I voluntarily will to die, and that part of me is immortal which so wills" (Barfield 2008, 52). What, though, of the "omphalos of the moral earth?" Barfield has in mind not simply the moral imperative to self-transformation but also Coleridge's argument that "Conscience is the root of all Consciousness, and a fortiori the precondition of all Experience; & . . . the Conscience in its first revelation cannot have been deduced from Experience" (Coleridge 1995, 837–8). My consciousness of death is grounded in my preconscious, primordial relation to those around me. The "will to die" is the "omphalos of the moral world" because it brings into my volition this insight about our essential interrelation, "always already" bound together.

The will to self-transcendence is also the will to truth, and the "outward motion of the will, unsupported by hope or desire, is itself the foundation of reason" (Barfield 2008, 54). The transformation of one's personality is distinct but indivisible from "the naked love of truth" present in "a soul whose structure [includes] some bare minimum of conscience, some at least momentary love of truth as an end in itself, with the self-extinction which that entails while it lasts" (Barfield 2008, 54). Just as for Heidegger the prospect of death is the fundamental feature of our Geworfenheit, or "thrownness," for Barfield the love for the truth is a love for that with which we are out of alignment. To that extent, love for the truth is also "seeking Another" (Barfield 2008, 55). Indeed, "the true will to self-extinction . . . is identical with the will to be another" (Barfield 2008, 55). That is as much as to say that "the *true* will to self-extinction and therefore the true love of truth, is identical with love itself" (Barfield 2008, 57). Thus, "love is the ultimate source of all meaning of the earth" (Barfield 2008, 57).

This reveals another paradox, however: if love is the source of all meaning, one cannot speak of it meaningfully. It too involves an "intuitive penetration" of the mysteries beyond the reach of discursive reason. "Pure love cannot be spoken or written of, it can only write or speak"; therefore, it is "impossible to speak of it without at once making it something other and less than itself" (Barfield 2008, 57). As Barfield put it during his "great war" with C. S. Lewis, because "this force [love] is at the core of all human conscious experience, it is impossible to speak of it. It is only possible to attempt to live it" (Feinendegen & Smilde, 118). If the will to death and the will to truth are the same, and the will to truth is the same as the pure love that is the source of speech, then love must exceed language in the same way that death does. Orpheus descends into love to recover Eurydice; Psyche lights her lamp to glimpse her beloved, Hades. Or to put it otherwise, love is an unheard verb that speaks the psyche into existence as listening, transforming personality: "Inspiration is at the same time Love and Self-knowledge" (Feinendegen & Smilde, 119).

If love constitutes the self, it cannot also be its effect; my personality is not an atomic unit that subsists and transforms independently of others. It is also "impossible to express in words . . . what is meant by 'being' another, when it is predicated of something which at the same time remains itself" (Barfield 2008, 57). The relation is unspeakable by discursive reason because it flouts its laws. It is the logic of metaphor, in which A = B. Predicates are identities, and vice versa. At the "mathematical limit" of the relation to others, one finds that "confidence in immortality and the relation to other beings are closely interconnected [because] their 'limits' coincide" (Barfield 2008, 57). Thus, one finds an integral, essential bond between the individual personality and its "relation to others." At the horizon where the will to truth, will to love, and self-transcendence converge, the atomic self becomes "a coinherence[5] of selves, a simultaneity of separateness and union, a being at the same time a part and the whole, of which the love, friendship and the *esprit de corps* that we know in the flesh are only faint and feeble shadows" (Barfield 2008, 57).

From this vantage, we can see why the equivalence of the "will to die" with "highest life" is also the "omphalos of the moral earth" (Barfield 2008, 52). The "coinherence of selves" that is the essence of moral experience requires it. Only so can Barfield maintain that "the moral law is mandatory, not theoretical. It is known immediately and intuitively and, if you deny it, there is only one answer: so much the worse for you!" (Barfield 2008, 51). The moral law is not a categorical imperative or "thou shalt not" but the pre-discursive experience of love as the "coinherence of selves," of the part as the whole. It is the poetic trope synecdoche taken as the most fundamental and comprehensive cognitive act and the most essential feature of one's moral life. If metaphorical identities hold between the will to death, the will to truth, and becoming another, there is an equivalence of part and whole that is the same as the moral law.

In "Destroyer and Preserver," Barfield explores the polar opposite to "pure love." His subject here is "the human relationship to evil [that] would appear to be changing" (Barfield 1932b, 145). Just as some, like Goethe—another apostle of love dear to Barfield—take up the imperative to "die, and become," so too an increasing number of people choose—like Dawson in Barfield's novel *English People*—"actively to take the part of the evil forces working in [them]" (Barfield 1932b, 146). Such a person "chooses evil, not because it is pleasant but because it is evil" (Barfield 1932b, 146). Whereas the person motivated by love wills truth and self-transcendence, this person affirms the "identification of the will with the forces of destruction" (Barfield 1932b, 146). In fact, ironically, one finds that in so asserting one's will it becomes hijacked:

> In the present case, one will perceive that it is not the mere awareness of forces, or even *impulses*, of destruction in one's own being, in one's own will, that is wrong. On the contrary, these are the mark of conscious strength. What is wrong is the inability to disentangle the Ego from these forces, the inability so to adjust the Ego that it shall use, instead of being used by them. (Barfield 1932b, 146)

Barfield points to Dostoevsky and Albert Steffen as particularly effective analysts of this newly prevalent form of consciousness. It is typified by "the rarified intellectualism, the nervous symptoms, the imbecile excesses of self-contemplation which characterize our age" (Barfield 1932b, 147). Above all, it involves "continually meeting *on all sides* this dread of the sharp outlines of self-consciousness, and the same consequent relapse into that vague semi-conscious 'life' whose function it is to build up the physical body without the co-operation of the conscious Ego" (Barfield 1932b, 147). The positive project in "Death" involves one's conscious effort at self-transformation, first by confronting the meaning of death itself. Here, as in Kierkegaard's and Heidegger's analysis, "dread" leads the hapless individual to flee the self-consciousness that it generates.

This state of mind—dread-ridden, anxious, fleeing from self-consciousness into an active engagement with evil—has its own trope. Not metaphor or synecdoche this time but irony:

> Underneath much of the speaking and writing that goes on to-day there is to be detected a ground-tone of vapid irony. It is an irony which does not know at the expense of what it is being ironical. Its object is to have no object. If it could it would prevent anything anywhere being taken seriously—even itself. (Barfield 1932b, 146)

This quintessentially modern form of irony is a "ground tone" beneath conscious utterance and action that expresses a will to untruth—not to lies but to the ungrounding and mocking of the question of truth itself. It destroys not by being explosive but by undermining any sense of integrity. Vapid irony, like synecdoche, is a mode of relation to others, to the wider world, and to oneself, a metaethical way of orienting oneself that has inescapable ethical consequences.

Barfield returned to the themes of these two essays in "Style" (1933), which was published six weeks after Hitler took control of the Reichstag. The essay—which in some ways anticipates George Orwell's "Politics and the English Language" (1946)—focuses primarily on literary sincerity, in which "style" refers not to affected mannerism but "the literary production of a man whose concern it is to express his thought, and succeeds in doing so" (Barfield 1933b, 84). This seemingly trivial issue matters to Barfield for its ethical implications. The affected style that depends on cliché produces the same corrosion of the soul induced by modern irony:

> *cliché* is simply the abdication by the ego of its prerogative of thinking what it speaks and speaking what it thinks. How is it that the result is not a mere babble of meaningless nonsense? Because, no sooner has the ego abdicated, but something else, a sort of synthetic ghost of previous uses of the words, steps into its place and preserves intact the hollow shell of superficial meaning. (Barfield 1933b, 85)

This eclipse may show up as "purely artistic insincerity," but even in this case because "things have been uttered which purport to be uttered by the ego, but which have in fact been uttered by something or somebody else. . . . moral blame attaches" (Barfield 1933b, 84). Just as the will to truth is also a will to transformation, insincerity is a betrayal of the self. The danger this poses requires that "the price of literary sincerity, like that of liberty, is eternal vigilance, and the writer is a man waging perpetual war against an enemy perpetually on the watch to cozen him of his own thoughts" (Barfield 1933b, 85).

Once one consciously begins the effort to attain true "style," one discovers that "the solution of the problems of style is really a way of initiation" insofar as "both may be conceived as a progressive disengagement of the not-self from the self" (Barfield 1933b, 86). In "polishing" one's style, one removes "existing stains and impurities" in order to reveal "the full beauty of the grain" (Barfield 1933b, 84). In this case, the wood is one's own thinking, gradually cleansed of the clichés that masquerade as one's thoughts, but that in fact hijack and satirize it. This is a kind of modern initiation because "by purging and purifying away the stains and irrelevancies which obscure it, the ego is laid bare, the true *Self* is found. And at the same time the discovery is made that this true Self is, from the earthly point of view, selfless" (Barfield 1933b, 86). Once again, the true self is selfless; the underlying impurity is the illusion of the atomic cogito. The positive moral imperative built into the "dialogue of one" that constitutes thinking is to be ever vigilant in one's conscious recognition that "to write what I have thought is to write what spirit has thought" (Barfield 1933b, 86).

3. Solovyov and Romantic Moral Philosophy

We are now in a better position to understand Barfield's relation to contemporary moral philosophy. With inevitable oversimplification and distortion, one can say that modern moral philosophy consists of three broadly defined groups: the "Hume" or emotivist group, represented most famously in the twentieth century by G. E. Moore; the "Kant" or rationalist group; and third, the "MacIntyre" or virtue ethics group. Alasdair MacIntyre has argued that since the Enlightenment not only academic moral philosophy but also public moral discourse in general has been in a state of attenuated collapse. "What we possess," he says, "are the fragments of a conceptual scheme.... We possess indeed the simulacra of morality, we continue to use many of the key expressions. But we have—very largely, if not entirely—lost our comprehension, both theoretical and practical, of morality" (MacIntyre 1981, 2). As MacIntyre sees it—and we already know Barfield would agree—Enlightenment philosophers such as Hume and Kant were responsible for consolidating the Cartesian picture of the isolated subject that must develop and justify its values from out of itself. However, the two major alternatives, emotivism and rationalism (which were given paradigmatic expression by Hume and Kant, respectively), could not be maintained consistently even by their major proponents. Emotivism undermines the very notion of negotiation and makes the arbitration of moral disagreements impossible, while rationalists have been unable to explain our motivation to obey the categorical imperative without admitting judgments of taste into the heart of their ethics.

But even the significant qualifications that Hume and Kant allowed did not render them immune from their opposites. Kant offered a devastating critique of what he called the "mixed doctrine of morals, put together from incentives of feeling and inclination and also of rational concepts" (Kant 65), on the grounds that it ultimately devolves into an either-or choice between the survival of ethics and its destruction. Such followers of Hume as Jacobi, on the other hand, impeached Kant with regard to the motivation for our ethical decisions. If goodwill cannot finally be reduced to the assertion of the moral law—if it requires instead the felt willingness to be benevolent—then Hume was right after all: rational judgments about ethical matters ultimately arise from, and to some extent at least are reducible to, simple feeling.

The upshot of this "moral disorder" is that we "simultaneously and inconsistently treat moral argument as an exercise of our rational powers and as mere expressive assertion" (MacIntyre 1981, 11). MacIntyre uses G. E. Moore's *Principia Ethica* as his first example of moral incoherence, which is also a useful focal point for this discussion as it was still the center of discussion in literary London as Barfield came of age. For MacIntyre, the awed and adoring reception of Moore's book is instructive, despite its central claims being at best "highly contentious" and at worst "*plainly* false" and "*obviously* defective" (MacIntyre 1981, 16). Its "great silliness" conceals the deeper truth that the Bloomsbury set "felt the need to find objective and impersonal justification for rejecting all claims except those of personal intercourse and of the beautiful" (MacIntyre 1981, 16). More important still, submission to Moore's supposed infallibility extended to much of the analytic tradition in ethics: "Moore's followers had behaved as if their disagreements over what is good were being settled by an appeal to an objective and impersonal criterion; but in fact the stronger and psychologically more adroit will was prevailing" (MacIntyre 1981, 17). The incoherent mishmash of Platonism, emotivism, and utilitarianism that Moore shored against his ruins did not bother his disciples because it reinforced the ideals they already cherished in private, as raised beds in their spoiled intellectual gardens. The "thin" thinking Barfield complained of in 1940 was present already in the first decades of the century, even in London's most urbane drawing rooms.

In the face of the disintegration of moral discourse, MacIntyre has argued (in Gerald Bruns's paraphrase) that "rationality is internal to specific cultures and traditions, meaning that there is no such thing as rationality except against a background of specific cultural narratives that show what it is for anything or anyone to be called rational" (Bruns 94). Barfield would agree with this, as he would with MacIntyre's countering the Enlightenment image of isolated ethical agents with the image of them as actors embedded in various cultural assumptions and practices that tell them what it means to be moral. For MacIntyre, "moral philosophy can only take place at the level of narratives of human judgments, not at the level of principles and rules that would guide judgment toward the right and the good" (Bruns 96). This is consistent with Barfield's conviction that cultures and periods of the evolution of consciousness can be so different as to offer incompatible, perhaps even incommunicable, experiences of the self and the bonds of community—that they inhabit, as he puts it, "different worlds."

MacIntyre turns to narrative as a solution to this problem, and his emphasis on the role of narrative in moral judgment has inspired philosophers and literary critics to explore whether or not, as Martha Nussbaum has it, "literary form is . . . separable from philosophical content, [or] is, itself . . . an integral part . . . of the search for and the statement of truth" (Nussbaum 3). For Nussbaum and MacIntyre, however, literary form seems to be limited primarily to ancient Greece and to realist and reflective fiction of the nineteenth century—*Antigone* and James's *Golden Bowl* are for Nussbaum models of moral deliberation but not, it would seem, *Kotik Letaev* or *The Four Zoas*.

Barfield, building on the premises provided by his metaphysic, works within a fourth school, of which he may be the only modern member, that we might call "Romantic" ethics. Under the influence of Coleridge and Steiner, Barfield, like MacIntyre and Nussbaum, turns to narrative and poetics to develop a robust account of moral judgment but is more radical in utilizing the ways in which tropes like metaphor and synecdoche offer forms of deliberation and interpersonal experience. This is not to suggest that Barfield is immune to the importance of reason and tradition. We have already seen that he was impressed by Lewis's *The Abolition of Man*, in particular its defense of objective reasoning as a bulwark against intellectual caprice. He also read Aristotle's *Nichomachean Ethics* and *De Anima* with Lewis, and the experience stayed with him long enough that he has Burgeon defend an Aristotelian argument for penal reform in *Unancestral Voice*. A brief consideration of the use Barfield makes of Aristotle helps to show what he would find congenial about the Thomist neo-Aristotelian virtue ethics espoused by MacIntyre and where he would find it too limited.

In chapter five of *Unancestral Voice*, during the debate over penal reform, Burgeon surveys a middle path between those who argue for the retributive and reformist views on criminal punishment, respectively. Burgeon "endeavoured to expound a more Aristotelian concept of 'retribution' and to distinguish it carefully from the Roman and Jewish one of retaliation" (*UV* 53). His goal was to show that "retribution was a satisfaction which society itself, as such, demanded; and that was a demand which it might well prove health-giving for the criminal to have to meet" (*UV* 53). Burgeon's audience remains unmoved by this gambit—preferring the comforts of the polarization to which it has become accustomed—but in the context of the essays of the 1930s that we have already examined, we can see the appeal. After all, how is one to move from the cynical, atomistic egotism implicit in vapid irony, from the corrosive effects of cliché-ridden insincerity, to the modern initiation that constitutes the will to self-transcendence? The virtuous Aristotelian balance Barfield proposes has the ameliorative effect of alerting the offender to her own hitherto unapprehended social bonds. It is a ritualistic cleansing at a social level in anticipation of an initiation that resembles catharsis, except that the agent is the center of her own tragedy, and catharsis is the harbinger of self-transformation for the agent, not the audience.

Barfield's response to the neo-Thomist movement spearheaded by Etienne Gilson helps to elucidate his views on the contemporary relevance of Aristotelian thought. He quotes approvingly from Gilson on the conformity of the mind to being but sees this as an experience that declines following the Middle Ages. "How different from ours," Barfield writes, "must have been the whole picture of the relation of man to the universe, which was latent in the background of the medieval mind" (*RCA* 246). The bulk of Barfield's essay illustrates the ways in which the modern era of the "consciousness soul" has grown alien to the affinity of the mind and being articulated by St. Thomas. We now must experience the relation to angelic beings neither as an "external divine staircase" (*RCA* 266) nor as "a poetic or allegorical symbol" (*RCA* 266). Rather, "*their life is the substance of our own wills. For the mind and the senses, the world is their finished work, from which they have withdrawn their being. In the individual human will they have their present existence*" (RCA 266). Barfield agrees with the metaphysical conclusion of neo-Thomism (as presented by Gilson, at any rate) but sees the model of reason and of the self that was championed and exemplified by Aristotle as out of step with modern consciousness.

In fact, it follows from Barfield's metaphysic that if one pursues the essence of reason to its logical conclusion, one arrives again at the paradoxical notion of the self as a synecdoche:

> Only in thinking—in pure thinking as distinct from an abstract chain of thoughts based on remembered sense-impressions—the individual human being functions, not as a skin-confined personality, but as anthropos. That is really the heart of the matter: that the less personal a man is—the less merely and egotistically personal—the *more* truly individual he is. That is of course a difficult thought; but if, as I am convinced, it is also the mystery at the heart of creation, it would be rather naïve to expect it to be anything less. It is also the reason why the method for investigating qualities, unlike the method of traditional science, must have a moral as well as an intellectual coefficient. (*RM* 180)

Because reason on its own leads the self beyond itself, Barfield need not be shy to embrace Objective Idealism in ethics as well as metaphysics. Barfield defended Lewis's argument for "the doctrine of objective values" in *Abolition of Man* because he was convinced by Lewis that "the whole doctrine of objective values" secures with it "the concept of a stable and objective humanity," something that has been "analyzed away during the period now closing, in favour of that other doctrine of objective stable entities, particulate in nature and literal in language" (Barfield 1964, 124). On the one hand, reason rightly safeguards a necessary sense of the self and its moral commitments as being objective, but on the other hand in the very process of doing so, it discovers that the objective self so secured exceeds conventional thinking and even itself.

Barfield found an argument more fully congenial to his own views in Vladimir Solovyov's *The Meaning of Love*, which he read between 1945 and 1951 and revisited in 1985. For in Barfield's view, Solovyov makes good on Coleridge's mostly unfulfilled promise to build a poetic ethics. Solovyov patiently and deductively argues that "the root of false existence consists in impenetrability, i.e., in the mutual exclusion of beings by each other" (Solovyov 188) and that "true life is to live in another as in oneself, or to find in another the positive and absolute fulfillment of one's own being" (Solovyov 188).

Barfield found a concept similar to Coleridge's "conscience" in Solovyov's "syzygetic." He quotes this passage in his introduction to *The Meaning of Love*:

> As for sexual love (in the sphere of personal existence), the single "other" is at the same time all, so, on its side, the social *all*, by power of the positive solidarity of all its elements, ought to manifest itself for each of them as a real unity, as the other living being which would fulfil him in a new and wider sphere. . . . This bond between the living human source (personal) and the unity-of-the-all idea incarnated in the social spiritual-physical organism, ought to be a living *syzgetic* relation. (Barfield 1985, 14)

It should be clear by now why Barfield was drawn to this passage, the climax of Solovyov's argument: it puts in philosophical language the picture of the human being as synecdochical microcosm that he found elaborated in detail by Steiner and that he dramatized in his Burgeon trilogy.

Barfield was struck powerfully enough by Solovyov's book that it became the occasion and the focus of an important essay of 1951, "Form in Art and in Society." He uses Solovyov for his own purposes, reading the Russian idealist through the lens of post-Romantic thought in a manner that resembles Hegel's threefold concept of freedom as the foundation of legislative, personal, and socioeconomic life.[6] Barfield's focus in the essay is on "the relation between form in art and form in human society" (*RM* 227). According to Barfield, "the establishment of a true relation . . . between part and whole in society is a problem of great practical urgency. Indeed it is a truism that civilization is threatening to break down because of man's failure to solve it" (*RM* 223). Like MacIntyre, Barfield diagnoses a crisis in contemporary culture. Where Macintyre focuses on breakdowns in moral discourse, Barfield highlights the relation of the individual to society as a whole. These problems are mutually implicating: one cannot discern the proper relation of the part to the whole without a discourse to describe it, and yet one cannot articulate a coherent moral discourse without understanding the relation of the part to the whole. More precisely, Barfield notes that while "the demand for social 'solidarity' and the conviction of its necessity are today realities" (*RM* 225) it is also the case that "the demand for individual liberty, spiritual as well as political, is no less real" (*RM* 225). The upshot, which, for example, runs through the formative debate between Robert Nozick and John Rawls, is that "unfortunately, it appears all too evident to most people that individualism is incompatible with collectivism and 'fellowship,' and that to propound as a good the unlimited expansion of individualism in any sphere would be to preach moral egoism and social anarchy" (*RM* 225). Barfield argues that a resolution to this dilemma cannot come from within either "individualism" or "collectivism" but only by fundamentally reshaping the mode of thought in which the ideas "individual" and "social" arise.

The essay begins with reflections on the nature of artistic form that will be familiar to those who have worked through the aesthetics of Kant, Schiller, and Schelling, and that was perhaps most present for Barfield in Coleridge's essays on "Genial Criticism," which were readily available in the Shawcross edition of the *Biographia Literaria*. "Artistic form," in this view, "may be resolved into a peculiar relation of part to whole, and of whole to part" (*RM* 218). The distinguishing feature of this relation is that an artistic object is a whole whose parts are not only highly individualized but also mutually interpenetrating. A part may struggle for, and in an unspecified sense even achieve, "independent life," but it nevertheless remains "a true part of the whole" (*RM* 217). No less than in his description of the imaginative apprehension of the parts of a metaphor, Barfield remains consistent with his Romantic predecessors in arguing that the apprehension of such organic artistic relations requires imagination: they are, as Barfield puts it, "the kinds of relation which the imagination, and only the imagination, detects between the parts and whole of a living organism, and both creates and detects between the parts and whole of a work of art" (*RM* 220).

Barfield makes use of the organic metaphor—which Solovyov builds deductively and literally—by applying it to the ways we can think about the relations of parts and wholes to each other. So, while romantic love may be the most obvious example of artistic, organic wholeness between people, Barfield follows Solovyov in extending it to social relations as such: "the love between two human beings . . . is true to its own essence only if it functions as a sort of biological cell, with the potentiality of expanding to the entire social organism" (*RM* 220). This is important because "organic" relations are neither external and contiguous, as they are in the inorganic realm, nor organized by an externally imposed idea—as in, say, the bureaucratic state—but by what Barfield, following Solovyov, calls "the all-one idea" (*RM* 220). External relations are those in which individuals of whatever sort—atoms, let's say, or Cartesian cogitos—remain individual by denying the interpenetration of other atoms or minds. Relation by arrangement builds external relations into itself, constituting wholes through the arrangement of parts, or the creation of new wholes through their rearrangement. The "all-one idea," by contrast, requires not merely "the greatest possible distinctness and self-sufficiency of its parts—provided only that we do not think of them as mutually impenetrable" (*RM* 221); not merely this, but even that "the ideal organic relation of part to whole is a sort of *identity* of the one with the other" (*RM* 221). Collective unity achieved by way of individual liberty, identical to "an 'organic' relation between part and whole . . . is usually called love" (*RM* 223).

This identity is a synecdoche in which the part and whole are not only identical but also reversible:

> Not only man in general, but each individual man "may *become* all" . . . as he lives and learns to do away with that inward boundary which severs him from the rest. . . . Thus, in the "all-one idea" realized, the part *is* the whole, not by merger, but on the contrary by intensive development of its true individuality or

> part-ness. Or rather the whole is the part; for, whereas when we think abstractly *about* being, as in the processes of logic and classification, the whole is predicated of the part, so that we say "A horse *is* a quadruped," in the actual *process* of being, the order is reversed, and the race or archetype *is* the species or individual—because it gives it being. (RM 222)

If we apply these claims to one of the most famous examples of predication, to say that "Socrates is a man" is not merely to say that manhood is a predicate of the subject, Socrates, but also that manhood is what gives rise to Socrates: Socrates is simultaneously an example of humanity and its epitome, as are we all. The individual is the archetype, and vice versa. Thus, the mutual penetrability that marks the part/whole relation applies not only laterally to each member, so that I am in metaphorical identity to every other member of my community, but also vertically to the whole of which I am a part, and that is a part of me.

Full grasp of this concept requires the exercise of imagination because it is "the image of a special relation between part and whole, which is neither serial nor spatial nor . . . hierarchical; the kind of relation, in fact, which the imagination, and only the imagination, detects between the parts and the whole of a living organism" (RM 220). Thus Barfield, like Eliot but for different reasons, affirms the contemporary relevance of Coleridge's clerisy:

> should *imagination*, as the Romantics tried to expound it, take as firm a hold of the minds of the intelligentsia (or clerisy, as I prefer to call them) as *judgment* did in feudal Europe, it would furnish the necessary mental foundation for a viable democracy. Necessary, because the existing foundation of Newtonian, atomic thought, can only be realized either in *laissez faire* or in totalitarian reaction from it. (RM 224)

The "Newtonian, atomic" thought of the contemporary intelligentsia makes it unable to reimagine society except between the extremes of "*laissez faire*" and "totalitarian reaction" because it either treats individuals as mutually exclusive atomic units or subordinates them to an abstract universal. Without the "imaginal" experience of the part as the whole, and of each individual as every other, "you cannot *have* an enduring society *at all*" (RM 225). In fact, "so far from individualism leading to social anarchy, the solidarity of your society will vary directly with the extent to which the individuals composing it become and remain individuals. If you are aiming at collective unity, you must also be aiming at individual liberty" (RM 225). Once again Barfield points to Steiner's *The Threefold Commonwealth* as expressing his own argument, though "this book has met with so little understanding principally because the ideas it expounds need, in order to grasp them, the kind of thinking and perception which is normally reserved today for the appreciation of works of art" (*RM* 225).

4. Imagining Liberty

Steiner's distinction between the cultural and legislative domains, which Barfield alludes to in describing the antinomy of "individualism" and "solidarity," is the subject of an essay he wrote not long after he finished *What Coleridge Thought*, "Participation and Isolation: A Fresh Light on Present Discontents" (1972). It is not concerned primarily with "culture" but with the "legislative" or rights domain. As the subtitle suggests, it is also an updating or correction of Freud's interest in the underlying conditions for current social tensions and problems. The intervening twenty-one years since "Form in Art and in Society" had brought great changes, of course.

For example, among the most notable features of a new phenomenon, the counterculture, was that despite its energy, it included "a great deal of bewilderment... and a great deal of that paralysis of the will which bewilderment engenders" (*RM* 202). Indeed, Barfield saw enervated confusion quite a bit. In contemporaneous essays, he warns that if we do not overcome the "force of habit" that leads us to assume that we are sealed off from the "outer world" by the boundary of our skin, we will "slide deeper into the morass of self-deception that is paralyzing our wills" (*RM* 162). In "Form in Art and in Society" he had already discerned that for the modern person the schism between the equally compelling motives to "solidarity" and "liberty" was "confusing his mind, weakening his will, and reducing him to a condition of impotent *malaise*" (*RM* 225).

This confused *malaise* is in part produced by the "mainly sensational media we've come to rely on for our news" (*RM* 202), a version of a complaint Barfield had been making for nearly fifty years, but the indifference of the "sensational media" to the truth is as much symptom as cause. The more profound cause of our torpor is the social alienation that springs from metaphysical rootlessness—an alienation from objectivity as such. On the one hand, there is "a growing demand on all sides and by every kind of human being for a greater share in the control of his own life and destiny" (*RM* 201); on the other hand, "there is another widely prevalent frame of mind . . . the impulse not only not to assume responsibility for the conduct of society but, as far as possible, to keep out of the whole rumpus" (*RM* 202). This contradictory state mirrors our intuition of metaphysical contradiction, responsibility for which falls upon Descartes for his "denial of participation ... [on which] the whole methodology of natural science is based" (*RM* 205). Barfield can demonstrate that "the human mind is not an onlooker on, but a participant in the so-called outside world" (*RM* 203), but the closest that most people come to absorbing this point or registering its practical implications is to think of participation as "some kind of aggregated or collective consciousness, some 'coenaesthesis,' or 'intersubjectivity,' or whatever new word may be found for it" (*RM* 204). The denial of participation, or reduction of it to anemia, amounts to a denial not only that "the world itself, the objective world ... is his self-consciousness displayed before him, so to speak, as his perceptions" (*RM* 204); not only this, but equally important in a time of social crisis, it also denies that "mankind is a real totality, as well as an abstract class of quantitative units" (*RM* 204). Over here, an impulse to individual freedom; over there, a demand for collective solidarity; in the midst, the need for, and denial of, a robust concept and experience of participation.

Hence it is difficult to know how to act on another new phenomenon, the demand for universal justice based on the felt perception of universal, inalienable rights. There is, he says:

> a third contemporary ideal, or demand, or complaint, or slogan, or warcry (they are becoming very much the same thing).... If *participation* and *alienation* are being very much insisted on, so, in the same breath is *equality*; or rather, the ideal of social equality is not so much insisted on as it is presupposed, taken for granted. (*RM* 207)

This calls to mind once again Macintyre's argument that incompatible accounts of justice prove intractable because they arise from and are embedded in conceptual systems that are themselves fundamentally incompatible. Aristotle and Hume use terms like "*arête*" and "sympathy" that reveal "the fundamental incompatibility of theories of justice framed in terms of one of those schemes with theories framed in terms of the other" (Macintyre 1991, 150). The implication is that "the history of philosophy as a form of rational inquiry is in such cultural and social orders embedded in the larger history of culture and society and will be, if too much detached from that history, in certain respects distorted or even unintelligible" (Macintyre 1991, 150–1).

The danger of this insight, of which MacIntyre and Barfield were equally aware, is an irreducible pluralism, not merely of values or ideals but also of the modes of reasoning by which one arrives at them. MacIntyre points to Isaiah Berlin as "the most systematic and the most cogent defender" of the view that "there is no such thing as 'the' contemporary vision of the world, there are a multiplicity of visions deriving from [an] irreducible plurality of values" (Macintyre 1981, 109). Barfield alludes to Berlin's most famous defense of this view in "Two Concepts of Liberty" when he identifies equality with "political liberty" and invokes Berlin's definition of negative liberty with the promise that:

> every single [person] is entitled to have assured to him his separate existence as an independent being, free of any such paternalist or authoritarian control of his choices, as was inseparable from the hierarchical construction of society, and free also from such other interferences as mass-disseminated propaganda disguised as news. (*RM* 212)

This paraphrases Berlin's definition of negative liberty as "the answer to the question 'What is the area within which the subject—a person or group of persons—is or should be left to do or be what he is able to do or be, without interference by other persons?'" (Berlin 2002, 169).

For Barfield, the purpose of liberty is to allow individuals to discover and unfold "the concrete realities of nature and human nature" (*RM* 215). Berlin, however, is leery of any single definition of human nature. Berlin points to Plato, Rousseau, Kant, Fichte, Hegel, and others—the idealist or essentialist tradition, broadly conceived—as holding a bifurcated picture of the self. One half is the "dominant self" that is "variously identified with reason, with my 'higher nature', . . . with my 'real', or 'ideal', or 'autonomous' self, or with my self 'at its best'" (Berlin 2002, 179). The other half consists of "irrational impulse, uncontrolled desires, my 'lower' nature, the pursuit of immediate pleasures, my 'empirical' or 'heteronomous' self, swept by every gust of desire and passion, needing to be rigidly disciplined if it is ever to rise to the full height of its 'real' nature" (Berlin 2002, 179). Furthermore, in the Platonic-Kantian-Hegelian tradition the supposed higher or "true" self is "conceived as something wider than the individual," indeed as "a social 'whole' of which the individual is an element or aspect" (Berlin 2002, 179). It is but a short step to ensure that "this entity is then identified as being the 'true' self which, by imposing its collective, or 'organic', single will upon its recalcitrant 'members', achieves its own, and therefore their, 'higher' freedom" (Berlin 2002, 179). Plato, Kant, Fichte, and the rest assume that "a rational (or free) State would be a State governed by such laws as all rational men would freely accept; that is to say, such laws as they would themselves have enacted had they been asked what, as rational beings, they demanded" (Berlin 2002, 191). As a consequence, "they all assume that in a society of perfectly rational beings the lust for domination over men will be absent or ineffective" (Berlin 2002, 192) and thereby ensure, paradoxically, that "liberty, so far from being incompatible with authority, becomes virtually identical with it" (Berlin 2002, 194). This terrifying result leads Berlin to conclude that "the belief that some single formula can in principle be found whereby all the diverse ends of men can be harmoniously realised is demonstrably false" (Berlin 2002, 214). The position that Berlin finally takes is that:

> pluralism, with the measure of "negative" liberty that it entails, seems to me a truer and more humane ideal than the goals of those who seek in the great disciplined, authoritarian structures the ideal of "positive" self-mastery by classes, or peoples, or the whole of mankind. It is truer, because it does, at least, recognize the fact that human goals are many, not all of them commensurable, and in perpetual rivalry with one another. (Berlin 2002, 216)

It is easy to see the challenge this poses to Barfield's picture of a flourishing society and human being. With the propaganda of the recent war still fresh in mind, Berlin is wary of pictures of society as "organic," the "vitalistic models of social life" (Berlin 2002, 189) sought for by Herder, Hegel, and Marx. Indeed, Barfield's picture of human flourishing, a will to truth and to love that culminates in the "coinherence of selves," may, when translated into political action, sound uncomfortably close to Kant's "kingdom of ends" or Hegel's "I that is we, we that is I." It is perhaps monolithic as well, "some single formula" as Berlin would have it, and therefore inattentive to the fact that "human goals are many." Barfield might respond that Berlin assumes without argument that the tradition of the "true" or "higher" self is false and drily ridicules the notion throughout his essay. He might also say that an idealist picture of the "true" self need not entail the coercive rationalism that Berlin suggests must follow. These objections are inadequate, though, for they leave unanswered how in a just society one can protect the pursuit of irreducibly various ends while also weaving the "coinherence of selves" that Barfield argues is our *telos*.

Barfield's solution to this dilemma, perhaps surprising given his general hostility to the analytical tradition, is to take an analytical approach: what does the word "equality" mean for ordinary language users today?[7] Equality essentially means two different and perhaps incompatible things: "numerical" identity and "replica" identity. The former is Aristotle's first rule of reasoning, that a thing is the same as itself (Socrates is Socrates; or, $A = A$). Barfield has little to say about it because it is "no relation at all. . . . To say that a thing is identical to itself is to say nothing about the relation because, for the purpose of a relation, you've got to have two or more things" (*RM* 208).[8] "Replica" identity is the more interesting to him in this context because it is the basis of the assertion of rights. This sort of equality, rigorously considered, entails that "the closer any two or more units come to being equal with each other in all respects, the truer it is to say that the only relation between them is their separateness" (*RM* 208). Furthermore, this replica identity is also the foundation of abstract reason:

> Now there is one thing to be noticed about the notion of absolute equality, or identity. It is the foundation of all merely *abstract* thinking. Abstract thought looks at a number of diverse and separate units—individual trees, or chairs, or human beings—and concentrates exclusively on the respects in which they appear identical with each other. That apparent identity is indeed precisely what it "abstracts" and gives a name to. And yet it is quite unreal. The diversity, the disintegration, is real; the integration is only a convenient fiction. (*RM* 209)

Barfield leaves unstated the obvious implication that our modern understanding of, and insistence upon, political equality is a part of the larger historical and social impulse belonging to modernity, or the "Consciousness Soul" age. Equality is one fruit of the alienation brought about by the Cartesian schism. Just as this split requires us no longer to experience nature as "a fecund and benevolent companion," but as "an inhuman and meaningless mechanism" (*RM* 210), so too do we now experience that "it involves the reduction of human relations to side-by-sideness . . . and so eliminates mutual participation" (*RM* 210). In the realm of political rights we are all identical, undifferentiated, insofar as we, by virtue of our shared humanity, enjoy the same legal recognition. People are "equal precisely in the regard that they are independent or, if you prefer, alienated and isolated from one another" (*RM* 212). Thus, the "principle of equality" is "both a curse and a blessing" (*RM* 210)—an "indispensable" blessing with regard to "the rule of law" but at the considerable cost of reducing our relations to contiguity. To focus exclusively on equality—or equity, as we might say today—is to embrace an "integration contradicted by disintegration" insofar as it at once obliterates our uniqueness and siloes us off from each other and so leaves "nothing to restrain everyone from having . . . negative feelings about everyone else" (*RM* 211).

How then to realize in a healthy way the "inexorable, almost universal, demand for equality" that "arises out of the deepest nature of human beings as they are *now* constituted" (*RM* 212)? The answer, for Barfield, involves addressing:

> the practical question . . . Is it possible to retain the kind of participation that makes human society possible without abandoning the relatively new principle of equality, of social equality? There are few more important questions because

the plain truth is that if it is *not* possible, democracy as an experiment has failed. (*RM* 212)

Barfield's answer returns us to the argument of his ethics: if we are to make a success of "democracy as an experiment" we must make a "conscious effort" to recognize and experience that "insofar as they genuinely participate with one another, human beings are *not* equal, because they are not merely side by side but are interpenetrating" (*RM* 212). As we are now aware, this requires us to develop moral imagination, for:

> the opposite of abstract thought is imagination, which deals not with identities, but with resemblances; not with side-by-sideness, but with *interpenetration*; and if we want to see the whole system of abstract thought, in which we're so deeply immersed, from outside of itself, so to speak, we must begin by seeing it in the light of imagination. (*RM* 209)

Here we have, in the moral and political spheres, the relation of poetic to rational principles in Barfield's poetics and of Reason to the Understanding in his metaphysics. Our abstract, "replica" identity is a necessary fiction in the legislative realm, bracketed on one side by "moral imagination" as the heart of cultural activity and on the other side by the unwitting altruism of the economic realm, for "the principle on which [the latter] is based is that of all for each and each for all, of each individual human unit participating in a vast whole, which we call industrial society" (*RM* 207).[9] In other words, Barfield agrees with the need in Steiner's "threefold social organism" to establish a radically democratic society and follows Steiner's dictum that modern societies become unhealthy when the legitimacy of any of the three spheres is denied or any of its members absorbed into one of the others. It is no surprise that Barfield alludes yet again to "the threefold sociology of Rudolf Steiner" or that he singles out for appreciation that Steiner:

> did not simply confront abstract thinking with its opposite, imagination (as many poets have done both in the Old World and in the New, as all the alienated do subconsciously, and a few of them explicitly), but whose genius succeeded in combining the two in an altogether new and intimate way. (*RM* 213–14)

Barfield's moral and political thought—with its differentiation into cultural/moral, political, and economic realms, as well as its combination of imagination and abstraction—plows the same field. Berlin, we might say, drew the wrong conclusion from his deep study of Romanticism: it leads not to fascism but to liberty.

6

Mysterious Potency

The Burgeon Trilogy

The Burgeon trilogy that Barfield published from 1950 to 1965 is perhaps the happiest accident of his career, though it seems in retrospect like it was inevitable all along. The most prominent strands in Barfield's philosophy are his poetics, historiography, metaphysics, and his leap into cosmology. In the Burgeon trilogy, he most fully synthesizes his poetic philosophy with his poetic practice, as well as dramatizing the progress from chaotic aestheticism through the articulation of an objective idealist metaphysic to the growth of the capacity to experience, not just theorize about, oneself and the world as a "primary symbol." More than that, it brings directly into his life the themes he discusses from the beginning: Barfield had considered the transformation of thinking as the modern form of initiation since the 1920s. In response to a crisis in his marriage during the 1940s, he created the persona G. A. L. Burgeon and wrote a series of satirical love poems that implicitly and explicitly address a woman named "Betty" as his muse, with no apparent thought of developing the persona into the protagonist of a novel, much less a trilogy of them; in fact, after finishing the first book he does not appear to have considered continuing its narrative for many years afterward. Burgeon undoubtedly surprised Barfield as much as anyone by becoming the protagonist of a trilogy consisting of *This Ever Diverse Pair* (1950), *Worlds Apart* (1963), and *Unancestral Voice* (1965). The trilogy records Burgeon's transformation, from the satirically hellish and destructive trials of the first novel, through the intellectual purgation of the second book, to the total transformation into "primary symbol" of Burgeon's deepest sense of self in the finale, as an emblem of the kind of transformation that Barfield believed the modern age demanded of each of us. Steiner, we recall, says that "Anthroposophy is a path of knowledge to guide the Spiritual in the human being to the Spiritual in the universe. It arises in man as a need of the heart, of the life of feeling; and it can be justified only inasmuch as it can satisfy this inner need" (Steiner 1973, 13).

This is an apt description of Burgeon, whose "life of feeling" undergoes a trial by fire across the three novels, confirming his late insight that "destruction is the precondition of every transformation" and that "transformation is most absolute . . . [w]ithin man himself" (*UV* 159). The process is evident in the three genres Barfield uses for the three works: *This Ever Diverse Pair* is a Menippean satire, *Worlds Apart* is a kind of Platonic dialogue, and *Unancestral Voice* is a fictional spiritual autobiography. Barfield sometimes referred readers interested in his metaphysics to *Worlds Apart* but he failed to mention that it is part of a trilogy of novels—in other words, that its philosophical claims are circumscribed by the poetic, or that *Worlds Apart* is in the broad sense poetic rather than simply didactic. As the climactic realization of Barfield's synthesis of his poetic practice and poetic philosophy, it is worth tracing the trilogy's organic unfolding, from existential despair through philosophical clarity to personal transformation and the personal integration of poetic cosmology.

1. The Burgeon Poems

Throughout the 1940s there were intimations of the book that Barfield would publish in 1950. For example, in the 1940 essay "Panic and Its Opposite," after commenting on the way that long practice of Anthroposophy makes one's writing "more and more entangled with our personal idiosyncrasies and accidents of our personal history," Barfield goes on to say that his essay "will be of interest to those who are physically and etherically so constituted as to be without what is called 'natural courage'" (Barfield 1940b, 1). Cowardice, we shall see, is a defining feature of Burgeon's character, abiding even to the end of *Unancestral Voice*. In 1942, Barfield republished his major essay "Equity," a topic that plays a large thematic role in the book, including a satirical-allegorical, quasi-divine embodiment of Equity as adjudicator in Burgeon's final dream vision. In "The Psalms of David" (1945), Barfield developed a theme that would again loom large in *This Ever Diverse Pair* and *Unancestral Voice* alike: that one must develop a "sympathetic understanding" for why the Psalmist and his audience could have a powerful aesthetic experience of "anything so dry and authoritarian as the Law" *(RM* 240). Barfield fully explores this dryness, indeed deadness, in the 1950 novel, but Burgeon only has the promise of "sympathetic understanding" at that point. Finally, in 1946—the same year that Barfield published the first of the "Burgeon" poems—he published another major essay with obvious relevance to his new authorial persona, "Poetic Diction and Legal Fiction." One could easily retitle the essay "Burgeon and Burden," with the proviso that Burgeon and Burden only satirically represent poetry and the law.

The years 1946–7 also witnessed the mysterious appearance of five poems by G. A. L. Burgeon in the *New English Weekly*, a prominent periodical sympathetic to the Social Credit movement and notable for publishing poems and essays by Ezra Pound and T. S. Eliot, among others, from the 1930s into the 1950s.[1] Barfield first uses the *nom de plume* "Burgeon" in these five poems.[2] One might say that "Burgeon" arises from Barfield much as Burden does from Burgeon at the beginning of *This Ever Diverse Pair*—that is, from the realm of "the Mothers," spiritual depths that coincide with the deeper layers of the unconscious mind. We find in the poems an indication of the existential crisis—"I must now write about something or die" (*TEDP* 4)—that would lead to Burgeon's "writing this 'diary', as I have not very accurately called it" (*TEDP* 120). In later years, Barfield was matter-of-fact that he shared his character's crisis:

> I can't say that during much of my life I've been aware of living in polarity, or that I thought formally in those terms. Looking back, it's quite true that there does seem to have been a rather marked element of it. It may be that there is in most human beings. It does come out, I think, very strongly, in the fact that I went into the law, law being almost by definition living and organic, or however you like to put it. And my being instinctively in the one and being compelled to live with my mind and activity very much in the other did lead, over a great part of my life, I suppose, to a kind of polarity as tension, very much as tension. And the tension at one stage became so violent that, together with other pressures, it very nearly resulted in a nervous breakdown; and I think I've always thought, looking back, that I avoided a nervous breakdown largely by writing that little book *This Ever Diverse Pair* and really in a way I did it more out of that impulse, or desperation, rather than having any hope of ever publishing it as a book. The characters Burden and Burgeon are embodiments or symbols . . . of a very real experience of polarity and tension in my own life. (Sugarman 21)

It is no accident that in these years of personal "polarity and tension" Barfield took a strong interest in Existentialist thought of Kierkegaard and Gabriel Marcel. Barfield was going through an existential crisis of his own, from the dichotomy of his legal and poetic careers to his marital woes and romantic entanglements. Barfield must have been aware that Kierkegaard suffered a similar "polarity and tension" in his own life, though the Dane resolved it differently. It is therefore unsurprising that Barfield adopted some of Kierkegaard's themes and techniques, including the ruse of publishing under a *nom de plume* with a quasi-allegorical name. The "violent" experience of polarity is also not unlike

Kierkegaard's paradoxes, though in the gap between polarity and paradox lies one distinction between Barfield and Kierkegaard.

Barfield's "Burgeon" poems are his initial creative efforts to master the violent upheavals of destructive polarity. The poems form two distinct groups. The first of these, published in quick succession, are "The Russet," "Semantics," and "Tradition in Poetry." "Cosmetics" and "The Doppelganger," published later and close together, form another group; taken together, the five slight poems indicate a speaker pockmarked with alienation and anxiety due to the inescapable experience of personal and cultural collapse.

The first three poems represent different forms of fallenness. "The Russet," which begins the sequence, reports the narrator's dream, in which Cupid becomes a Satanic figure who offers the speaker's "love" an array of apple slices on a "pewter platter" (Barfield 1946a, 217). That Burgeon would dream of Eve's temptation in a classical Eden is not surprising—in *This Ever Diverse Pair* he reports having *Paradise Lost* on his bedside table (*TEDP* 91). In this dream, he is a helplessly innocent Adam, cut off from the sensory delights of "touch" and "taste" that open before his lingering, nodding, love, the pun on "nodding" indicating both her willing assent and her own dream state. The archaic diction of the poem—"winged," "accoutered," "pedlar," "dan," and so on (Barfield 1946a, 217)—further emphasizes that the speaker has been left behind, as if he were the narrator of Marvell's "The Garden" but had himself been abolished to a green thought in a green shade.[3]

"Semantics" pursues the same theme of a fall but this time as a broader cultural disintegration. The speaker looks back to those "strange men with straight noses" who "*made* music"—music as such, not this or that musical composition—and had direct visionary experience of the "divine ladies, nine ladies" (Barfield 1946b, 6). Though there is no rich visual description as in "The Russet," the setting is the modern one "down centuries thrice ten" from that of visionary and creative majesty, and the intervening eras have been marked by steep decline. The ironic tension of genuine former fertility and current sterility is nicely captured in the pun on the Muses's "printless fall / Of their dancing breaks" (Barfield 1946b, 6)—at once their spiritual dance and their unpublished or unwritten collapse, the deteriorating succession also recorded in the sequence "from 'Muse' . . . 'music' . . . 'musical' . . .," analogous to the increasing alienation and abstraction that Barfield notes in *History in English Words* from "human" through "humane" and "humanitarian" to "humanitarianism" (*HEW* 193).

Burgeon completes the first set of Burgeon poems with "Tradition in Poetry." If the speaker of "The Russet" seems impotent and abject, and that of "Semantics" nostalgic and melancholy, this one rages against *vers libre* and all it represents. The sequence of three poems moves from an Edenic garden through thousands of years to a desiccated present moment. This poem imagines and quotes an exponent of free verse, who punningly critiques Burgeon's "Attic mould." The speaker confesses a "heart that's choked with grief" (Barfield 1946c, 47); he seeks "swift relief" from "ancestral voices" and yet seems unable to evoke this heritage in his own voice. He is reduced to stating "*I wandered lonely as a cloud—*, / Hymn, Ballad, Nursery Jingle" (Barfield 1946c, 47). He intuits the presence of "Betty, and the Muses" in the evening hours, having steeped in these old forms, but he cannot do any more with them than he did in the first two poems. "Betty" is more quotidian slang than a Beatricean archetype for feminine beauty. He confesses, in a possible reference to the opening lines of *The Unicorn*, that "my hand's unsteady / And, by the Dog, I need old wine / Because I'm drunk already" (Barfield 1946c, 47). If the language of modern poetry has collapsed, so has Burgeon himself; like the narrator of *The Unicorn*, he is a confused wanderer—what does he have to offer, in his drunken state, but the "old wine" of which he stands in need? To the fall of the potent image in "The Russet," and of musical meaning in "Semantics," we can add the fall of poetic language itself in "Tradition in Poetry." The record of Burgeon's impotent isolation is all but complete.

The two final poems in the quintet are narrated from this fallen perspective and themselves constitute a dichotomy. They feature the return of "Betty" from "Tradition in Poetry." "Cosmetics," the title of the fourth poem, encapsulates this debasement insofar as cosmetics etymologically is the art of "cosmos," arrangement. The claim that the artist "can divine" the "living feature" of "pure Nature" beneath "the dross all purged away" (Barfield 1947a, 189) hints at the Neoplatonic image of the artist as semi-divine revealer/maker on a cosmic scale. Burgeon's deployment of this mighty rhetoric in the service of convincing "Betty" to remove her makeup so that he can see "that gash you call your mouth" puts all this in bitterly ironic relief. Betty is correct to call him "quaint" when his idealism devolves into clichéd, vague, and tautologous praise of her "dear dear beauty and high spirit" (Barfield 1947a, 189).

Nor does Burgeon seem to believe his own rhetoric, as he reverses himself in the next and final poem, "The Doppelganger." He is again aware that surface and depth diverge in his beloved but replaces his ironic-prophetic confidence in his visionary discernment with mock-fraught self-doubt at the "strange dichotomy" and "mental disputation" that erupts when "the Betty in my mind / Meets Betty on the station" (Barfield 1947b, 105). The speaker is troubled to "see them side by side, those two / And match them both together" (Barfield 1947b, 105). Ideal

Betty is no longer the living feature of pure nature, though, and the two Betties cannot be properly merged, or the "dross" one removed; instead, the "eye" is more discerning than the "heart" and accuses the latter of hiding within its "fancy" her flaws "there and there . . . / And *there*" (Barfield 1947b, 105). The heart does not respond to the eye's damning catalogue, nor does the speaker succeed in his effort to ensure that "the first one fades away . . . / And melts into the second." The poem ends ambiguously: "I lose my head and hear it say: / 'She's sweeter than you reckoned!'" (Barfield 1947b, 105). The speaker at the end is presumably, but not obviously, the heart, making a feeble response to the sharp, accusing eye. The speaker has indeed lost his head: the first three poems of the Burgeon cycle record various forms of spiritual and artistic loss; the final two poems reflect the fundamentally schizoid upshot of that loss, at the level of artistic perception. Burgeon cannot meaningfully distinguish truth from error, beauty from ugliness, virtue from vice. The "doppelganger" of the poem's title is not one of the Betties but the speaker's "eye" itself, tormenting his heart with its lacerating and unanswerable observations. It is no wonder that the Burgeon we meet at the beginning of *This Ever Diverse Pair* is on the point of personal collapse, against a backdrop of sociocultural meaninglessness and intellectual incoherence.

2. *This Ever Diverse Pair*

The Burgeon poems are the backdrop for the first book of the trilogy, *This Ever Diverse Pair*. Burgeon's use of the form fits squarely within the discussions of the form by Northrop Frye and Mikhail Bakhtin that remain widely influential today.[4] For example, Burgeon makes use of a number of genres in addition to straightforward narrative: poetry, song, a mini-play, legal prose, epistles, dream vision, and so on. Burgeon almost invariably uses these forms for comic effect, with no regard for verisimilitude. Rather, the forms and their unpredictable combination introduce fantasy, allowing the free exploration of philosophical concerns, psychological extremes, and moral crises, while maintaining a light, satiric tone. One senses the seriousness beneath the light surface, but the lightness remains inviolable and essential. Burgeon's characters, including himself, are caricatures that embody intellectual attitudes or dispositions that mirror those of Burden and himself.

The use of a *nom de plume* to tell a story of personal and cultural alienation, Burgeon's persistent sense of dread and self-consciousness (and the apparent link between them), the mutual hostility of the aesthetic and the legal/ethical, and the problem of faith, all bring to mind Søren Kierkegaard, whose reputation and influence flourished at mid-century.[5] Kierkegaard seems to have been on Barfield's mind as he worked on his novel. In "The Time-Philosophy of Rudolf Steiner" (1955), Barfield singles out Kierkegaard and Gabriel Marcel as representatives of "Christian Existentialism" who carry "a weighty, almost crushing, sense of *responsibility* in face of the universe." Barfield envisions someone like Kierkegaard who:

> sees a poster inscribed with the words, "It all depends on me." And he takes the words to heart. Read a few pages of Kierkegaard, and you are suddenly brought up with an almost horrifying shock: "Good heavens—this man really means what he says!" And then, just possibly, you may feel rather ashamed of yourself. (*RCA* 260)

The same mood of anxious responsibility pervades *This Ever Diverse Pair*, suggesting that by 1950 Barfield had read *Either-Or*, *Fear and Trembling* and *The Sickness Unto Death* (probably in Walter Lowrie's 1941 translation of the latter two and the joint translation of the former by the Swensons and Lowrie, published in 1944). In particular, Barfield dramatizes Kierkegaard's themes of the aesthetic and ethical life central to *Either-Or*, of dread and self-consciousness central to *The Sickness Unto Death*, and *Fear and Trembling*'s contrast of the "knight of infinite resignation" who embraces universal ethical demands (embodied and satirized by Burden), and the Pauline "knight of faith" that Burgeon unwittingly struggles to become.

Before he turns to the narrative proper, Burgeon places before us epigraphs from the Pauline epistles that alert the attentive reader to these Kierkegaardian themes.[6] However, even this is not as simple as it seems. The first edition of *This Ever Diverse Pair*, published under Burgeon's name, has two of them; for the second edition (1985), published under his own name, Barfield added one more epigraph and the lines of Meredith's sonnet from which he derived the title of his book. Furthermore, in the first edition the Pauline epigraphs are quoted in Greek; only in the second edition did Barfield add translations, from the King James Version. The original readers of the first edition, published by "Burgeon," must make the translations and attributions on their own, but when Barfield takes over he adds content, context, and translations. All of this raises complex questions about authorship and agency that render still more complex the central thematic concerns about authorship and selfhood of the book itself, and indeed of the whole trilogy.

Each of the epigraphs appears to be self-sufficient. The original 1950 examples are: *Because the law worketh wrath...* and *Nay, I had not known sin but by the law.* They illustrate Burgeon's state of mind and the limit of his vision, what he is able to recognize about himself, and his remaining tasks regarding self-knowledge. The original two epigraphs point to the anger and sharp self-consciousness brought about in Burgeon by his experience of "the law" and to the awareness of sin as being generated by the law. In short, they point to the paradoxical quality of a law-bound moral sensibility: that the law creates the very quality it brings to the soul's consciousness and judges as deadly to the soul itself. The first epigraph, added in 1985, points to the final result of this morally catastrophic quandary: the death of the soul itself. In this, Barfield seems to follow Kierkegaard, who in *Either-Or* presents the quasi-Kantian antinomy of the aesthetic and the ethical, with the promise that only a "leap of faith" can bridge the gap between the particular impulses of the senses and the universal demands of the law.

The wider context for these epigraphs, indicated by the use of ellipses, reveals another layer of meaning. Burgeon ends the first epigraph with the limit of his vision, "wrath." Here is what he does not fully understand, so cannot include:

> Because the law worketh wrath: for where no law is, there is no transgression. Therefore it is of faith, that it might be by grace; to the end the promise might be sure to all the seed; not to that only which is of the law, but to that also which is of the faith of Abraham; who is the father of us all. (Romans 8:15-16)

Whereas Burgeon understands the wrath generated by the law to describe his own existential crisis, Paul's meaning is that the wrath is divine and follows necessarily from the creation of the law. Those who are bound to the law are bound to wrath, which one can only escape when one transcends the law itself by means of faith, which is the true legacy of Abraham. This central idea of Kierkegaard's *Fear and Trembling* eludes Burgeon completely.

The other epigraph Burgeon chose for the 1950 edition, also from Romans, further illustrates the limits of his vision. In this case, he misses or ignores that Paul contrasts Christ with the law, as a look at the somewhat context of the epigraph illustrates:

> Wherefore, my brethren, ye also are become dead to the law by the body of Christ; that ye should be married to another, even to him who is raised from the dead, that we should bring forth fruit unto God. For when we were in the flesh, the motions of sins, which were by the law, did work in our members to bring forth fruit unto death. But now we are delivered from the law, that being dead wherein we were held; that we should serve in newness of spirit, and not in the

oldness of the letter. What shall we say then? Is the law sin? God forbid. Nay, I had not known sin, but by the law: for I had not known lust, except the law had said, Thou shalt not covet. But sin, taking occasion by the commandment, wrought in me all manner of concupiscence. For without the law sin was dead. For I was alive without the law once: but when the commandment came, sin revived and I died. (Romans 7:4-9)

Lodged within this passage is the phrase that so struck Burgeon ("Nay, I had not known sin but by the law"). Once again, he has grasped it in too sentimentally aesthetic, too narrowly self-absorbed, a way. He has seized on Paul's point that consciousness of the law conjures sin into being, anticipating that he will unconsciously conjure forth Burden in a dream. Here Burgeon ends, stuck between the "aesthetic" and "ethical" stages. He misses the contrast of the law with "life" and "the body of Christ," as he had with "faith" in the previous epigraph. Indeed, he misses Paul's still wider purport, the contrast of the "spirit" with the "flesh," and the transformation of the meaning of "flesh" through Christ's incarnation. As we shall see, transformation of our understanding and experience of the relation of the spiritual to the physical return as themes in *Worlds Apart* and *Unancestral Voice*, respectively.

The Pauline epigraph that Barfield added in 1985, which he placed first in the new edition, illustrates this dynamic yet again. The omission is perhaps most striking in this case. The epigraph is: "For I through the law am dead to the law . . ." The passage in fuller context is:

For I through the law am dead to the law, that I might live unto God. I am crucified with Christ: Nevertheless I live; yet not I, but Christ liveth in me: and the life which I now live in the flesh I live by the faith of the Son of God who loved me, and gave himself for me. (Galatians 2: 19-20)

Burgeon (if we can still credit him with epigraph selection in 1985) puts a period at the end of the first phrase, neglecting entirely the life unto God. He thereby also misses what, in part, this life consists of: crucifixion with Christ, the substitution both of Christ for "I" and of "faith" for "flesh," and the transformative self-sacrifice that epitomizes both acts. We might say that Burgeon's melancholic attachment to his own suffering, bound to the wheel of the "law," dictates his inability to see beyond his selections. He is a would-be aesthete who is also an unwilling knight of infinite resignation, unable to be reborn as a knight of faith. This is another way of saying that he fails to see his implicit challenge or goal, and that his narrative records his intuitive effort to resolve, or transform into a productive polarity, the sterile dichotomy of aestheticism and legalism to which he binds himself. As the novel's author and first-person voice, Burgeon's aesthetic sensibility of course is primary; the legal perspective of Burden arises from his depths, with the need to make the transformative leap of faith that would enable him to understand the epigraphs that preface his own narrative.

The narrative arc across which this dialectic plays out is from an initial state of crisis, through various manifestations of this initial state, to a climax and its subsequent peaceful resolution. As so often in Barfield's creative work, including the contemporaneous poems *Riders on Pegasus* and *The Unicorn*, this linear narrative also has a chiastic structure. The book's eleven chapters mirror each other thematically such that the last mirrors the first, the penultimate chapter mirrors the second chapter, and so on, with the middle (sixth) chapter acting as an unpaired pivot of this elaborate set of polarities. Thus, the first chapter begins with Burgeon's underlying despair and fear of imminent death and his concomitant assertion of control over Burden and ends with the dream in which Burden appears for the first time; the last chapter is a dream that establishes equity between Burgeon and Burden and resolves into a hopeful new life with Burden's proper integration. The second chapter focuses on a meaningless dispute that is unresolved and forgotten, while the parallel tenth chapter recalls and resolves the dispute between Burgeon and Burden. The third chapter centers on the dysfunction of Burgeon and Burden amidst an all-too-casual divorce dispute; its balancing chapter is the climax of the book as a whole—the looming divorce of Burgeon and Burden becomes all-too-serious as a possible murder/suicide pact. The fourth chapter centers thematically on the problem of inattentive, thoughtless sensation (in the form of Euphemia, her father, and Burgeon himself); its parallel eighth chapter includes a satirical Platonic vision of the "Absolute Solicitor" that indicates Burgeon's readiness to attend to spiritual sensations. The fifth chapter, "Rhemataophobia," transitions from the pain of sensation-drenched inattention to the painful intellectual effort required to understand meaningless speech; the balancing seventh chapter, "Cestuis Que Trustent," features the reestablishment of trust via a first consideration of equity and the first positive aesthetic experience of the narrative, a Madonna-like young mother. The central and unpaired sixth chapter, the most famous of the novel because it offers a fictionalized portrait of C. S. Lewis, has as its themes the redemption of language and the conjunction of artistry and generosity. This central salvation of language, beauty, and community makes possible the positive, healing developments of the second half of the novel; it may be Barfield's most touching testimony to the saving grace of friendship.

The novel has three core themes woven into this framework—the split psyche, the problem of meaning, and equity—each of which folds into the others. The ultimate resolution of the split psyche, for example, is the restitution or creation of intrapsychic equity, which Burgeon's newfound capacity to experience meaning makes possible. Likewise, the ways in which the episodes symbolize problems in the relation of Burgeon to Burden, and vice versa, indicate that the broader problem of inequity as it arises in the legal realm is the outer form of spiritual divisions within the individuals caught up in its tensions; and correlatively, those who experience such a split are sure to find themselves running into problematic social relations where equity is an issue. Inequity is the outer form of the split psyche; and the split psyche is in the individual what inequity is for society as a whole. "Meaning," meanwhile, is the necessary condition for the psychic healing of the individual and the establishment of equitable social relations; the loss of the sense of meaning individually and culturally guarantees individual and social collapse. It is therefore fitting that the central episodes and mediating chapters of the novel dramatize Burgeon's crisis over meaning, just as the first third is taken up with anxiety and the last third with the discovery and internalization of equity.

The book's initial crisis is the problematic integrity of Burgeon and Burden. We have already seen that the cycle of Burgeon poems traces the collapse of sentimental aestheticism that mirrors the enormous personal and professional pressure that Barfield felt in his own life. The collapse of Burgeon's aestheticism in the poems is a negative confirmation of the aesthete's insight[7] in Part One of *Either-Or* that:

> One need only consider how ruinous boredom is for humanity, and by properly adjusting the intensity of one's concentration upon this fundamental truth, attain any desired degree of momentum. Should one wish to attain the maximum momentum . . . one need only say to oneself: Boredom is the root of all evil. Strange that boredom, in itself so staid and stolid, should have such power to set in motion. The influence it exerts is altogether magical, except that it is not the influence of attraction, but of repulsion. (Kierkegaard 1959 1, 281)

Burgeon, at the end of the poem cycle, is in the throes of this sort of boredom, disenchanted with the sensory as such, all delicate feeling reduced to self-satire. Burden, the embodiment of legal, ethical, and cultural dutifulness, arises from the depths of Burgeon's psyche at this moment of existential *ennui*. In one of the "upbuilding" discourses he wrote after *Either-Or*, Kierkegaard suggests that the aesthetic falls into crisis because it consists of passive "wishing" and cannot make the leap into "willing" that characterizes faith. In *The Sickness Unto Death*, Kierkegaard further elaborates that in the interval between passive, aesthetic "wishing" and the "willing" of faith falls the shadow of "dread" that is positive insofar as it alerts one to one's state of crisis: though existential dread is a painful symptom of one's misalignment with oneself, it is also, in its painful sharpness, irrefutable evidence of a spiritual existence independent of the senses and their charms.

At the height of his crisis, in chapter 9 ("Crisis"), Burgeon seems to reflect an awareness of Kierkegaard's ideas, ruminating on the relation of will to fear and despair:

> People talk of the courage of despair, but has anyone ever seriously investigated the relation of fear and will? I believe it is remarkably close. If over a fairly long period you dislike and shrink from nearly everything you have to do, you are also conscious of willing positively *everything* that you do. (*TEDP* 90)

The relation of fear to volition has been part of Burgeon's consciousness from the beginning. He begins his narrative with the realization that he is responsible for willing—"worst of all, I find that nearly all the decisions have to be made by me" (*TEDP* 8)—and a concomitant recognition of his fearfulness. "I woke up—feeling a little afraid" (*TEDP* 9), he says, after the dream in which Burden appears for the first time. The book as a whole is, for Burgeon, "my declaration of independence. I always thought I should be able to keep that, but now I am afraid" (*TEDP* 5).

The crisis has many aspects. Some are particular to the intrapersonal dynamics of Burgeon and Burden, the former embodying will and imagination (*TEDP* 8), the latter responsible for memory, rigor, and routine.[8] Burgeon emphasizes, with a faintly absurd grandiosity in comparing himself to Faust, that he "deliberately called him forth from obscurity—summoned him, as it were, from the realm of the Mothers, and set him up in space and time" (*TEDP* 4–5).[9] Even so, Burden's first appearance in a dream surprises Burgeon, as does his "present bewilderment" at this "sort of Frankenstein" (*TEDP* 5). It is perhaps a telling irony that Burgeon identifies himself with Faust and mistakes the monster for the creator in Mary Shelley's novel. His self-alienation is not the result of birthing Burden; rather, Burden appears dialectically as the embodiment of the alienation from which Burgeon already suffers. Prior to, and during, the act of evoking Burden, Burgeon finds himself alienated, semi-conscious, and troubled.

Burgeon only subsequently discovers that his discomfort also regards an underlying inauthenticity concerning his vocation—that is, the legal/ethical pole opposite his aestheticism. Burgeon recognizes that "some sort of crisis is approaching" (*TEDP* 82) when "the endless procession of troubles and the pressure at which we are working" mount such that "somewhere inside something is quivering practically the whole day now. I think it is the expectation of little blows and bruises" (*TEDP* 82-3). The true crisis soon erupts over a debate about casuistry. Burgeon wonders "how do you distinguish the honest from the dishonest?" in response to Burden's claim that casuistry is "the science of applying general moral principles to particular cases" (*TEDP* 85). This alludes to the origin of casuistry in the resolution of cases of conscience by medieval "Courts of Conscience," an issue that looms large when the topic of equity arises, as it soon will. It both sharpens and widens to negotiation as a whole the problem of dishonesty that Burgeon finds in his profession:

> I suppose a starting price is the price one just dares to hope the other fellow may turn out to be green enough to pay. If he *is* green, it seems to me it must be dishonest. His greenness makes you a sort of trustee for him. If he is not green, then perhaps it's not dishonest—but—oh, how *silly* it is! God, what a way for a man that stands upright between the earth and sky to use the spirit that is in him! (*TEDP* 87-8)

Burgeon's complaint here, of course, is not simply about socioeconomic equity but also about the intrapsychic economy of himself and Burden: each stands in dishonest, inequitable relation to the other, and the tension reveals his own lack of personal authenticity. Interpersonal relations of any kind involve implicit or explicit negotiations, which seem to entail a lack of authenticity. This is the source of fear and anxiety that plagues him throughout the satire.

When Burgeon comes to recognize the close connection of fear to will, he has a further, liberating insight into personal authenticity:

> When you do get a chance to relax completely, this purely volitional self, reacting from the normal condition of strained exertion, makes itself felt in surprising ways. You find it is still there, though it is not doing anything—this mysterious unknown whose whole function is, precisely—*doing*! . . . I am not saying that your will necessarily becomes stronger, only that at such times you become very conscious of it. It upholds you; you seem to float on it as on a sort of buoyant, hyaline sea. You recognize the faint quivering of that sea, though it is no longer within you. "God," said Epictetus, "hath entrusted me with myself: He hath made my will subject to myself alone and given me rules for the right use thereof." Can one imagine a more awe-inspiring discovery than this, that in doing so He entrusted me with *more* than myself? (*TEDP* 90)

In this moment, Burgeon sees past his fearful, anxious, and inauthentic relation to himself and Burden such that he is able to help Burden overcome his own anxiety in the face of death (*TEDP* 92–3). The passage calls to mind Kierkegaard's discussion of the authentic and inauthentic self in *The Sickness Unto Death*. Burgeon's experiences the "awe-inspiring discovery" that when his will "is still there, though it is not doing anything" he feels that "you seem to float on it as on a sort of buoyant, hyaline sea" that is identical with "God." This is reminiscent of one of Kierkegaard's more abstract definitions of self's authentic alignment with itself: "This then is the formula which describes the condition of the self when despair is completely eradicated: by relating itself to its own self and by willing to be itself the self is grounded transparently in the Power which posited it" (Kierkegaard 1941 [2013], 271).

If only the healthy self relates itself to itself by willing to be itself, thereby floating (as Burgeon would have it) in a "buoyant, hyaline" relation to the divine, such healthy, despair-free spirits are vanishingly rare. Kierkegaard's description of the despairing self also neatly fits Burgeon and the whole psychomachic nature of the book. Kierkegaard begins *The Sickness Unto Death* with a famous definition of the self:

> Man is spirit. But what is spirit? Spirit is the self. But what is self? The self is a relation which relates itself to its own self, or it is that in the relation [which accounts for it] that the relation relates itself to its own self; the self is not the relation but [consists in the fact] that the relation relates itself to its own self. Man is a synthesis of the infinite and the finite, of the temporal and the eternal, of freedom and necessity, in short it is a synthesis. A synthesis is a relation between two factors. So regarded, man is not yet a self. (Kierkegaard 1941 [2013], 269)

It is not difficult to read the whole book as Burgeon's attempt to relate "two factors," himself and Burden, though even then remaining somehow fragmented and "not yet a self." In fact, Burgeon fits Kierkegaard's description of despair, insofar as he feels "despair at not willing to be one's own self" (Kierkegaard 1941 [2013], 270) and that "the self cannot of itself attain and remain in equilibrium and rest by itself, but only by relating itself to that Power which constituted the whole relation" (Kierkegaard 1941 [2013], 270). Burgeon's struggles with Burden are attempts at self-equilibrium by willing himself to be himself. That self-relation is only possible through relation to "that Power which constituted the whole relation" renders the process enormously complex. Beneath the light surface of Burgeon's satire, we see the deadly serious problem of despair faced not only by Burgeon but by all of his readers.

Burgeon's first step along the path to authentic self-relation is by way of the problem of meaning, which appears most vividly in chapters 4–6. They describe a dialectical arc similar to that of the novel as a whole, from the cheerful meaninglessness of Euphemia's appropriately happy but empty speech, through the fearful, painfully self-aware torment Burden undergoes and analyzes in "Rhematophobia," to the earned happiness of "The Things That Are Caesar's." Chapter 4 offers a good example of the braiding of the novel's major themes. It begins from Euphemia's perspective, which is startled into alertness by her father's impatient "are you attending?" (*TEDP* 28). Euphemia has not been attending, because she is taken up with "how agreeable everything looked!" (*TEDP* 28).[10] Immersed as she is in sensation, Euphemia, like Janet Trinder at the beginning of *English People*, follows a train of associations similar to some of those satirized by Jane Austen, including "how handsome" (*TEDP* 29) she finds Burgeon/Burden. When the focus shifts to the male characters we find that they too, despite their image of themselves as decisive and focused, are aesthetes with wandering minds: Euphemia's father feels remorse that "he had just spoken too harshly to his daughter for the same offence" (*TEDP* 29), and Burden repeatedly shouts at Burgeon for the same reason, compelling Burgeon to "drag . . . my attention dutifully back to the piece of transparent blue paper" (*TEDP* 35). Moreover, just as Euphemia's immersion in meaningless inner and outer sensations propels her cognitive drift, so too Burgeon's mind paddles about, considering the patrilineal prejudice that underlies the will he is reading and the whole history of aristocracy and empire that it works to support. The question of "equity" arises (*TEDP* 32), and Burgeon attempts to pursue it "back to the Root" (*TEDP* 32) but must give it up because "there is nothing whatever to show identity" (*TEDP* 35). Burgeon's aestheticism and Burden's legalism are unable to solve the immediate problem of what is equitable for poor Euphemia because they founder on the linked issues of attention, meaning, and identity.

In the next chapter, "Rhematophobia," the issue of meaning and identity sharpens to a point of crisis. This time the focus is on Burden's, not Burgeon's, distracted attention:

> Just as a complicated mathematical formula is a system of brackets within brackets set out in space, so Burden's mental life of attention and concentration is chopped up into a series of interruptions within interruptions extended in time. Day after day after day appears to him in retrospect as a series of frustrated attempts to pick up the broken thread of what was to have been the main business of the day before. (*TEDP* 37)

Poor Burden suffers a parody of the ethical life, his dutiful attention to the law blown apart by the forces that would bring it to his attention. Burden's mechanomorphic legalistic thinking is tormented by meaninglessness as much as Burgeon's sensitive aestheticism. Burgeon's empathetic appreciation of Burden's mental life grows from his insight that:

> Generally speaking, it is the meanings of words and the tone in which they are spoken which are the cause of pain. I have only lately realised that mere words, as such, irrespective of tone or meaning, mere quantity of utterance apart altogether from its quality, can inflict as much pain as a rebuff or a cold reply to an affectionate question. (*TEDP* 36)

The neologism Burgeon invents for the title of the chapter tries to capture the "fear and hatred of the spoken word" that is the "most alarming effect" of this new sensitivity. Burgeon suspects this has become a "chronic affliction" in the whole of society, driving the universal alienation of "nothing but supper, silence, and bed" (*TEDP* 38). We are all driven into isolation by "the effort required to convert sound into meaning and to unite that meaning . . . with the meanings of previous words and of those which are to follow" (*TEDP* 39). The alienation of all from all makes rendering sense exhausting, destroying the most tender threads of society, even "to avoid the children" and "my best friends—as entertaining and affectionate friends as a man could ask" (*TEDP* 38). Burgeon's pain separates him from even the most rudimentary forms of ethical obligation and social relation—family and friendship—even as sensation only yields the painful impression afforded by meaningless speech.

It is all the more remarkable, then, that Burgeon finds salvation via friendship in the next chapter. From the sharp pain of grasping even basic meaning in "Rhematophobia," Burgeon finds in his friend Ramsden the counterimage to alienation in the novel's main themes. Ramsden expresses himself in language that would seem "to the eye of any third party either meaningless or idiotic, but pregnant symbols to us of a period of intellectual intercourse long since woven into the stuff of our lives and taken up into whatever we can claim of wisdom or insight" (*TEDP* 45). Moreover, Ramsden's generosity with meaning extends to a compulsive generosity with the large profits his books make, to the point of near bankruptcy (*TEDP* 49). Ramsden stands before Burgeon as the artist of meaning and of instinctive equity, an archetype of the healing Burgeon must find in his own way.

Burgeon's felt perception at the call to authenticity that he should "wake up sometimes and take a hand in law and in life" (*TEDP* 94) leads, paradoxically, into a deeper sleep and two dreams. These bring to a head the themes of divorce and equity that have come up as problems throughout the narrative, the former a central theme as well of the ethical letters by "Judge Vilhelm" in *Either-Or*. Both dreams lean heavily on the law but the second, about equity itself, is the more important—indeed, the judge has "the countenance of Equity" itself (*TEDP* 119). Equity is the title and subject of an often-reprinted essay by Barfield. Key for our purposes here is that Barfield finds in the evolution of "courts of conscience" that conscience "implies a state of knowledge either shared with or at any rate considered in relation to *another* being. . . . [and] that this 'knowing with' another (which, reduced to its lowest terms, is the bare admission that there *is* another being) is firstly, an act of will, and secondly, that it is the basis of self-consciousness" (Barfield 1932b, 143). We are reminded once again of Kierkegaard's distinction between the wishing of aestheticism and the willing of authentic self-relation, though in this case the similarity is due to the shared roots of Barfield and Kierkegaard in German idealism.

At the heart of self-knowledge and authenticity is the paradoxical truth that one achieves them in and through one's relations to others. When Burgeon discovers, in his first authentic moment of self-reflection, that "He entrusted me with *more* than myself" (*TEDP* 91), he has a Coleridgean intimation that conscience precedes self-consciousness. The judge with the countenance of equity reveals Burgeon's anxiety-driven mechanisms for escaping himself—conflict-aversion, dishonesty (*TEDP* 118)—and then in a practical way brings Burden into Burgeon's willing itself. This is a true partnership of the aesthetic and the ethical, unlike the stark dichotomy presented by Kierkegaard. *Either-Or* simply presents them as equally unfulfilling alternatives, with no possibility of harmony. Barfield's commitment to Coleridge's "tautegory" enters here as a model for intrapsychic equilibrium. Because Burgeon is able in a dream-like way to bring himself and Burden into tautegorical relation, "the whole *modus operandi* of the partnership has been greatly improved. We have even worked out its application to details—such as the drafting of affidavits" (*TEDP* 120). Burden, as a result, disappears in another dream, not vanquished but integrated into Burgeon's sensibility. Burgeon's discovery of consciousness as a predicate of conscience coincides with—is equivalent to—his experiences of authenticity, equity, and meaning itself. The satire ends on the ambivalent note that "I turned my face grimly to the Office. And the effort of doing so awoke me with a jerk" (*TEDP* 120). Burgeon has not yet become a "knight of faith," is not yet beyond "either-or," has not yet made the leap into complete transformation. Even so, when Burgeon awakens he is past the worst of his existential collapse.

3. Worlds Apart

The backdrop for *Worlds Apart* (1963) is "the growing sense of meaninglessness" that "amid all the menacing signs that surround us in the middle of the twentieth century, [is] perhaps the one that fills thoughtful people with the greatest foreboding" (*RM* 11). This no doubt reminds us of the openings sentences of "The Rediscovery of Meaning" (1961). It also captures the existential mood and themes of *This Ever Diverse Pair*, but in the thirteen years it took Barfield to resurrect Burgeon in *Worlds Apart*, the character had changed. Instead of starring in another Menippean satire, Burgeon is at the center of a quasi-Platonic dialogue in which Burden never appears (though he does return in *Unancestral Voice*). The mood, though lively, is thoughtful and deliberative—there are no emotional upheavals, only a contest of ideas among characters with varied levels of interest in, and engagement with, the conversation. However, because the narrative structure is more complex than Barfield indicates in retrospect, one should look somewhat skeptically at Barfield's comment thirty years later that the book is "essentially an attempt to refute criticisms" (Schenkel 33).

Unlike *This Ever Diverse Pair*, Barfield published *Worlds Apart* under his own name, with Burgeon as the first-person narrator of events. Burgeon invokes "my friend Owen Barfield" (*WA* 13), who does not appear in the book but whom Burgeon refers to at several points.[11] Alas, says Burgeon, though "Owen Barfield" "could not unfortunately be one of us" he "kindly composed" the dialogue from "the tape-recording of what passed between us during our (to me) memorable weekend" (*WA* 13). Why Burgeon, the published author of *This Ever Diverse Pair*, should need to enlist the help of "Owen Barfield" to author this book goes unexplained, which is doubly odd given that Burgeon says that the book composed by "Owen Barfield" is "a very different matter" (*WA* 13) from what it would have been if he had written it. Indeed, "Owen Barfield," arranging and working outside the voice of Burgeon, seems to include numerous implicit and explicit references to his own books and ideas through the course of his retelling. As we shall see, this is significant, not only insofar as the dialogue form is a model of the act of thinking but also in that the narrative structure itself becomes a symbol *of* thinking, even as Burgeon argues (or "Owen Barfield" has him argue) that the symbol is instrumental *to* thinking. Thus, "Owen Barfield" emerges as a central symbol in the book, all the more important for never appearing directly in it; his active role in structuring the narrative is emblematic of the symbol's dynamic action in self-consciously participatory thinking.

We shall return to "Owen Barfield" as symbol later, in the context of Burgeon's theory of the symbol.[12] For now, it is enough to say that the three days in which the conversation takes place constitutes a kind of initiation in which each of the participants is invited to follow "the principle of initiation," which is to say to "actually become a different kind of man" (*WA* 202).[13] The definition Sanderson offers here seems to echo that of Mircea Eliade, whom Burgeon quotes approvingly earlier in the book (*WA* 121): "'Initiation' means, as we know, the symbolic death and resurrection of the neophyte or, in other contexts, the descent into Hell followed by the ascension into Heaven" (Eliade 1961, 49). Perhaps only Burgeon is, in the end, able to begin this process (or rather, to continue what he began in *This Ever Diverse Pair*), which he will still more fully achieve in *Unancestral Voice*. Burgeon has become simultaneously more and less of a freestanding character: he no longer claims any authorial standing, yet he does not merely participate in a semi-autobiographical psychomachia free from the need for verisimilitude. Barfield replaces the conventions of Menippean satire that govern *This Ever Diverse Pair* with those of Platonic dialogue, ripe for the kind of literary and allegorical interpretation common from the neo-Pythagoreans to Ficino.[14]

For example, the host of characters may be viewed as types no less than as "realistic" characters. In some cases, their names have clearly allegorical significance: the depth psychologist is "Burrows," the dour positivist is "Dunn" (a punning name as well as an allegorical one), the eager young rocket scientist is a "Ranger," the evolutionary biologist is "Upwater," and the sharp interrogator who exposes logical error is a "Hunter." "Burgeon," of course, is an imperative that Burgeon feels sharply. The physics professor "Brodie" is indeed stuck in place, as at least one speculative etymology of his Gaelic name would suggest. Finally, "Sanderson" is largely, if not entirely, the clear conquering victor of the dialogue as well as the intellectual son of the book's overall metaphysical hero, Rudolf Steiner.

The book as a whole, then, is a quasi-allegorical philosophical dialogue that follows the pattern of initiation that Steiner and Eliade describe, from an initial period of purification, to a suspension between worlds, and a final symbolic "resurrection" with a new knowledge that promises a new way to live. This theme is important to Barfield for the same reason that, as Eliade describes it, "interest in occultism" in the modern West has led to the flourishing of "a considerable number of occult sects" including "the Theosophical Society, Anthroposophy, Neo-Vedantism . . . [and] Neo-Buddhism" (Eliade 1958, 133):

> initiation lies at the core of any genuine human life. And this is true for two reasons. The first is that any genuine human life implies profound crises, ordeals, suffering,

loss, and reconquest of self, "death and resurrection." The second is that, whatever degree of fulfillment it may have brought him, at a certain moment every man sees his life as a failure. This vision does not arise from a moral judgment made on his past, but from an obscure feeling that he has missed his vocation; that he has betrayed the best that was in him. In such moments of total crisis, only one hope seems to offer any issue—the hope of beginning life over again. This means, in short, that the man undergoing such a crisis dreams of new, regenerated life, fully realized and significant. This is something other and far more than the obscure desire of every human soul to renew itself periodically, as the cosmos is renewed. The hope and dream of these moments of total crisis are to obtain a definitive and total *renovation*, a renewal capable of transmuting life. Such a renewal is the result of every genuine religious conversion. (Eliade 1958, 135)

Worlds Apart takes up this theme of initiation in multiple ways. It suggests not primarily a personal crisis for Burgeon but one for the whole of Western civilization, a crisis of intellectual chaos that demands not just the integration of "Burden" into each individual but also a new *Weltanschauung* and the new life that might come with it. As will become clear, Burgeon comes closest to achieving this, though without total success, even as the creative figure of "Owen Barfield" looms in the background as magus. The first half of the book—through the middle of the second day—involves a purification of worldviews, by means of a Blakean "consolidation of error." The conversation vividly reveals a crisis of Western culture due to the mutual contradiction and inherent inadequacy of the various contemporary *Weltanschauungen*. When Sanderson begins to take over in the second half of the book an alternative begins to emerge, though others contest it and raise questions that Sanderson and Burgeon are unable to answer. At the end of the book, Burgeon and Hunter find themselves fundamentally changed, the latter despite himself.

Near the end of the book, Sanderson says that Burgeon "staged the dialogue" (*WA* 178) of the previous day in order to drive home how difficult it is, once one is intellectually convinced, "really to *accept*" that, as Burgeon puts it:

> the whole conception of my mind sitting safely in my body and looking out through its senses on to a universe which is *not*-mind, and with which my own mind has therefore no connection except through the senses, is an impossible one. The whole picture is an illusion, and I myself called the whole apparatus, on which this much-prized "solitude" is based—a spectre. (*WA* 178)

Though Burden does not make an appearance in *Worlds Apart*, the "spectre" is a version of him and links this book with some of Barfield's other creative works. Like Los's Spectre in Blake's prophetic poems, and the malignant voice in Barfield's early novel *English People*, it is the demon or contagion that needs to be purified and assimilated if he and our culture are to overcome the paralysis of imagination that is the sickness unto death. In this sense, although the spectre is not a character, it also parallels the roles of Hades, the Furies, and Burden in *Orpheus*, *Riders on Pegasus*, and *This Ever Diverse Pair*, respectively. The first half of the book is taken up with consolidating and dispatching it.

The conceptual essence of the spectre is "the idea of a mindless universe" (*WA* 88). This idea manifests in two ways. The first and most deeply rooted in our most basic assumptions is a positivistic understanding of the "correspondence" theory of truth, that true propositions must agree with verifiable states of affairs, that these states of affairs are known to us through the senses, and that the material world exists independently of our senses in a way that aligns with them more or less exactly. The second, more recent but more pernicious, is that the there is no world "behind" the senses because in the opposition between the mental and the physical, only the physical exists: the mental and all its predicates are epiphenomenal and therefore ultimately unreal.

Distinguishing between the "familiar" nature we experience through the senses and the "concrete" world of matter that underlies it, Burgeon describes the spectre's first form this way:

> We assume that familiar nature is and was there without the help of either the conscious or unconscious mind. But this assumption is ruled out, *both* by ordinary psychological analysis . . . *and* by physical science. It is a delusion and, when we project it back . . . into the past, I call it a "spectre." (*WA* 114)

This is a condensed version of the account Burgeon presents in his Platonic pastiche with Brodie:

> [T]here is a real earth, investigated by physicists, which is the fact of the matter and the external reality, and which is independent of men's minds and senses, and there is also a semblance or appearance depending on or constructed by the eyes and other senses and the minds of men, and these are not two earths but one and the same earth. . . . [S]o there can be no externally real second earth, resembling the appearance, except that it was not constructed by the minds and senses of men, but came into existence of its own accord. . . . [I]n very truth . . . any such second earth could be no more than a kind of spectre, which the inventive mind or brain of man has capriciously interposed between itself, the constructor, and the world of nature which it confidently tells us is its "construct."

> And such a spectre does not and cannot exist even *now*, but is a mere figment of man's bemused imagination. (*WA* 85)

In earlier chapters, we explored the metaphysical implications of this older or popular form of materialism. Here, Burgeon's critique is that it undermines itself if taken to its logical conclusion—the psychology of perception and classical physics lead to the cul-de-sac of an infinite regress of worlds. Of particular significance here, though, is the alienating effect such an assumption must have. The "inventive mind" interposes the spectre between itself and the "world of nature" such that the latter becomes "a mere figment of man's bemused imagination." Even Hunter, the theologian modeled on C. S. Lewis, must "assume the spectre" because he embraces "the purest positivism" that "knowing nature" has nothing to do with "knowing God" (*WA* 206). So too with the "insect-like" narrators invented by Henry James and Virginia Woolf, infected with an alienated "self-consciousness which is at once too subtle and too cumbrous. . . . Fussy and restless—compelled to be so by the limited reach of its feelers" (*WA* 192).

The Charybdis to this Scylla is the less pervasive but even more insidious positivism represented by Dunn, a kind of anti-philosopher who has "given up wondering" because he is "more inclined to sleep" (*WA* 144). His drowsiness is primarily brought on by the "veritable orgy of subjectivism" (*WA* 92) that led to the "two earths" impasse—in other words, Dunn, like Burgeon and Sanderson, rejects the dualism to which popular materialism leads. He embraces instead the linguistic analysis typified by Gilbert Ryle, John Wisdom, and A. J. Ayer (*WA* 98). "The confusion," he says, "on which the whole issue—or rather the whole supposed issue—between materialism and immaterialism is based, arises from ignorance, or forgetfulness, of the rules governing the use of language" (*WA* 93). Specifically, Dunn rejects any use of language that violates convention and that cannot avail itself of empirical verification. He concludes that such words as "mind" are meaningless because they cannot be empirically verified. Thus, while according to Dunn "the business of philosophy is common sense" (*WA* 54) he also considers the "most reliable observation" of the whole first day to be that "there is nothing to talk about" (*WA* 42), even if the latter violates the common sense that is the "business of philosophy."

It is perhaps unsurprising that all of the other participants reject Dunn's position as an unfruitful and contradictory dead end. Hunter rejects as circular Dunn's argument that "the normal use of words is the way in which they are commonly used in talking about things it is possible to talk about" (*WA* 96), while Ranger rejects as a violation of common sense that when Hunter and Upwater discussed the ontological status of "familiar" and "inferred" nature, "they were not in fact talking about anything" because "that is a thing it is impossible to talk about" (*WA* 97). So too, Sanderson and Dunn clash over the nature of mathematics. For the former, it is "pure thinking free of any perceptual element" (*WA* 140) and for the latter it is "a skill we have to learn like any other skill—by perceiving and handling things" (*WA* 141). Burgeon, for his part, rejects Dunn's contention that language can be cleansed of its symbolic function. Burgeon also claims that Dunn's philosophy "*is* a system of assumptions; assumptions of all sorts, including in particular that historical assumption of the origin of mind from a mindless universe, of which we have been talking here" (*WA* 105). Finally, Sanderson concludes that Dunn's attempt to enforce "rules for the use of language" is along with the project of behaviorists "in destroying all variation" and geneticists in "deliberately controlling heredity" to "arrest all further evolution; the freezing of the human spirit into immobility at the outset of its path to maturity" (*WA* 111).

Though united in rejecting Dunn's physicalist reductionism, his interlocutors do not seem to have a convincing alternative. Where Dunn reduces matter to sensation, and mind with all other abstract nouns to meaninglessness, everyone else is trapped in an existential dilemma. Burgeon suggests without objection from the others that Erich Heller's *Disinherited Mind* shows that "what he calls 'the loss of significant external reality' was not a blessing—and is proving a catastrophe" (*WA* 180). Sanderson adds that Sartre's version of Existentialism found an audience because it brought this crisis to consciousness:

> The Existentialists are sharply aware of the causal nexus between the absence of significant external reality on the one hand—and the presence of human freedom on the other. They see the one as correlative to the other; and they feel the full weight of the responsibility which this freedom brings. But because they are blind to the roots of human freedom in the whole evolution of human consciousness, they feel crushed by the weight. They claim that man is responsible for all that exists, and yet the creature that bears this responsibility is for them a hollow void. (*WA* 180)

By the middle of the second day, the group has consolidated the error of common-sense materialism; with the exception of Dunn, they have agreed that the alienation it produces is "*the* curse, *the* experience which menaces, more and more with every decade that passes, our civilization and even our sanity" (*WA* 179). This is the null point of their shared *katabasis*, from which they and our culture must arise to a new life.

In nearly the last words of the conversation, at the point when Hunter and Dunn form an unlikely alliance over the assertion that "knowing nature" has nothing to do with "knowing God," Sanderson and Burgeon cement their own alliance with a definition of the symbol in relation to knowledge:

> As to knowledge of nature and knowledge of God, if knowledge is the doing of a jig-saw puzzle with atomic events, there is no more to be said. But if it is really a participation through the symbol in the symbolized, it is a different matter. . . . Suppose that Burgeon and I are right: then, in the meantime, nature *is* the unconscious, represented. And if that, or something like it, is the case, I submit that our knowledge of nature is very relevant indeed; for it is only by ceasing to regard nature as a spectre that we can hope to inherit her as a kingdom. And it is only in that kingdom that our common destiny can be fulfilled. (*WA* 207)

Sanderson's summation contains a great deal. He intends it as an antidote to the "spectre" that has haunted their conversation. It also brings together ideas Burgeon and Sanderson developed independently over the previous days. Key concepts include participation, the symbol, and the equivalence of nature to the unconscious. I will not here enter into metaphysical discussion too deeply but will focus on the views of Burgeon on the symbol and Sanderson on the phenomenological approach to nature as indicative of a shift toward "initiated" consciousness.

Burgeon introduces the "symbol" as a response to the subtle interplay of Dunn's behaviorism and Hunter's dualism. Dunn believes "the difference between animal and human responses can be summed up in one word: *delay*" (*WA* 44), a point that Dunn makes at all due to "the cleavage Hunter mainly stressed . . . between nature . . . and thinking" (*WA* 44). Burgeon, in a quite general way, and confessing himself to have in mind "a jumble rather than a coherent system" (*WA* 45), follows his intuition that "anyone who is interested in the *genesis* of poetry—the art of poetic composition—finds himself pondering on the mystery of thought at its *emergent* stage—the point at which it first appears, perhaps very simply and vaguely, in the poet's consciousness" (*WA* 45). Burgeon, referring to Cassirer, Langer, and Jung, argues that our experience of "familiar" nature is due to the "pre-conscious organizing of perceptual experience" through the conversion of "percepts . . . into *systems* of concepts, before we even know we have been hit by them" (*WA* 48). Burgeon follows Cassirer and Langer in describing this "specifically human activity" as "the 'symbolic transformation of experience'" (*WA* 47); and, that "the most elaborate and universal system of symbols we know is language" (*WA* 47–8). Burgeon likens the way language preconsciously synthesizes the concepts and percepts that make up experience to Coleridge's "primary imagination." The first steps in overcoming the malign influence of the spectre are to recognize the failure of positivist metaphysics and to recognize in full clarity the symbolizing intellect's fashioning of familiar nature through the medium of language.

Burgeon, in tandem with Sanderson, gradually develops the argument that only such a "presentational," as opposed to "representational," epistemology can overcome the two dualisms: the chasm between mind and nature and the corollary split between "familiar" and "inferred" nature. On the second day, for example, Burgeon resists Burrows's attempt to reduce "the characteristic symbols that we find in ancient myths and in many modern dreams to their physical origin" (*WA* 120) because this obviously embraces the "spectre" of the mind-free outer (or inner) world that Burgeon seeks to overcome. Burgeon argues instead that "such reduction is inconsistent with the very nature of the symbol" and consequently that if you "dip into the *Vedas* you often no longer know whether you are reading about birth and death, summer and winter, or breathing in and out . . . [b]ecause symbolic language—and all language is symbolic—can signify all these rhythms at the same time" (*WA* 121). Burrows correctly sees in myths a connection to natural processes, but the spectre obscures his vision: he should have concluded that the multivalence of mythological and dream symbolism points to the common origin of inner and outer worlds, inner and outer rhythms, as belonging to a shared "presentational" symbolizing activity that underlies inner and outer perception.

The archetype of this common origin is the "paradise-imago." It is "*the* symbol *par excellence*" not only because it is "so universal" and "has so many ramifying significances" (*WA* 124) but also because:

> You will never understand symbols until you have grasped that pre-historic man in his unconscious goes back, not to the animal kingdom, as the nineteenth century fondly imagined, but to a paradisal state when there was no death, because there was no matter. (*WA* 124)

Correlative with this, as Barfield points out in *propria voce*, is that "all known forms of the Paradise Myth represent Nature as implicated in the fall of man from his paradisal state. They all contain or imply a kind of magical sympathy between Man and Nature, which made this inevitable" (*RCA* 273). This nostalgic longing is part of the symbolist tradition as a whole. For example, it is essential to Baudelaire's aesthetic that:

> art . . . "is born of the absence of paradise, but of the memory of paradise: more precisely, it is both the absence and the memory of paradise, and that is why

Baudelaire can find in it the best proof of our immortality—of the immortality of our soul, attested by the *reminiscence*." (Richardson 229)

Just as the "paradise-imago" points to an original union of nature and mind, the fall-imago implies the sundering of the two.

For Burgeon, positivism represents the nadir of this split. The upshot of overcoming nineteenth-century positivism and its underlying neo-Lockean epistemology is the vision of an alternative picture of the "evolution of consciousness" that is instrumental in replacing the spectral image of mind emerging from the mindless. Burgeon is unable to develop the full metaphysical implications of his point, but he offers a kind of parallel between the evolution of language and the emergence of consciousness from nature:

> I am only inclined, very tentatively, to see an analogy between ideas about nature and ideas about language. By analysing a lot of languages the older philologists got down to a sort of bedrock that they called the "roots of speech." That was all right; but then they went beyond that and started saying that these roots exist as words, and that they were the first words from which all language originated... . The nineteenth-century philologists—as has been said by someone who knows more about it than I do—"mistook elements for seeds—and called them 'roots'". . . . Well, I sometimes wonder if the "particles," or whatever, are the "roots" of nature in the same sense only that the grammatical roots are the roots of speech. (*WA* 90-1)

Two things are worth noting here: first, an anticipation—"Owen Barfield" appears to have smuggled in a quotation from his own book, *Poetic Diction*, but to have avoided self-reference by having Burgeon describe him as "someone who knows more about it than I do." I will return to the role of "Owen Barfield" later. For now, Burgeon's hesitancy is more relevant. He has already rejected the evolutionary picture of the "mindless" universe, but he is unwilling or unable to commit to an alternative metaphysic—not yet having heard what Sanderson has to say. Rather, he offers "very tentatively" an "analogy" between particles of speech and particles of nature.

This is not to say, though, that he will simply take on whatever metaphysical principles Sanderson provides. He will instead keep to the end a hermeneutical humility. Precisely because symbols preconsciously mediate or create what we experience as familiar nature:

> it is only people living in the same period and, broadly speaking, in the same community, who inhabit the same world. People living in other periods, or even at the same period but in a totally different community, do not inhabit the

same world about which they have different ideas, they inhabit different worlds altogether. (*WA* 172)

This is one point of disagreement between Sanderson and Burgeon, a disagreement that points to a limitation in Burgeon's development, as it seems to indicate a shadow of the spectre in the form of cultural relativism.

Sanderson provides crucial support for Burgeon in his effort to disentangle from what Barfield would later term the "residue of unresolved positivism." Whereas Burgeon primarily focuses on the philological evidence for the evolution of consciousness—the universal system of symbols from which we derive all sense of ourselves and the cultural and natural worlds to which we belong—Sanderson's interest is in the role of symbol and imagination in the sciences. For him it is:

> the less surprising that Burgeon here and others should find in the persistent image of paradise the symbol of symbols, or that they should detect that image not only in actual myth and symbol, but also in the face of nature herself—when it is seen *as* a face and not simply stared at as a spectral mask with nothing, or what have you, behind it. (*WA* 198)

Sanderson is unfazed by Burgeon's iconoclasm because he has long treated the symbolist cosmology, that for Burgeon is merely nascent, not as a theoretical construct or philosophical system but as the framework for scientific observation and experimentation. For Sanderson, "the human body, its form and its functional drives" (*WA* 198) is itself a symbol: "our own bodies are themselves symbols in your sense, and perhaps the most characteristic and powerful symbols known to us" (*WA* 121).

Sanderson, in other words, collapses the distinction between literal and symbolic levels of meaning not by reducing the symbol to a spectral substratum but by making the multivalent symbol the most primary level of meaning and experience, the "root" and "particle" that Burgeon tentatively indicated earlier.[15] Whereas Burgeon reaches first for the "paradise-imago" to find his way to the phenomenon, Sanderson finds in the body itself the "symbol of symbols" because even the dullest human being is a multivalent image of paradise. Thus, Sanderson claims that "when we speak of investigating anything scientifically, it signifies that, instead of resting content with a phenomenon as presented to us, we go on to inquire into its *provenance*" (*WA* 141). This provenance is not a theoretical construct or assumption of mechanical causality but a close attention to the metamorphic transformation of what is latent in the phenomenon and its spatiotemporal setting: "in the first place it involves *looking* at the phenomena open-mindedly, without at that stage obtruding any theoretical cerebration, conscious or unconscious, and letting them speak to you for themselves" (*WA* 146). As Burgeon quickly notes, "it's the same with the symbol—if it's a genuine one. It is only when you attend to it wholeheartedly instead of speculating on what is behind it that—that you really *reach* what is behind it" (*WA* 146).

To train oneself to experience all phenomena as symbols in this sense requires a transformation of consciousness, which comes about in attending to our own faculties in the same Goethean manner that Sanderson advocates. For example, just as overcoming the dualist mutual exclusion of spirit and matter leads one to appreciate the "'coincidence of opposites' in the meanings of symbols" (*WA* 127), so too:

> the next step which evolution is calling for is something quite different. Once the new, brain-focused centre is created, its whole relation to the periphery changes. In a way it again *becomes* the periphery—or is capable of doing so. By contrast with Heraclitus, *we* can only participate in the "ether" in what you might call an "adult" way. This means, not merely looking outward into it and feeling the way it works in nature, including ourselves, but also looking inward *with* it and *understanding* the way it works in nature. That's what I meant when I spoke of turning our idea of space inside out. (*WA* 135–6)

For Sanderson, space is itself an idea—to turn it inside out, and so to invert the "provenance" of the phenomenon, is to invert one's own consciousness so that what one directly experiences as consciousness, as center, becomes periphery, and vice versa. Thus one adds a new and deeper dimension to the "felt change of consciousness" induced by an effective metaphor and returns to the metaphysics of microcosm and macrocosm that Barfield would continue to explore in works like his environmental novella *Eager Spring*.

Moreover, this transformation of brain-based literalism correlates for Sanderson with the raising of the unconscious into consciousness. For him, "the 'contradiction' between spirit and matter is of the same kind as that between conscious and unconscious; and if you want to learn more about the relation between spirit and matter, the first thing you come up against is the relation between spirit and space" (*WA* 127). This conclusion follows from the denial of any absolute division between mind and matter. If it is the case that thought and phenomenon are interwoven, and that the phenomenon has no material substratum, then there is "a participation of the knower *in* the unconscious thinking that is going on in nature. That is only achieved by contemplating [phenomena] in concentrated mental activity, but without at the time thinking *about* them. Then they begin to explain themselves" (*WA* 145). The feeling of growth and decay, expansion and contraction, of center becoming periphery and vice versa, correlates with the interpenetration of the conscious and unconscious poles of the psyche:

> Consciousness and unconsciousness are mutually exclusive; but the mutual exclusion of two opposite poles is resolved in the tension between them and the motion it begets. In the case of the spiritual polarity between conscious and unconscious the motion begotten is rhythmic—it finds expression in the course of time and the various rhythms of nature. (*WA* 197)

One harnesses this "concentrated mental activity" by, first, "systematically training" the faculty of attention through meditative exercises (188); then, one practices "a systematic cultivation of feelings—feelings evoked by selected images and symbols, for instance, and feelings about the processes of nature and her appearances" (188). One thereby develops the capacity to "*use* one's feelings as a means to perception; to treat *them* as a precision instrument for investigating quality, just as we take enormous pains to develop external precision instruments for investigating quantity" (*WA* 188). In this way, we learn to "'read' [spring and autumn] rather than merely perceive them, for the inner processes of growth and decay which they express are qualitatively part of our perception. . . . [W]e experience, both in observation and feeling, the alternate expansion and contraction, which characterizes the growth-process itself" (*WA* 189–90).

This is not to suggest that Sanderson completes a metaphysic that Burgeon could only begin. Sanderson admits that "by and large the complaint is justified" (*WA* 201) that he relies too much on Steiner's authority, and he concedes to Hunter that his position includes contradictions that he hopes to solve with the blanket claim that "almost everything to do with thinking is a paradox" (*WA* 175). Within the initiatory framework of the book, Sanderson's goal is not to produce a comprehensive metaphysical deduction but an explanation and example of transformed vision, of the expansion of the literal center to the periphery of the symbol. In this way, he and Burgeon answer the malaise of Sartre's existential alienation, and in the case of Burgeon it is only because he has met Kierkegaard's challenge that he is able to do so. If to resurrect the dead literal phenomenon into a living symbol is also to raise the unconscious into consciousness, it is in addition to exchange the "hollow void" for the recovery of "that inheritance in the realm from which it stemmed, a realm beyond the brain and the senses" (*WA* 180). In making this exchange, "the solitude, the disinheritance, the loss of significant external reality, is a catastrophe; but it is so only as being born is a catastrophe" (*WA* 181). Sanderson makes this point as if speaking directly to Burgeon at the end of *This Ever Diverse Pair*, though it now applies to the mass of Western, industrial, positivist humanity, just as it is Barfield's account to himself of the leap from metaphysical deduction to poetic cosmology.

It is easy to forget, within this complex clash of ideas, that the dialogue has a narrator: "Owen Barfield." Perhaps we are tempted to forget about him because we are unsure what to do with him. Recall Burgeon's first reference to him:

> Few, if any, people are capable—at all events in our time—of conversing in the manner which has become traditional in philosophical dialogues from Plato to Brewster and Lowes Dickinson; and not many even of those who can think well and coherently have the faculty of clothing their thoughts *ex tempore* in linked and properly constructed sentences.... It will be obvious then to the reader that the tape-recording of what passed between us during our (to me) memorable weekend is, in form though not in substance, a very different matter from this book which my friend Owen Barfield, who could not unfortunately be one of us, has kindly composed from it, with such additional help here and there as my memory afforded. (*WA* 13)

Beneath what appears to be a cloying surface, including an allusion to Plato's famous self-referential absence from the *Phaedo*, this passage raises complex and important questions. "Owen Barfield" is not quite a character in the book—his presence behind the scenes is silent, but his influence is explicit and enormous. As composer of "this book" he fashions Burgeon's own first-person voice, including the attestation of "Owen Barfield's" kind help and the help offered by his own memory. And yet, "Owen Barfield" cannot be equated with the holder of the book's copyright, who was not friends with his fictional creation and could not be invited to a fictional retreat weekend. "Owen Barfield" is an example of an "arranger," a critical concept used in *Ulysses* scholarship "to designate a figure who exercises an increasing degree of overt control over his increasingly challenging materials" and who is not the equivalent of the narrator or a character, though may overlap with them (Hayman 70). This creates interpretive difficulties around seemingly simple passages. Consider the following: "Ranger paused for a moment and smiled with a disarming modesty" (*WA* 15). In the fictional context of the book, is this observation the fruit of "Owen Barfield's" imagination, Burgeon's memory, or some combination of the two? It would not be available from the tape recording that is the basis for "Owen Barfield's" work but does not seem to be the fruit of Burgeon's memory either.

"Owen Barfield" also includes references to himself with more or less subtlety throughout the book. We have already seen that he has Burgeon refer to him with rotund modesty as "someone who knows more about [philology] than I do" (*WA* 91) before he quotes from *Poetic Diction*. Sanderson also seems to have read "The Rose on the Ash Heap," presumably in manuscript (*WA* 19), and he has absorbed *Poetic Diction* or one of Barfield's contemporaneous Anthroposophical essays deeply enough that he can refer without need of further explanation to "concrete, sense-free thinking" (*WA* 175). Sanderson has also closely read *Saving the Appearances*, though "Owen Barfield" is discrete in having him refer to "'collective representations', as I believe they have been called" (*WA* 173). Balancing this modesty, though, are overt and ambitious inclusions. The most significant for our purposes is this:

> What are you going to call this pre-conscious organizing of perceptual experience, which gives us the world as we actually and consciously experience it? Coleridge called it "primary imagination." My friend Barfield called it "figuration." Langer . . . calls it "formulation." Both of them, and Cassirer and many others, agree that it is the same activity as the activity which we call, when we *are* aware of it—*thinking*. (*WA* 48)

Here indeed we have an indication of why Owen Barfield creates "Owen Barfield"—the latter's constitution of the scene and the dialogue from the tape-recorded percepts itself symbolizes the "pre-conscious organizing of perceptual experience." "Owen Barfield," who arranges the book from the periphery, is the "symbol of symbols" at its center, the self-aware participated thinking valorized by Sanderson, for whom description and creation are the same thing. The creation of "Owen Barfield" out of Owen Barfield is an example of self-positing final participation, an instance of the principle of initiation that the book demands. It does not matter in the end that Burgeon and Sanderson cannot deliver on their metaphysical ambitions, as the book's most important act is the creation of "Owen Barfield," who stands in relation to the book as the "spiritual world" does for Sanderson: "By 'spiritual world' I mean an immaterial realm beyond space and containing it, from which the physical world is brought into being" (*WA* 198). Indeed, we can go further: Owen Barfield creates "Owen Barfield," who holds up Burgeon, Sanderson, and the others as mirrors in which, like the demiurge, he sees and shapes himself. So too, for Sanderson:

> [H]uman consciousness is the mirror in which nature surveys herself. . . . The past remains latent in the present, perhaps in something the same way as it does in the meaning of a word. I don't think I can be more precise. I could

not be without beginning to speak of hierarchies of creative beings, and there is obviously no time for that, even if you wanted it. (*WA* 194)

Unancestral Voice takes up where Sanderson leaves off, not by merely speaking of "hierarchies of creative beings" but by introducing them as characters whom Burgeon experiences directly, at the peripheral center, or central periphery, of inner space.

4. *Unancestral Voice*

In the same interview in which Barfield describes *Worlds Apart* as "an attempt to refute criticisms" (Schenkel 33), he says he wants to concentrate not on "the justification of there *being* a Steiner" but on "the *results* of his spiritual researches," though he was "frightened" that "one had to say to some extent how the narrator got these illuminations from the Meggid" (Schenkel 32). The shift from the philosophical elaboration of an Anthroposophical metaphysic dramatized in *Worlds Apart* to a more practical focus on "results" brings a corresponding simplicity of narrative structure. Though Barfield was "frightened" to create an overtly mystical narrative, he did so anyway, along with an equally overt narrative voice. For the first time, Burgeon is not the narrator of a Burgeon story; rather, we have an omniscient third-person narrative almost objective enough to defy the role of "narrator," though this disarming simplicity is also deceptive.

Unancestral Voice, despite its metaphysical daring, does not engage in metaphysical debate. Instead, it mirrors the arc of Barfield's intellectual biography by making the leap from metaphysics to cosmology and revealing that that leap was the *telos* of his philosophical labors all along. Burgeon seems to take the tentative conclusions of *Worlds Apart* for granted; the whole action shifts from the philosophical disagreements of that dialogue to divergent paths of initiation. D. H. Lawrence offers the most prominent of these different paths. Barfield begins the book with a chapter in which Burgeon discusses with his allegorically named interlocutors Rodney (pro-Lawrence) and Middleton (neutral) his own visceral distaste for Lawrence. That might have been the end of it, but Burgeon's preoccupation with Lawrence extends across the whole of the book and so across years of narrative time. Burgeon's initial ridicule of *Apocalypse* as ignorant and incoherent (*UV* 13–14) yields to the recognition that he had at least to some extent misjudged Lawrence. After Burgeon's encounter with what he calls the Meggid—the spiritual voice that Burgeon experiences as "within" yet "other than" himself—it becomes clear that he and Lawrence experience and offer two different forms of "potency," and for the rest of the book he tests his own experience and understanding against that of Lawrence. These are not two competing philosophies or worldviews but two esoteric paths of initiation.

Lawrence, like many of their generation, shared Barfield's interest in occultism. He revised *Women in Love* extensively after reading Madame Blavatsky's *The Secret Doctrine* and the occultist J. M. Pryse's *The Apocalypse Unsealed*[16] and was "deeply influenced by Wagnerian and occult thought" (Surette 1993, 29). Lawrence's *Apocalypse*, which along with *Lady Chatterley's Lover* is the touchstone for Burgeon's reflections, was written as an introduction to Frederick Carter's *The Dragon of the Alchemists*. It takes for granted Pryse's thesis that *Revelations* involves an "initiation into death and rebirth" (Lawrence 1976, 67). Burgeon seems to pick up on all of this and understands Lawrence to have written occult books that promote an occult path of development.

The famous closing passage of *Apocalypse* confirms Lawrence's "crass, though deeper" (*UV* 106) understanding of instinct:

> we are unnaturally resisting our connection with the cosmos, with the world, with mankind, with the nation, with the family. . . . *We cannot bear connection.* That is our malady. We *must* break away, and be isolate. We call that being free, being individual. Beyond a certain point, which we have reached, it is suicide. Perhaps we have chosen suicide. Well and good. (Lawrence 1976, 125)

Burgeon shares Lawrence's preoccupation with cultural, indeed global, suicide, though he is more understated. Part One of *Unancestral Voice* is an extended illustration of the unbearable burden of connection, as it manifests in sexuality, adolescence, and prison reform. This fear of connection, according to the Meggid, is a form of self-protection in the face of the "deep-hidden and hitherto unconscious . . . fury of destructive force" (*UV* 159) that resides at the core of every modern "civilized" individual. The doctrine of materialism itself "is founded in fear" (*UV* 160) because it denies the substratum of "potency" or energy that is equivalent to "this destructive impulse and this chaos" (*UV* 160) that humanity harbors.

Thus far Lawrence and Burgeon (or the Meggid) have a similar diagnosis of the existential, perhaps apocalyptic, ills facing contemporary humanity. Lawrence's solution of a self-consciously unselfconscious paganism, his neo-Nietzschean celebration of power, is anathema to Burgeon and the root of their disagreement. As Barfield puts it in a contemporaneous essay, "the history of Paganism is the history of the human Spirit slowly emerging from the Spirit of nature, and still dreamingly aware of its former union. We are becoming more and more alive to this as a fact of history" (*RCA* 299). The famous closing passage of *Apocalypse* is worth quoting in full because Burgeon carries it into his sleep in the first chapter and struggles to metabolize it for the rest of the book:

> What man most passionately wants is his living wholeness and living unison, not his own isolate salvation of his "soul." Man wants his physical fulfilment first and foremost, since now, once and once only, he is in the flesh and potent. For man, the vast marvel is to be alive. . . . Whatever the unborn and the dead may know, they cannot know the beauty, the marvel of being alive in the flesh. The dead may look after the afterwards. But the magnificent here and now of life in the flesh is ours, and ours alone, and ours only for a time. We ought to dance with rapture that we should be alive and in the flesh, and part of the living, incarnate cosmos. I am part of the sun as my eye is part of me. That I am part of the earth my feet know perfectly, and my blood is part of the sea. My soul knows that I am part of the human race, my soul is an organic part of the great human soul, as my spirit is part of my nation. In my own very self, I am part of my family. There is nothing of me that is alone and absolute except my mind, and we shall find that the mind has no existence by itself, it is only the glitter of the sun on the surface of the waters. (Lawrence 1976, 125–26).

There is much in this ecstatic conclusion for Burgeon to celebrate. Its rapturous statement of the identity of the senses with the spirit and of the individual with the cosmos is consistent with the message of the Meggid. After all, when the Meggid maintains that "the relation between yourself and nature is, not a relation between your body and all else in nature, but the relation between yourself on the one hand and, on the other, your body, as at once a part of nature and her epitome" (*UV* 114), Burgeon answers that "Lawrence, with his ignorance and his inkling, was at least one of the few" (*UV* 114) who concurred with the Meggid. Lawrence's Dionysian identification with the cosmos is a more elaborate version of the microcosm/macrocosm identification made by the Meggid.

Yet in avoiding what the Meggid calls the "Great Tabu," Lawrence falls into another error: he concludes from his celebration of the flesh that "the mind has no existence by itself" and indeed is merely an epiphenomenal "glitter of the sun on the surface of the waters." For Lawrence, this is the fissure and flaw that runs through St. John's *Apocalypse*. The "pagan manner of thought" is evident in the "old plan" of its vision, but since "the Jews have a moral instinct against design" they "spoilt the beauty of [the] plan by forcing some ethical or tribal meaning in" (Lawrence 1976, 55). Lawrence supports the anti-Semitic thrust of his argument with a scathing indictment of the Christian Logos:

> So the Logos came, at the beginning of our era, to give men another sort of splendour. And that same Logos today is the evil snake of the Laocoön which is the death of all of us. The Logos which was like the great green breath of spring-time is now the grey stinging of myriads of deadening little serpents. Now we have to *conquer* the Logos, that the new dragon gleaming green may lean down from among the stars and vivify us and make us great. (Lawrence 1976, 94)

Lawrence's provocative rhetorical stance—in league with the dragon of cosmic vitality against the grey Logos of self-alienation—is of a piece with his critique of modernity as anti-nature, anti-flesh, and anti-sexual, thereby denying the "potent" ecstasy of cosmic oneness.

Lawrence looks forward to the "lovely green dragon on the new day" that will "come, come in touch, and release us from the horrid grip of the evil-smelling old Logos!" (Lawrence 1976, 96). This is the predicament and liberation of Lady Chatterley:

> Today, the best part of womanhood is wrapped tight and tense in the folds of the Logos, she is bodiless, abstract, and driven by a self-determination terrible to behold. A strange "spiritual" creature is woman today, driven on and on by the evil demon of the old Logos, never for a moment allowed to escape and be herself. The evil Logos says she must be "significant," she must "make something worth while" of her life. (Lawrence 1976, 95)

The "evil Logos" denies modern women fulfillment and encourages them to take up a self-empowered yet self-alienated individualism. This project, which belongs to both men and women, is another aspect of the existential dilemma and a part of the spiritual crisis of modern industrial democracies: "when you start to teach individual self-realization to the great masses of people, who when all is said and done are only *fragmentary* beings, *incapable* of whole individuality, you end by making them envious, grudging, spiteful creatures" (Lawrence 1976, 120). These isolated entities believe themselves to be individuals "equal" to each other, each asserting power over the other: "But a democracy is bound in the end to be obscene, for it is composed of myriad disunited fragments, each fragment assuming to itself a false wholeness, a false individuality. Modern democracy is made up of millions of frictional parts all asserting their own wholeness" (Lawrence 1976, 123). Lawrence's promotion of a neo-Pagan celebration of the "green dragon," of the "eternal vital correspondence between our blood and the sun" and "the cosmos [as] a vast living body, of which we are still parts" (Lawrence 1976, 29), is a path of individual transformation and the only solution to the ills of alienation, meaninglessness, and endless dysfunctional bickering that plague modern democratic societies.

Unancestral Voice starts from the same premises—that the need for self-transformation is a necessary step in overcoming meaninglessness and alienation, and that our crippling social ills grow from these problems—but is otherwise the inverse of Lawrence's vision. Against his anti-Semitism, Barfield finds inspiration in Jewish mysticism; against demonizing the "evil-smelling old Logos" he celebrates the Logos as underlying both the "potency" Lawrence seeks and the evolution of consciousness that yields our contemporary alienation; against Lawrence's reduction of the spirit to the flesh, he sees the flesh as a vital aspect of the spirit; and he affirms the reality and necessity of the conscious individual as the site of the self-transformation by which humanity can regain the experience of itself as the epitome, the microcosm, of the vital cosmos.

We are now in a better position to appreciate Barfield's decision to opt for mild omniscient third-person narration as opposed to the first-person perspectives of *This Ever Diverse Pair* and *Worlds Apart*. *Unancestral Voice* counters both alienated subjective fragmentation and the dissolution of the self into the noumenal wonder of the living cosmos. One might say that *Worlds Apart* did that by introducing "Owen Barfield" as a character who represents the individual as the living symbol of the microcosmic demiurge. In *Unancestral Voice*, Burgeon is both an individual character in the book—central but only one among many—and the peripheral and transpersonal consciousness that holds the whole story. At the same time, one major arc in the narrative is the manner in which Burgeon becomes indivisible from the Meggid, an entity with a still more individual voice that speaks through and within him—a spiritual voice, moreover, that claims a universal or third-person perspective on issues of pressing concern to Burgeon and those with whom he converses. At the level of narrative structure, Burgeon increasingly becomes the third-person perspective that narrates his story; he simultaneously becomes the Meggid, who narrates much of the story from within him, and claims precisely the individual-yet-universal perspective that increasingly becomes Burgeon's own.[17]

This anti-Lawrentian picture of *participation mystique* is already present in seed-like form in the first chapter of *Unancestral Voice*. Rodney, Middleton, and Burgeon engage in a muddled conversation about the recent obscenity trial of *Lady Chatterley's Lover*, muddled because it is not altogether clear what is at stake. Initially, they "get . . . cluttered up" (*UV* 11) attempting to distinguish and classify obscenity, lust, and disgust, and then in doing the same with reticence and hypocrisy. The conversation becomes more impactful for Burgeon when Lawrence's themes distill into the question whether "potency . . . is to be equated with sex" (*UV* 14), especially considered in the light of the evolution of consciousness. Burgeon argues with particular energy that Lawrence "never even dreamed of" the importance of the latter in considering the former, thereby relegating all that is not of the flesh to "sex in the head" (*UV* 14).

Burgeon, as we noted, takes into his sleep the long passage from *Apocalypse* that contrasts flesh with mind. It produces the ironic effect that Burgeon discovers what is true potency for him when he wakes in the morning, in the subtle change in his own consciousness: "his mind wide awake . . . [but] also quite empty," Burgeon cultivates a mildly creative attitude toward the previous night's conversation, "a good state of mind to cultivate if one were trying to write a play" (*UV* 16). In this receptive state, a gentle form of what he defined in *Poetic Diction* as "concrete thinking," he for the first time experiences the presence of the Meggid as "thoughts which were 'given' . . . naked of words" (*UV* 16). Those that crystallize into language, and so into full consciousness, though "without any effort being required on his part," are: "*interior is anterior*" and "*the transforming agent*" (*UV* 16). These are followed by a series of associations, in which Burgeon meditates (again without conscious effort) on: first, lines from the *Carmina Burana* about postcoital lassitude; second, his overly energetic reaction to and misjudgment of Lawrence; third, recent changes in Western consciousness resulting from transformations in "the front part of the brain and at the same time in the organs of reproduction" (*UV* 17); finally, that consciousness is the object or patient of the "transforming agent" whose existence has just been disclosed to him.

The two halves of the first chapter, then, disclose the two paths of initiation that Barfield sees open to modern Western humanity: firstly, Lawrence's celebration of ecstatic union with the living cosmos through immersion in the flesh and the concomitant dissolution of individual consciousness; and, secondly, Burgeon's revelation within consciousness itself of a spiritual visitor who discloses knowledge as a different kind of potency, as it rises from the depths of the unconscious through layers of partial awareness into language. This process mirrors the "adept's process" outlined by Werblowsky, of moral purification, followed by sense-free thinking, the imagination of the spiritual world through the contemplation of the "En Sof" (Werblowsky 69). We already anticipate that knowledge *about* the "transforming agent" is instrumental to transformation, and that the patient who receives this knowledge is stimulated by it into agency; in fact, that the transformation must involve at least in part a metamorphosis from patience into action.

The history of Burgeon's relation to the Meggid offers a telling window into his development. Even referring to the voice as "the Meggid" is misleading, as is referring to the voice as "him," though Burgeon does so throughout the book. Burgeon's ostentatiously arbitrary choice of "the Meggid" as a name for the voice recalls the apophatic tradition of Dionysius the Areopagite, the traditional author of *The Divine Names*: the name "Meggid" is divine precisely because it foregrounds its inadequacy. On the final page, the voice claims many names, including Batkhol, Daimon, Khochmah, Sophia, Theosophia, names that arose "articulately only in the mysteries and through the sibyls, the prophets the masters" (*UV* 163). The voice then declares that "I am that *anthroposophia* who, by whatsoever communications howsoever imparted she shall first have been evoked, is the voice of each one's mind speaking from the depths within himself" (*UV* 163). It appears, then, that Burgeon's specific reference to the voice as "*he*" (*UV* 27) is a mistake only corrected on the book's final page.[18] As the narration has been omniscient and in the past tense, this final revelation has been withheld strategically.[19] This makes sense because it is also Burgeon's own record of a final revelation of identity with a voice that is both omniscient and personal, an identity that in the book's final words expands to include the reader:

> But what you shall do shall be taught you not by me, neither by my masters. You may only receive it direct from the Master of my masters; who is also their humble servant, as each one of them also is mine; as you—if your "doing" should be only a writing—will strive to be your reader's, and as I am yours. (*UV* 163)

Christ stands behind Anthroposophia as the "Master of my masters" and the "transforming agent" who at once unifies, transforms, and inspires not only her but also Burgeon and, if only through anticipation, the reader. The book in our hands has indeed been authored by Burgeon, who has fulfilled the task set before him by the voice; and the reader, having finished the book, is herself transformed, in such a way that transformation, unification, and inspiration are identical. These mutual interactions of creation and reception remind one that while "this indwelling of the *Shekhinah* in man also accounts for such mystical phenomena as maggidism" (Werblowsky 157), the Maggid are (as Barfield again noted in a marginal comment in his personal copy) both visiting spirits and human creations—inner sensation and imaginative creation, metaphysics and poetic cosmology, meet at the horizon point in human souls where the *Shekhinah* indwells.

The Meggid's self-identification as "that *anthroposophia*" is a reference to what is for Anthroposophists one of Steiner's most important lectures, the so-called

"Christmas Conference" lecture in which he presented the "Foundation Stone" meditation.[20] This lecture includes one of Steiner's few notable references to Anthroposophia as a spiritual being, woven into his presentation of the meditation. It is not difficult to understand why it would come to Barfield's mind as he created "the voice." Steiner says that the transformation needed to meet the ills of our time will only happen when "our hearts are enlivened through and through by Anthroposophia" (Steiner 1990, 70), and this happens when "out of the signs of the present time we may renew, in keeping with our way of thinking, the ancient word of the Mysteries: 'Know Thyself'" (Steiner 1990, 68). The self-knowledge Steiner has in mind is precisely that in which the individual is a synecdoche or microcosm of universe.[21] The spiritual seeker cultivating a relationship with Anthroposophia along the path of self-knowledge will:

> recognize himself as an individually free human being within the reigning work of the gods in the cosmos, as a cosmic human being, working for the future of the universe as an individual human being within the cosmic human being. Out of the signs of the present time he will re-enliven the ancient words: "Know thou Thyself!" (Steiner 1990, 71)

Out of such work, says Steiner:

> will you found . . . a true community of human beings for Anthroposophia; and then will you carry the spirit that rules in the shining light of thoughts . . . out into the world wherever it should give of its light and of its warmth for the progress of human souls, for the progress of the universe. (Steiner 1990, 77)

It is plain that Burgeon follows the path laid out by Steiner: he too seeks self-knowledge, no longer through Kierkegaardian inner conflict, or deliberation on the metaphysics of the self, but by experiencing himself directly as a microcosmic epitome of "the cosmic human being" that is one with, or comes to expression by way of, "the reigning work of the gods in the cosmos." In this sense, self-knowledge is the same as the two aims of the Jewish mystics identified by Werblowsky, which Barfield again noted in a marginal score: the exaltation and redemption of the exiled Shekhinah and communion with God (Werblowsky 58).[22]

As we consider the narrative voice of the book, then, we are far from Lawrence's picture of "potency." The book's conclusion brings back to mind Burgeon's experience of the conversation about Lawrence. At that early stage, Burgeon recalls Lady Chatterley's sarcastic rejection of "the supreme pleasure of the mind" that is "merely messy and doggy" in favor of "sheer sensuality" (*UV* 29). This in turn reminds Burgeon of the Courtly Love tradition, at which point "Burgeon felt that the Meggid had begun to speak" (*UV* 29) about the relation of "potency" to the evolution of consciousness, in particular that "that mysterious potency . . . reach[ed] the heart and the blood and from there began to manifest itself in a new way, a way of which the Greek world has as yet no experience—and of which Lawrence and most of the twentieth century *no longer* had any experience" (*UV* 29). Burgeon, or Anthroposophia, sees this "potency of feeling" as "sex in the heart" (*UV* 31) as opposed to Lawrence's famous dictum of our alienated "sex in the head." In the movement further "into the loins," Lawrence was correct to see a kind of "awakening" and to "divine . . . the truth that, although it was within him, it did not belong to him. It was his surviving real link with the cosmos, out of which even his separateness had been born" (*UV* 31).

Lawrence's error, however, is to see in "the logos . . . the insipidity of intellect, because intellect had no potency" (*UV* 32). The Meggid gives Burgeon a contrary insight:

> At last it was clear. The potency had become his own in order that he, having become himself, might give it back to the logos, whence it had descended, leaving behind it an impotent shell. . . . Either down into animalism or back into the "logos"—of which Lawrence knew nothing, which Lawrence found insipid. (*UV* 32–3)

Lawrence and his followers are right to see "insipidity" and "impotence" in "the only kind of thinking they recognized; the kind that had brought about the industrial civilization in which they were all embedded from childhood and which had seared the sensitive soul of the child Lawrence instead of simply murdering it" (*UV* 33). They are wrong, however, to limit thinking to this instrumental role.

Burgeon's unfolding relation to Anthroposophia is one way to consider the potent transformation of intellect. Initially, the voice appears to him as the Maggid appeared to Joseph Karo, as a teacher and responder of questions (*UV* 22). Gradually the relation becomes more nuanced, as "when the encounter came, it came of its own accord" (*UV* 45). This yields to a "new development in his intercourse with the Meggid" (*UV* 50), namely that instead of "occasional encounters" punctuating "ordinary life," it now:

> was all beginning to remain much more present to him. Instead, it was sometimes an effort to concentrate, in forgetfulness of the Meggid, on ordinary activities.[23] He found himself preoccupied with problems that arose out of what he had "heard." So that, in a sense, the testing was going on all the time. (*UV* 50)

As Burgeon begins to think more deliberately—from the standpoint of the Meggid, as it were—he recognizes that the voice, "though not wholly inaccessible to specific questions, preferred to choose his own times and occasions for the most important things he had to say" (*UV* 51). Burgeon recognizes that the voice now speaks in, not through, him:

> And it was at this point that he first realized that the Meggid himself was now speaking in him. How long that had been going on, he could not say, for it was definitely "in" and not "through"; there was no question of his being used as a sort of microphone; and yet it was almost as much like hearing someone else speak as it was like speaking; and this because his lips were uttering, and with the confidence of personal experience, things which he must indeed have thought, but could not possibly say he *knew* from experience, since he had not lived them, or had never lived up to them—had never taken them seriously, as he took, for instance, eating and drinking seriously. (*UV* 86–7)[24]

This new experience, of distinction without division, is at the heart of Burgeon's sense of self. After "many months" in which the voice has been absent, it is a "startlingly clear perception, a moment of intellectual vision" (*UV* 84). Burgeon's intellect is becoming potent in a subtler way than Lawrence would allow, attuned to the *energia* at the threshold of consciousness, for the first time taking intellectual vigor as seriously as the vitality of the flesh.

This new intimacy between Burgeon and Anthroposophia becomes the norm for him: "for some time now Burgeon had been aware that the Meggid was, in effect, speaking in him. He was the less surprised to hear his own voice propounding things he did not even know that he knew" (*UV* 101). It is perhaps also the less surprising that in this state of differentiated self-awareness the voice is able to share a clearer understanding of Burgeon's "persistently obliterated" conception of the "transforming agent" and its role (in Burgeon as an individual and in Western humanity as a whole) in "that recent and still proceeding emergence from a quasi-instinctual life of the mind into a vigilant one" (*UV* 106). Lawrence returns yet again in this moment, as Anthroposophia distinguishes her use of "instinct" from his:

> There should be no danger of your taking the word 'instinctual' here in the sense in which biology speaks of "instinct" nor even with the crass, though deeper, overtones which it bore for such a mind as Lawrence's. They were no merely physical energies that still helped to sustain the men of the preceding age. They were beings. I spoke then only of the being whom we called Gabriel, but behind him, active in him and one with him, are ranged all the hierarchies of his fellow

beings in the spiritual world. And so it is still for sleeping, though not for waking, humanity. (*UV* 106)

As Burgeon becomes aware of Anthroposophia's voice within his own, he learns from that voice of "all the hierarchies" resonant within her, that are therefore also "active in him and one with him"—Anthroposophia refers to Gabriel here, but her words apply no less to Burgeon himself. This is the potency of which "waking" humanity stands in need, rather than the "crass, though deeper" celebration of the flesh advocated by Lawrence.

This experience of a personal voice speaking and thinking within his own becomes the norm for Burgeon: "in the course of the years, the information that had come to him from the Meggid and his own thoughts and reflections had become so inextricably involved with one another that it was almost impossible to disentangle them" (*UV* 147). At this point, Burgeon gives his most detailed phenomenological account of his spiritual encounters with the Meggid:

> It may be tedious, but is perhaps advisable, to repeat once more—that the dialogue-form is a kind of travesty of what actually happened between Burgeon and the Meggid. That is the somewhat undignified penalty that has to be paid for putting into words drawn from ordinary experience (and there are, after all, no other words) an experience that is not ordinary, inasmuch as it is beyond, or rather behind language, taking place in the realm whence the very faculty of transforming experience into words is derived. (*UV* 150)

The paradoxical problem of describing the leap, like that of a subatomic particle, of prelinguistic experience across the event horizon into language applies no less to the inner life than it does to the outer world. The metaphor of the dialogue is a travesty because Anthroposophia is a voice within Burgeon himself—within, yet distinct, like Athena at the source of the "fountain" of thought in Barfield's poem *Riders on Pegasus*. Burgeon's use of the passive voice here illustrates the problem: who, exactly, possesses "the very faculty of transforming experience into words"? This is the mystery and paradox of selfhood: Burgeon has autonomous integrity, has potency, even has repeated lives; but, his "I" is sustained by the "Thou" of Anthroposophia that itself both contains and is sustained by "all the hierarchies." The individual is an infinity of beings, each of which is active in every other and all of which are present at the leap into language.

This paradox of multiplicity-in-unity, of "Thou" in "I," of receptivity that is activity can also be considered spatially: *where* is the "realm whence the very faculty of transforming words into experience is derived"? What is the space of the "logos," that is to say, of the "transforming agent"? The abstract discussion of space in *Worlds Apart* is now direct experience for Burgeon. The very concept of space is the fulcrum that makes sense of the interior otherness of the voice that speaks through, and then in, Burgeon. First, Burgeon's assumptions about interiority require correction from the Meggid:

> You are using the term "interior" to yourself, he said, as if it meant deeper and deeper inside your body. In fact, it means almost the opposite. When I said "interior is anterior," I was not using it in that way. I can best put it by saying that I meant by "interior" nearer to where you eventually found *me*. You ought to know better than to think that this "interior" is so situated that it can be reached by more and more infinitesimal dissection. . . . If you are still disposed to make a sheet-anchor of "interior is anterior"—add to it, as a rider, that "Space is both interior and exterior." (*UV* 45)

The Meggid's concern to shift Burgeon's understanding of "interior" to space itself, as opposed to the body, is of a piece with the "Great Illusion" in *Worlds Apart*, that "the relation between yourself and nature is, not a relation between your body and all else in nature, but the relation between yourself on the one hand and, on the other, yourself as at once a part of nature and her epitome" (*UV* 114). One part of Burgeon's divergence from Lawrence is the latter's failure to appreciate that the felt sense of "interior" captured in the alienated awareness that we are shipwrecked in our own bodies is not merely a calamity but a by-product of the evolution of consciousness that includes some recompense. Lawrence wishes to obliterate interiority itself in ecstatic union with the living cosmos. The other-yet-inner voice that visits Burgeon encourages him to shift, not destroy, his understanding of the "interior."

Thus, Burgeon is well-prepared when he meets Flume, who queries the nature of space as understood by the advance guard of theoretical physicists. Flume posits that it is a "characteristic of imagination that it apprehends spatial form, and relations in space, as 'expressive' of non-spatial form, and non-spatial relations" (*UV* 127). This in turn accommodates the presence of quantum particles with no extension. Perhaps, then, physicists must abandon Newtonian space and in addition to the "3N dimensional space of their equations (to which no sort of actuality could be attributed)" posit "a negative, or perhaps a potential, space, for which they had no model and therefore, as yet, no equations" (*UV* 130). The upshot of this pragmatic but comprehensive reimagining of the nature of space is a fresh imagination (once again, courtesy of an inspired Flume) of the human being as microcosm and a practical way in which to overcome the Great Illusion. Speaking of his physicist audience, Flume says:

> Others chose to be sarcastic about a space in which the part contains the whole, or the centre the periphery. . . . Is it mere folly to suggest that we are being forced to cultivate a mode of thought capable of grasping such a relation between whole and part? Or a mode of space itself which we have not yet apprehended, leading us perhaps to the source from which space originated? . . . What *kind* of source can there be for the complex interacting rhythms of energy, of which we now find that the physical universe consists? What other can it be than a system of non-spatial relationships between hierarchies of energetic beings? And how can we obtain access to their realm, unless we learn somehow to think of them without the help of models? (*UV* 143)

Flume's inspired comment brings to full consciousness much of the interior action of the book. Considered spatially, Burgeon's mind is the arena that contains Anthroposophia, who contains "all the hierarchies," which in turn contain and emanate from the Logos who is also Christ, the "transforming agent." Considered from another perspective, Burgeon, Anthroposophia, Gabriel, and all the individual entities that constitute the hierarchies are synecdoches of the macrocosmic hierarchical pantheon. Or, put still otherwise, Burgeon's mind is the center around which the hierarchies revolve—in narratological terms, the character at the center of the narrative, and of our concern; and, he is at the same time the periphery, both as narrator and as the container of hierarchies. Considered as an activity, Burgeon is the "physical universe" produced by the "hierarchies of energetic beings"; but, Burgeon's active imagination is one of those energetic beings: his activity is a kind of reception, and his receptivity is a kind of action. Such is the living thinking demanded by Barfield and Lawrence alike, a movement beyond the dead "help of models" on which modern humanity has come to depend and which hastens us toward extinction.

Burgeon's path to this experience is not smooth. His first encounter with a materialist obstructer is with his old nemesis Burden. Burden made no appearance in *Worlds Apart*, having taken up his assigned domestic duties at the end of *This Ever Diverse Pair*. He has little in common with his earlier incarnation but instead plays a tempter or threshold-guardian role. Soon after Burgeon's first encounter with Anthroposophia, Burden appears, sounding much like Dunn in *Worlds Apart*, to convince him that the voice is a delusion. Burden quotes Hamlet and declares that Anthroposophia's initial pronouncements—"*interior is anterior*," "*the transforming agent*"—are simply "Words! Words! Words!" because each of them "really doesn't mean anything at all" (*UV* 24). In conventional fashion, Burden supplements his linguistic positivism with a demand for a verification principle and pairs it with a reliance on Darwinian evolutionary theory. Burden objects to Burgeon that "when you get to using words like 'immaterial' and 'consciousness', you are by definition outside the sphere of verification" (*UV* 25). Having ruled out of bounds Burgeon's characterization, Burden claims to defeat him by reducing his experience to "the complicated subjective meanderings of the brain" (*UV* 23).

Burgeon responds to Burden on two fronts, which contain rather than defeat him. On the one hand, he argues that neither the proposition that the brain produces consciousness nor the opposite can be proven—it is a kind of antinomy, each equally strong or feeble in its persuasive power. His second, more powerful, response is at the meta-level of narration itself. Burgeon asserts his power over Burden by acting as arranger of their conversation—he strips it of "inevitable interruptions and tedious repetitions" (*UV* 23), a role similar to the one "Owen Barfield" had in *Worlds Apart*. In recounting to Burden their history, he claims, "when we had that dust-up twenty years ago, I pointed out—*rightly*—that it was *I* who originally brought *you* into existence" (*UV* 26). In fact, as Burden must recall (his emphasis on "rightly" protests too much), he said in *This Ever Diverse Pair* that "I am responsible for the professional existence, *almost* for the existence at all, of Burden" (*TEDP* 4; my emphasis). Finally, Burgeon notes as he closes his episode with Burden that "after this initial flare up, the Burden element in Burgeon gave no more trouble; at least, it gave no more on *this* issue" (*UV* 27). What other issues Burden might have raised, we will never know because Burgeon chooses not to include them. As if to emphasize his creative control, Burgeon assures us that the presence of Burden does not presage "Burgeon's psyche sprouting a whole galaxy of invisible companions" (*UV* 23). This is obviously tongue in cheek: Burgeon's psyche will soon sprout its own celestial hierarchies. His more serious point in all of these controlling moves is to offer an implicit *riposte* to Burden—his creative consciousness does matter, his interior is anterior, his imagination is the transforming agent that gives rise to, and maintains control of, Burden and all that he represents.

Burden's discouraging, distracting, and reductive influence makes him a kind of emissary of Lucifer and Ahriman, obstructing spiritual forces from Steiner's cosmology who work to hinder the beneficent influence of the "transforming agent" and the celestial hierarchies. Burgeon is suitably struck by the revelation of their work. In fact, none of the voice's teachings makes a deeper influence than this one:

Nothing from his intercourse with the Meggid had left a deeper impression on him than that disclosure of the part played by the two adversaries. He never lost sight of this and he was astonished by the repeated vestiges he found of their chronic influence in eliminating men's awareness of the immaterial transforming agent and, where possible, eliminating the operation of the transforming agent itself. (*UV* 74)

Anthroposophia describes Lucifer's effort, similar to Chimaera's in *Riders on Pegasus*, as being "to preserve the old form unaltered from generation to generation, to nullify, in fact, the work of the transforming agent" (*UV* 67), while Ahriman strives, like the gorgons in that poem, to:

> hasten the extinction of the old form, if he could; but he would see to it that the new form, which replaced it, was no longer the creation of the transforming agent, but some caricatured invention of his own—something harder, something *pre*-mature. Between them they would seek to eliminate the transforming agent altogether. (*UV* 67)

The voice introduces here a nearly apocalyptic theme of the confrontation of demonic forces with Christ, the transforming agent. After all, potency consists of "different kinds of forces" and these are "only the end-product of [the] activity [of] . . . different beings" (*UV* 39). Among these are the celestial hierarchies, including not only Gabriel and Michael but also Lucifer and Ahriman working in opposition.

One indication of the ubiquitous presence of Lucifer and Ahriman is that they show up, either directly or by implication, in each of the book's three sections. They come up first in the ethical/political first part of the book, again in the second, *Weltanschauung*, section regarding evolution and reincarnation, and by implication in the third section, in the controversy over scientific method. The first of these, the social/ethical influence, can serve as a model for the working of Lucifer and Ahriman. Burgeon prepares us for their introduction in the previous chapter, about adolescence, in which he describes a different polarity, that of Gabriel and Michael. The voice instructs him that they too have worked together throughout the evolution of consciousness, the former most recently directing "the earnest gaze of mankind" to "dwell on the full meaning of the word *incarnation*" not merely (with a sidelong glance at Lawrence) in reference to "human flesh, or even only to flesh" but to "the whole world of nature, in so far as that is perceived through the senses" (*UV* 40). This "Gabrielic impulsion" during the Renaissance fostered "the growing warmth of enthusiasm for a purely physical science" (*UV* 41).

Left to itself this would yield "a thinking determined by the brain alone" (*UV* 43), but the Gabrielic impulse was more recently joined by the advent of the "Michael age" (*UV* 45), which seeks to combat the Ahrimanic acceleration of the "earnest gaze of mankind" into materialism. "At its best," the voice says, "it *is* 'without prejudice'—but also without potency. It is impotent. Is not that what you are all discovering? Is not that what Lawrence discovered?" (*UV* 44). Anthroposophia, "one of the least of Michael's servants" (*UV* 44), helps Burgeon to develop "non-physical thinking about the non-physical" (*UV* 44) and thereby aids him in overcoming Burden's materialist cynicism: "forces that can create by incarnating—are they impotent? You must distinguish. Non-physical thinking about the physical is still of the brain. Non-physical thinking about the non-physical can become *wholly* non-physical. It can become those very forces" (*UV* 44). This is the path to the "total transformation" that the voice demands: "Will you not now see that total transformation, *true* transformation, can come only from a transforming agent that transforms itself, and that it is to the 'laws' of that self-transformation that the phenomena said to be governed by chance point your inquiry?" (*UV* 155).

The corollary of the process of transformation pursued through "non-physical thinking about the non-physical" is Burgeon's recognition that his anterior interior consists of a multiplicity of beings: "My task is to teach you to recognize and name the contours of the interior which you already dimly see, that is, the beings of whom it consists" (*UV* 60). Indeed, "the time presses" because Burgeon already "[has] access" to the spiritual realm, is "there already" (*UV* 39) along with the rest of humanity. Because "the recognition grows more unavoidable, the struggle to evade it will grow more desperate, the verbal subterfuges more trivial" (*UV* 61). The voice gives Burgeon a "viaticum"—that is, a provision for a journey—to foster the Michaelic thinking that balances the efforts of Lucifer and Ahriman to pull him from the path of transformation:

> And ponder deeply these thoughts which I leave with you now as a viaticum: Evolution is the process by which a past form, or past condition, is transformed into a future one. Lucifer seeks to preserve the past from dissolution; Ahriman to destroy it utterly and substitute his own invention; Michael to transform it through death and rebirth. (*UV* 61)

Burgeon indeed takes these sentences as a mantra: "to say that he knew by heart those farewell words from their last encounter is an understatement. They had long since become a part of him" (*UV* 96). The viaticum itself is an agent in Burgeon's death and rebirth, of course, the initiatory process that has been underway since *This Ever Diverse Pair*; for, after all, "Burgeon, too, was evolving" (*UV* 75).

Burgeon's evolution includes a revisiting, at a higher level, of the Pauline existential themes of *This Ever Diverse Pair*. His reflections suggest that he has continued to meditate on the issues raised by his experience, just as his threshold-crossing encounter with Anthroposophia suggests that although he is unfamiliar with basic Anthroposophical methods and concepts, his weekend retreat with Sanderson and the others has continued to deepen in the interval. Kierkegaard and St. Paul reappear in the middle section of the book, during his cruise with Grimwade and Chevalier. This inevitably brings to mind *This Ever Diverse Pair*, though primarily by way of contrast: Burgeon has already made the "leap of faith" out of despair that caused his crisis in that book. He is now in a position to comprehend the Pauline epigraphs that preface the first book in the trilogy, though he admits "I, too, feel afraid" (*UV* 160), and receives from the Meggid Kierkegaard's insight that "some in the West at least begin to be dimly aware that there *is* this abiding fear, this haunting anxiety, at the root of their being" (*UV* 160).

Kierkegaard comes to mind as Burgeon tries to articulate a concept of evolution or transformation distinct from that of Grimwade (and, by implication, Lawrence):

> Grimwade is not interested in participating; he is only interested in disappearing. That is the whole difference between East and West. It is the whole difference between Orientalism and Christianity.... If I am right, the transition from East to West—signified the change that was taking place in human consciousness *from* awareness of a sort of *residual* participation in the Divine Mind, or creative Spirit, *to* an awareness only of *exclusion* from that participation. But . . . it is that very exclusion which gives to a man his separate, independent existence. It is this that bestows its inviolate *integrity* on his personality, for good or ill. What was Kierkegaard's phrase?—"Directness is paganism." Residual participation is at best instinctual—sibylline—mediumistic. But once a human self has been emancipated from instinct to the extent of being fully aware of its own existence—if it *then* seeks to resume its unity with the Divine Mind, it first has to die. There is no other way. (*UV* 100)

Burgeon's recollection of Kierkegaard here is telling. His paraphrase suggests he has in mind Kierkegaard's long discussion of "truth as subjectivity" in *Concluding Unscientific Postscript*. The essence of Kierkegaard's account is that "objectively there is no truth; for an objective knowledge of the truth of Christianity, or of its truths, is precisely untruth. To know a confession of faith by rote is paganism, because Christianity is inwardness" (Kierkegaard 1963, 201). Kierkegaard offers a phenomenology complementary to Burgeon's, a recognition that the leap into the abyss is the same as a conscious encounter with the transforming agent, and requires, as it does with Orpheus, an initiatory descent into the underworld: one must die out of "instinct" into a free and self-aware "participation in the Divine Mind."

At the end of the paragraph in which he leans on Kierkegaard, Burgeon also recalls St. Paul, again as a reminder of the need for death and rebirth. "I do not see how we can understand Christianity otherwise," he says, "than as the opportunity given to human souls to unite themselves with the Spirit; and *not* with a Spirit which takes care not to be born, but with a Spirit that dies *and is reborn*. What else but that does St. Paul really insist on?" (*UV* 100). Burgeon again places himself and Kierkegaard in the Pauline lineage of initiatory death and rebirth that is required of us both individually and collectively if we are to address the social ills that preoccupy Part One of the book.

After this conversation, St. Paul comes to Burgeon's mind again, as he and the Meggid discourse on the rejuvenation of energy that occurs with sleep:

> there was, after all, no more mysterious transformation than this nightly one of the fagged and jaded into the active and energetic. How could one ever hope to understand the transformation of matter into energy, of the heaviness of matter into the weightlessness of energy, without seeking also to penetrate this? For this *was* the transformation of matter into energy; only it was the inside of it. (*UV* 104)

The voice arrives at this moment to aid Burgeon's reflections, leading him through a picture of reincarnation as sleep and awakening writ large and of the "obliteration" by "Lucifer and Ahriman" of our "awareness" not only that "evolution is transformation" but also that "complete transformation entails the persistence of an immaterial transforming agent" (*UV* 106). This part of the discourse culminates in Anthroposophia's assertion that knowledge of Christ, the transforming agent, can help people to overcome the Luciferic/Ahrimanic pull away from the path of transformation:

> for this grace *today*, they need knowledge as well as virtue—the knowledge that he, whom they are finding, and will not recognize, as the transforming agent in nature, is also the ultimate energy that stirs in the dark depths of their own wills; and that all else that stirs there is the work of the one adversary or the other. (*UV* 114)

At this moment, Burgeon rounds back to the epigraphs that preface *This Ever Diverse Pair* by equating the transforming agent with "the *energeia* of which St. Paul so raptly speaks" (*UV* 114). As Burgeon is clearly aware, Paul uses *energeia* in a multifaceted way.[25] It represents (in the King James translation) the "work" or "force"—one might say "potency"—that transforms our "vile body . . . unto his glorious body" as well as "the working of Satan with all power and signs and lying wonders." Perhaps most relevant to the themes of *Unancestral Voice* is *energeia* as the inner transforming power that is the same as divine inspiration: "I was made a minister, according to the gift of the grace of God given unto me by the effectual working of his power" (Ephesians 3:7). And: "whereunto I also labour, striving according to his working, which worketh in me mightily" (Colossians 1:29). And: "Buried with him in baptism, wherein also ye are risen with Him through the faith of the operation of God, who hath raised him from the dead" (Colossians 2:12). For Burgeon, Paul is the archetypal example of the thoroughly initiated person such that he carries within him, as another will within his will, the power of the Logos who operates "behind him, active in him and one with him" (*UV* 106).

These observations about St. Paul align with Barfield's contemporary statements about him. For example, in "Man, Thought and Nature" (1961) Barfield points directly to the passage from Galatians he used as an epigraph for *This Ever Diverse Pair*. Since the epigraph was added in 1985, we might say it prefaces the whole trilogy:

> Rudolf Steiner described his Theory of Knowledge as "a Pauline theory." He never tired of quoting St Paul's words from the Epistle to the Galatians: "Not I live, but the Christ liveth in me." And he made it very clear that it is only on these terms that his path of knowledge can be followed. His Spiritual Science in fact is not anthropocentric but Christocentric. And it follows from this that the end of the path can never be reached by one or two men here and there, but only by all men in fellowship and communion. In the end, it is not this or that man, but only man himself, in whom the Spirit of nature can fully rise again to life. (*RCA* 309)

From the standpoint of the later Barfield, Burgeon is on the way toward, and unwittingly seeking, the "Christological" path in which the act of knowing itself is a kind baptismal event. Five years earlier, in *Saving the Appearances*, Barfield also referred to "the Pauline maxim: 'Not I, but Christ in me'" (*SA* 158) as a harbinger of "a new impulse towards final participation" that some people—including Burgeon, presumably—are attempting to make "a living experience" (*SA* 158). A few pages later, Barfield correlates Paul's vision with the effort to counteract "the sin of literalness" (*SA* 162), having brought Paul's "earnest expectation" into contact with "Novalis's gloss: *Man is the messiah of nature*" (*SA* 160). If Burgeon is to transform his thinking in this way, he must follow the path of Kierkegaard in rejecting the conventional Christianity Burgeon maintains in *This Ever Diverse Pair*. This also entails a universal, fully inclusive, "fellowship and communion." The sterile vision of "perfect" nature in "Cosmetics" and battle to the death of Burgeon and Burden are far from this vision.

All of these insights, which have a bearing on our retrospective reading of *This Ever Diverse Pair*, have their seed in Barfield's earliest reference to Paul's vision:

> Let us look at the human being for a moment, as St. Paul, for instance, regarded him. For St. Paul the human being is really two men, the old man and the new. The old Adam dies in each soul, as Christ brings to birth in it the new regenerate Adam. For many of us this picture has been renewed in a very remarkable way by Rudolf Steiner; but what is especially characteristic of spiritual science is its revelation of this birth of the new out of the old as a *process*. It is a process which is based on the rhythmic alternation in man of dying echoes of the old consciousness and premonitory experiences of the new. And according to Anthroposophy the free will of man and the grace of God in this matter do not express themselves in some sudden emotional conversion or salvation by means of which the old is alleged to have been destroyed for ever and the new created, intact and perfect, out of nothing, in the twinkling of an eye. Grace would not be itself, if it were theatrical. Rather they work, within the rhythmic system, gradually emphasising the new direction more and the old less. The new all the time is growing *out* of the old rather than in its despite, and the old Adam is not violently denied, but lovingly redeemed. (Barfield 1933a, 11)

Here too Barfield sees Anthroposophy as a modern form of Pauline vision. In this case, he emphasizes the divided nature of the human being and the need to integrate one into the other through a gradual, rhythmic process by which what Burgeon thinks of in "Cosmetics" as "dross" is "lovingly redeemed." In this redemption, "free will" comes to harmonize with "grace" in the form of faith, which itself is a loving and transformative activity, rather than an acquiescence to dogma. It is the death and rebirth of Burgeon in the imagination of his readers, the redemption of the literal by the individual imagination into a microcosmic symbol, such that "the centre of the Universe may well turn out to be the point where any observer is stationed" (*UV 156*).

Appendix

The five poems by "G. A. L. Burgeon" have not been reprinted since their original publication in 1946–7. It is worthwhile including them here, in their original order of appearance:

THE RUSSET

I dreamed I saw the wicked winged Child,
Accoutred like an old, bent pedlar,
Offering my love a pewter platter, piled
With codlin, crab and medlar,

Jonathan, Ribston, Pearmain, Golden Drop,
Nonsuches, Nonpareils—"O dip in
"Your dainty hands, my duck," he cried, "Ah, stop
"And stoop, and pick your pippin!"

Next, lip to ear, I heard dan Cupid say,
As, torn twixt Reds and Greens, she lingered
And, pursing wary lips in wise assay,
Those happy apples fingered:—

"The great green cooker's shiny-smooth to touch—
"That Bramley's crisp—" (she prodded)
"But this dry-looker tastes the sweetest—much!"
She laughed . . . and bit . . . *she nodded!*

(October 10, 1946)

SEMANTICS

Strange men with straight noses,
    Dead many years ago,
Made music—
       And why strange?
    Oh, not merely minstrels, no!

They *made* music!
    Made music?
  Made "music": saw and heard
Divine ladies, nine ladies
  Sent dancing in a word
Down centuries thrice ten . . .
  And still—
    Well?
        the printless fall
Of their dancing breaks, glancing
  From "Muse" . . . "music" . . . "musical" . . .

                      (October 17, 1946)

TRADITION IN POETRY

"Why choose so much this Attic mould,
"These quick staccato rhymes?
"It takes more plastic forms to hold
"The content of our times.

"A modern poet roams at ease:
"He neither rhymes nor rages—
"All your sonorous cadences
"Are echoes of past ages!"

You sapient ass, of *course* they are!
My fathers they've been haunting
Since Latin grew vernacular
For troubadours to chant in.

From cell, court, coffee-house they crowd,
At Albion's Rout to mingle:
I wandered lonely as a cloud—,
Hymn, Ballad, Nursery Jingle.

The bursting heart that's choked with grief
Or too too much rejoices
Turns, like a child, for swift relief
To deep ancestral voices.

Let sober men bring forth, with pains
Of labour, in the study

Echo-emancipated strains
More subtle, and more muddy:

But I—when the hour is waxing late
And dangerous wings enfold me—
The steady throb of Six and Eight
Is mighty to uphold me;

When Fancy tugs and sways—in fine,
'Tis true my hand's unsteady
And, by the Dog, I need old wine
Because I'm drunk already!

(November 14, 1946)

COSMETICS

Only the artist can divine,
Beneath her accidents, pure Nature,
Crystal in rock, or gold in mine,
Behind the mask of living feature.

The truth once caught, he bids it stay
And how he scrapes and how he bothers
Until, the dross all purged away,
It's extant for himself and others!

So, in those days before I won
Some slight concessions with a sonnet,
When (our acquaintance scarce begun)
Your face had still more paint upon it,

Let it be blushed through North and South
That I'm the man (I take much credit)
Who, past that gash you called your mouth,
Still "saw" your lips, your face, and read it.

Could my poor songs avail but this—
To teach your heart how ill they merit
Insult by over-emphasis,
Your dear dear beauty and high spirit!

What if between you and your glass
They crept one day—oh, not to upbraid!—I

Would have *you* whisper: "What I pass
"Must not demean so praised a lady!"

You taunt me with "old-fashioned," "quaint":
No, not a whit! I'm not so petty.
My dear, *charming* to see paint—
But much more charming to see Betty!

(March 13, 1947)

THE DOPPELGANGER

A strange dichotomy I find
Of mental disputation,
Each time the Betty in my mind
Meets Betty on the station.

At first, while we say how d'you do
And talk about the weather.
I see them side by side, those two
And match them both together.

"Look there and there!" says eye to heart,
"And *there*—your fancy hid that!
"Admit your memory took her part!
"You rather overdid that!"

Like snow that first one fades away
And melts into the second:
I lose my head and hear it say:
"She's sweeter than you reckoned!"

(July 3, 1947)

Notes

Introduction

1 See, for example, Frye 5, 179.

Chapter 1

1 Personal correspondence.
2 I am aware of the difficulty, but I guess not sufficiently so, in finding the right substantive to capture the writers and artists associated with Bloomsbury. On the challenge in deciding on "set," "group," "circle," or some other term, see Rosenbaum, 1–20.
3 The fact that Barfield revised *Poetic Diction* from his B.Litt. thesis at Oxford complicates the chronology. Oxford was not then in the practice of keeping theses, and it is not among Barfield's papers. As a result, it is difficult to know in many cases what he wrote when, and what revisions he made. Parts of what became *Poetic Diction* appear in print as early as 1922.
4 Barfield also singles Bell's concept for critique in "The Form of *Hamlet*" (1931). See *RCA* 124–5.
5 Eliot was aware that the disagreement was at least in part performative. As Seamus Perry reminds us, Eliot's distinctions are so contrarian and idiosyncratic that "his deploying of the categories often has a scarcely concealed comedy" (Perry 224).
6 For discussion of this dispute see: Goldie, *passim*, and Harding, 25–43.
7 Barfield refers to Graves's *Of English Poetry* when he notes that "nobody, as far I am aware, except for Robert Graves, has attempted to apply the teachings of psychoanalysis to the serious purposes of imaginative criticism" (Barfield 1923c, 524–5).
8 About Shaw, Barfield had this to say at the time: "And yet these great Victorians—Shaw, Galsworthy, Zangwill—cannot for the life of them create a single living character. Their plays are big and comprehensive. But through the midst of them blows that horrible chill blast of disillusion, like the waning of youthful passion. We sit down, as it were, with a bump and say to ourselves coldly: 'This is not about men and women; it is about ideas'" (Barfield, 1923c, 327).
9 In *Poetic Diction*, Barfield singles out Hardy as a bad poet who created a large number of false or accidental metaphors (*PD* 198).

10 Earlier in the year, Barfield reviewed Santayana's *Little Essays* (edited by Logan Pearsall Smith) enthusiastically, praising its author as "easily the greatest living critic" while also lamenting that "he understands romanticism—but he does not trust it; hence it is disconcerting for a romantic to observe how well he understands it" (Barfield 1921b, 729–30).
11 See Goldie 49–51.
12 Jewel Spears Brooker has shown that by 1926 Eliot pushed back the loss of unified consciousness from Donne's era to Dante's (Brooker 2018, 105–16). This may reflect Eliot's reading of *History in English Words*, which makes a similar argument. Eliot published Barfield in the July 1923 issue of *The Criterion*. A year earlier, as he was preparing to launch the journal, Eliot wrote that "its great aim is to raise the standard of thought and writing in this country by both international and historical comparison. Among English writers I am combining those of the older generation who have any vitality and enterprise, with the more serious of the younger generation, no matter how advanced, for instance Mr Wyndham Lewis and Mr Ezra Pound" (Eliot 2009 1, 710). Eliot undoubtedly considered Barfield one of "the more serious of the younger generation" and sought to cultivate him as a potential member of the group that included Pound and Aldington. He primarily had Yeats in mind as representative of the vital and enterprising older generation (see Kelly 202). It is fitting, then, that in the July 1923 issue of *The Criterion*, the first contribution is from Yeats, followed by Barfield.
13 Barfield's formulation recalls Shelley's claim, discussed below, that "every original language near to its source is the chaos of a cyclic poem."
14 Of course, Richards in later years had much to say about metaphor, and Barfield capitalized on his distinction between "tenor" and "vehicle."
15 The phenomenological metaphysics implicit in these passages from Coleridge and Steiner is the subject of Chapter 3.
16 This sentence incorporates two negative images from *Orpheus* and *Riders on Pegasus*: the monotony of Hades and Medusa's mineralizing gaze.
17 Barfield's unhappiness with Coleridge's coinage may have been influenced by his reading of Logan Pearsall Smith: "A chance appellation like *romantic*, for instance, or a metaphor like *inspiration*, are much more convenient names than a term like Coleridge's 'esemplastic power' for the imagination, which attempts to explain its working" (Smith 1925, 131).
18 See: Eliot 2021, 2: 227, 232, 329, 806, 824.
19 For a recent study that takes issue with this picture of the abject Eliot, see Kennedy.
20 It is well established at this point that the fundamentally comic-ironic aesthetic of Joyce and Yeats has more in common with Barfield's diagnosis than with Eliot's fatalistic description.

21 Archeologists are more likely to speak of an "Aryan migration" today, though scholars are not unanimous. See: Bryant and Patton.
22 It is worth recalling that if Schuchard is right that Eliot wrote the jacket blurb for *Poetic Diction*, he had also read or at least was familiar with the thrust of *History in English Words*: "Mr. Owen Barfield has already shown, in an earlier book, how fascinating is the story of the growth of meaning in words. In POETIC DICTION he is really using this key to unlock the inner secret of poetry. 'The full meanings of words', he writes in a fine passage, 'are flashing, iridescent shapes like flames— ever flickering vestiges of the slowly evolving consciousness beneath them' rather than 'solid chunks with definite boundaries and limits, to which other chunks may be added as occasion arises'. This metaphorical enrichment, which words undergo, is much more than a device of the human mind to amuse itself; it is a progress towards the true understanding of life. The argument, absorbing in itself, is illustrated with much curious detail, and enlivened by pungent criticism of other theories."
23 This description will remind many of Vico's similar account of *sapienza poetica* in general and in particular the example he gives of "poetic thinking" as identifying Jove with thunder. Barfield, though, had not heard of Vico until a few years after *Poetic Diction* was published: "I still recall rather vividly the surprise, slightly tinged with embarrassment, with which, a few years after it was written, the highly original author of *Poetic Diction* learned that early in the eighteenth century a man called Giambattista Vico had propounded something he called 'sapienza poetica' as the earliest form of human thought" (*PD* 219).
24 Barfield would retain his conviction that a renewed appreciation of the Middle Ages was of paramount importance: "the whole purpose of [*Saving the Appearances*] is to show that its spiritual wealth can be, and indeed, if incalculable disaster is to be avoided, *must* be regained" (*SA* 85). The Courtly Love tradition is central to Barfield's last major work, the novella *Eager Spring* (1985).
25 The American pragmatist C. S. Peirce also locates the Realism/Nominalism debate as pivotal for Western culture, reverberating even into the present. On the harmony of Barfield's ideas with those of Peirce, see Maddelena.
26 This image brings to mind not just Lawrence's physicality and the tradition of imagery around the Immaculate Conception but more specifically also recalls Yeats's "Leda and the Swan," published in *The Dial* in 1923, then included in *The Tower* in 1928, just as Barfield was shopping to Eliot his own long poem titled *The Tower*.

Chapter 2

1 Space prevents me from demonstrating that the unity of Barfield's thought itself forms a unity with his practice as a poet, novelist, and dramatist. I have written a

companion volume about Barfield's major poems, plays, and fiction that attempts to do justice to Barfield as an artist—both his poetic philosophy and his philosophical poetry are rooted in the way his "intense experience of poetry reacted on [his] experience of the outer world" (*RCA* 18).

2 Berlin's first major essay on Vico, "The Philosophical Ideas of Giambattista Vico," appeared in 1960 from an Italian publisher. This appeared in revised form in 1976, as *Vico and Herder: Two Studies in the History of Ideas*, a book that surely interested Barfield, given his long-standing fascination with Vico and Herder.

3 See, for example: Clark, Kelley, and Macksey. Barfield refers with approval to Lovejoy's *The Great Chain of Being* but does not seem to have considered Lovejoy's neo-Lockean epistemology.

4 Barfield's early distinction between the "fundamental base music" of iambic pentameter and the individual poet's departures from it is an example in the poetic process of what occurs here within thinking as such.

Chapter 3

1 The opening sentences of Nelson Goodman's *Ways of World-Making* could nearly have been written by Barfield: "Countless worlds made from nothing by use of symbols—so might a satirist summarize some major themes in the work of Ernst Cassirer. These themes—the multiplicity of worlds, the speciousness of 'the given', the creative power of the understanding, the variety and formative function of symbols—are integral to my own thinking" (Goodman 1). The primary difference in viewpoint between Goodman and Barfield is that, from the standpoint of the latter, the former pays insufficient attention to the "antecedent unity" and "the given," on which symbol-use and world-making depend, perhaps because Goodman, despite the deep impact of Cassirer's thought upon him, is insufficiently alert to the presence and importance of the evolution of consciousness. Though Barfield's metaphysics is close to Cassirer's, Barfield repeatedly emphasizes what he sees as Cassirer's most important contribution to modern thought: "the researches of Cassirer and others into the origin and growth of language destroy . . . the prevalent notion that there was a once literal language with exclusively objective (non-human) reference, as surely as the cloud-chambers of microphysics destroy the prevalent notion of stable material particles" (Barfield 1964, 124–5).

2 For fuller discussion of Barfield's reception of Steiner's philosophical writing, see Fischer. Michael Wilson, the translator of the edition of *Philosophy of Freedom* used here, cites Barfield's *Saving the Appearances* in his introduction and lists Barfield among those "who have helped and advised me with suggestions for

the translation" (Steiner 1964, xxii). Barfield commented specifically on how he related Steiner to Coleridge as his own views developed: "Steiner . . . wrote two or three books in which he justified his position philosophically. The best known of these is called *The Philosophy of Freedom*. . . . That book, more than any other, enabled me to overcome my own unresolved positivism intellectually; and also to see that Coleridge had done the same, and how he did it. There's a very close connection there I think between what Steiner meant to me and what Coleridge did" (Sugarman 16).

3 Michael Vincent Di Fuccia goes too far in claiming that "a majority of Barfield's thought is taken directly from Steiner and Coleridge" (Di Fuccia 10). This assessment, combined with his further claim that Coleridge "followed a Platonic scheme" (Di Fuccia 11), misleads him into a mistaken understanding of Barfield's poetics and metaphysics.

4 Barfield's introduction to his edited translation of Steiner's *Von Seelenrätseln* makes clear that he placed Steiner in the lineage of Brentano and Husserl. See Steiner (1970, 14–16).

5 This is not to say that Steiner and Husserl have identical definitions of the given, only that they have the significant overlap entailed by family resemblance.

6 Barfield notes the relevance to positivism of Steiner's notion of the given: "This brings us to his other use of the term 'given'—according to which it coincides with the pure percept, prior to all conceptual determinations whatsoever—to that element in experience which is *wholly* perceptual. Let us call it here the 'net Given'. It is important to be clear that the Given is never actually experienced 'net'. Thus, the net Given is something which a philosopher is concerned with, not as knower, but as epistemologist. This is a distinction Positivism fails to observe" (*RCA* 320–1).

7 Steiner also anticipates Cassirer, who wrote in 1925: "What is commonly called the sensory consciousness, the content of the 'world of perception'—which is further subdivided into distinct spheres of perception, into the sensory elements of color, tone, etc.—this is itself a product of abstraction, a theoretical elaboration of the 'given'. Before self-consciousness rises to this abstraction, it lives in the world of the mythical consciousness, a world not of 'things' and their 'attributes' but of mythical potencies and powers, of demons and gods" (Cassirer 1955, xvi).

8 Heidegger's most famous discussion of technology is *Die Frage nach der Technik* (1954). Barfield is unlikely to have read it in the original German the year before this essay was published. The first English edition appeared in 1977.

9 See Griffin for a helpful discussion of this pivotal moment.

10 Barfield's response to Sartre is consistent with that of Gabriel Marcel, whose work he quotes with approval in this essay. Marcel's first book was a comparison of the philosophies of Coleridge and Schelling, and he at one time planned to translate *Saving the Appearances* into French. For his response to Sartre, see Marcel.

11 The chronology of Cassirer's reception is complicated: Cassirer did all of his writing before or during the Second World War, but it was only translated into English in the years after it.

12 Barfield showed an unsteady grasp of Cassirer's work on 28 March 1964, when he wrote to Philip Mairet at Faber & Faber: "Have you come across Cassirer's excellent little book on the Cambridge Platonists (mainly): 'The Platonic Renaissance in England' – now alas out of print? Is the Theory of Knowledge, of which you speak, Vol. 1 of the 'Philosophy of Symbolic Forms'? I confined myself to Vol. 2, on Language, and did not read that nearly so fully as I should have wished to do. But, as one gets older, with less and less time left, one has to be more and more selective. I have made a note to look up the book on Kant, Rousseau and Goethe, which I have not come across." Barfield's relative ignorance of Cassirer's oeuvre is indicated both by his unfamiliarity with *The Theory of Knowledge* and by his forgetting that the first volume of *Philosophy of Symbolic Forms* is about language and that volume two focuses on mythic thinking.

13 It is possible that Barfield gleaned from Cassirer's account his understanding that "the philosopher Schelling maintained that mythology represents the repetition in the human spirit and consciousness of the processes of nature" (*RM* 28). It is also worth noting that Barfield, unlike Cassirer, does not disavow Schelling, whom he viewed as having merely fallen out of fashion.

14 See, for example, *WCT*, 257 n. 20.

15 Steiner also described his philosophy as a form of objective idealism: "For us, the so-called experience that positivism and neo-Kantianism would so much like to present as the only sure thing is precisely the most subjective. And in showing this, we establish *objective idealism* as the necessary consequence of an epistemology that understands itself" (Steiner 1993, 1). Barfield also described Steiner as defending "objective idealism" (*RCA* 313).

16 Beyond providing Barfield a means to articulate his own metaphysic, Barfield's account of Coleridge helps to recover Coleridge for the post-Kantian idealist movement as a whole, in alignment with Beiser's understanding of the history of the movement: "The subjective played a diminishing role in German idealism as the post-Kantian idealists realized that the Kantian transcendental subject plays a residual role in the constitution of experience, whose objectivity ultimately depends upon its universal and necessary normative structure. The history of German idealism is therefore more the story about the progressive unfolding of neo-Platonism. Ironically, its ultimate heirs were the Marburg neo-Kantians Hermann Cohen, Paul Natorp, and Ernst Cassirer" (Beiser 2002, 6).

17 For a good orientation to transcendental deduction as a form of argument, see Stern. My own thinking has been most informed by an essay by Charles Taylor, "The Validity of Transcendental Arguments," which Stern does not include in his bibliography: See Charles Taylor (1995, 20–33). Taylor is especially useful because he sees transcendental argumentation at work in late Wittgenstein, Heidegger,

and Merleau-Ponty in ways that parallel typical Barfieldian methods of argument as well. Taylor's conclusion is that "transcendental arguments turn out to be quite paradoxical things" because "they prove something quite strong about the subject of experience and the subject's place in the world; and yet since they are grounded in the nature of experience, there remains an ultimate, ontological question they can't foreclose" (Taylor 1995, 33). As we shall see, this is consistent with Barfield's view that polarity resists final deduction and that it can only be grasped in the end by "intuitive penetration" or imagination.

18 It is worth noting the full context of Corbin's definition, as the author of *Saving the Appearances* must have become very alert when he read it: "Let us look . . . at the course of action which phenomenological enquiry accomplishes. It is connected essentially with the motto of Greek science: *sôzein tà phainómena*, saving the appearances. What does this mean? The phenomenon is that which shows itself, that which is apparent and which in its appearance shows forth something which can reveal itself therein only by remaining concealed beneath the appearance. Something shows itself in the phenomenon and can show itself there only by remaining hidden. In the philosophical and religious sciences the *phenomenon* presents itself in those technical terms in which the element '-phany' from the Greek, figures: epiphany, theophany, hierophany, etc. The phenomenon, the Greek *phainómenon*, is the zâhir, the apparent, the external, the exoteric. What shows itself within this *zâhir*, while itself remaining concealed, is the *bâtin*, the interior, the esoteric. Phenomenology consists in 'saving the appearance', saving the phenomenon, while disengaging or unveiling the hidden which shows itself beneath the appearance. The *Logos* or principle of the phenomenon, phenomenology, is thus to tell the hidden, the invisible present beneath the visible" (Corbin 4–5).

Chapter 4

1 Barfield collected many but not all of the articles that supplement and lead to *Saving the Appearances* in *Romanticism Comes of Age*, which Barfield dedicated to "my many friends in the Anthroposophical Movement."
2 For an introductory, by no means exhaustive, account of Modernist interest in esotericism, see Surette (1993).
3 The etheric, astral, and I bodies are similar Aristotle's delineation of nutritive, sensitive, and rational souls, respectively.
4 For an informative overview of Steiner and Anthroposophy, see McDermott (1995). For a selection of Steiner's writings with a helpful introduction by McDermott, see Steiner (2009). For a dense and substantial overview, see Easton (1982).
5 When the essay was collected in *Romanticism Comes of Age*, Barfield changed the title to "Speech, Reason and Imagination."

6 Steiner's terms for the threefold soul are sentient, intellectual (or mind), and consciousness. They correlate with three eras in the evolution of consciousness.
7 Barfield split the essay into "On the Consciousness Soul" and "On the Intellectual Soul," placing his essay on *Hamlet* in between them, when he published *Romanticism Comes of Age*.
8 Easton says that "what makes eurythmy a new art, totally different from dancing, even dancing that makes extensive use of the hands and arms . . . is that it is speech and music *made visible*, using the human being himself as their instrument" (Easton 253).
9 Barfield's use of the term "Imaginative Soul" presumably refers to Steiner's use of it: "in the person who is developing spiritually, the consciousness soul is being changed into the *imagination soul*" (Steiner 1997, 193).
10 For a classic analysis of how this regress appears within, and remains unresolved by, German idealism, see Henrich.
11 The present victory of materialism coincides with the present "rulership" of Michael because nonparticipation is the condition for free thinking implicit in final participation. Michael, in other words, is a fitting symbol for the resurrection of thinking in the form of imagination.
12 There is some indication that Eliot would not have put Steiner in Yeats's company with mediums and palm readers. Perhaps under the partial influence of Barfield and Ernst Lehrs, Eliot claimed that "I think the present time will spontaneously lead to something like the separation of individual human beings from time's events. They will stand on their own feet, and from their innermost being they will seek new paths, spiritual paths. It seems to me that Goethe, for example, had a compass of consciousness which far surpassed that of his nineteenth-century contemporaries. Rudolf Steiner expressly upheld this, and I do too. In a certain connection, atomic science has a meaning, namely inasmuch as it is in the hands of men who are in no way able to cope with it. It has no importance whatsoever for the progress of mankind. I see the path of progress for modern man in his occupation with his own self, with his inner being, as indicated by Rudolf Steiner" (quoted in Wilson 335n).
13 Barfield's enduring fascination with the Middle Ages is further confirmation of Umberto Eco's thesis that "modern ages have revisited the Middle Ages from the moment when, according to historical books, they came to an end" (Eco 65), and that these returns typically occur during periods of sociocultural crisis or transition (Eco 74).

Chapter 5

1 During the "Great War" with C. S. Lewis, Barfield distinguished his definition of truth from that of his friend: "To me it is not a sort of accurate copy or reflection

of something, but it is reality itself taking the form of human consciousness....
This inspiration-imagination is, for me, the source of *meaning*. I am not quite sure what relation you postulate between *truth* and *meaning*, but I suggest that it is the existence of meaning which discriminates truth from truism" (Feinendegen & Smilde 44, 48).

2   See, among many others: MacIntyre (1981), Dupré (2005), Charles Taylor (2007), and Pfau (2013).

3   In 1938, Barfield wrote to the editor of *The Spectator*:

>   A morning and an evening paper of different political complexions both assure me that the "plan" agreed on between Mr. Chamberlain and M. Daladier is complete surrender to Hitler. Not only is the Sudetenland to be ceded to Germany but Czecholovakia [*sic*] is to be compelled to sever her alliance with Russia with the object (for what other is conceivable?) of placing her wholly at the mercy of her new "guarantor." I suppose it must be true. I am still rubbing my eyes, as I am one of those who had retained the belief that there were depths below which this country would not sink. I now see that the abyss is bottomless.
>
>   Hitherto I have not been a pacifist, but I take it that for every Englishman who is also a Christian the pacifist case is henceforth proved. It must be the duty of a Christian to be willing to die; it *may* be his duty to kill (even by modern methods) in order that wrong may not prevail. To flatter violence, acquiesce in fraud and aid extortion for the purpose of avoiding these evils and afterwards to face up to them in the cold cause of self-preservation may be the instinct of an animal. Only a lunatic could imagine it to be his duty. (Barfield 1938a, 482)

4   "Death" was published for the first time in 2008 but was written in 1930 with a view to publication in Eliot's *Criterion* as "one of 'a series of six or seven essays of predominantly ethical character'" (Barfield 2008, 45).

5   Barfield undoubtedly found the word "coinherence," which would later be a key term in Charles Williams's writings, in Coleridge's *Biographia Literaria*: "For to us the self-consciousness is not a kind of *being*, but a kind of *knowing*, and that too the highest and farthest that exists for *us*. It may however be shown ... that even when the Objective is assumed as the first, we yet can never pass beyond the principle of self-consciousness.... Or we must break off the series arbitrarily, and affirm an absolute something that is in and of itself at once cause and effect ... or rather the absolute identity of both.... [W]e must arrive at the same principle from which as transcendental philosophers we set out; that is, in a self-consciousness in which the principium essendi does not stand to the principium cognoscendi in the relation of cause to effect, but both the one and the other are co-inherent and identical" (Coleridge 1983 1, 285). Barfield here deploys the term in the spirit of the "Essay on Faith," to apply to the "I-Thou" relationship that is also the polarized form of the Absolute.

6   For Solovyov's debt to Hegel, one might start with Alexandre Kojève's *The Religious Metaphysics of Vladimir Solovyov*, which is of historical interest in its own right.

7 Barfield would undoubtedly take a great interest in the way that today the meaning of "equality" is being absorbed into "equity."
8 The implications of this sort of identity for Barfield's reflections on love and selfhood are obvious and compelling—in the end, as we have seen, self-identity is anything but simple, as it either metamorphoses into A = B, I = Thou or withers on the vine due to alienation. For the metaphysics of the self, numerical identity proves illusory.
9 Barfield follows Steiner's argument that the distribution of labor in the modern global economy entails that each individual works for the benefit of others, not for themselves: tailors make suits for others, not themselves, using thread made for them by others who do not purchase it themselves. Barfield and Steiner describe this as a kind of unconscious altruism, with the proviso that the motivation is not strictly generous.

Chapter 6

1 See Stough.
2 See the appendix at the end of this chapter for the complete published Burgeon poems. Barfield wrote many other implicit and explicit "Betty" poems that he did not publish, now in the Barfield papers at the Bodleian Library.
3 Marvell's poem was on Barfield's mind as he wrote "Poetic Diction and Legal Fiction" (*RM* 50).
4 Menippean satire is notoriously difficult to define, and proposed examples of the genre most often tend to share in common the controversy of their inclusion. Barfield never opined about the genre and of course cannot have known what Frye or Bakhtin had to say about it, predating the former and unaware of the latter, who was then still untranslated. For useful introductory comments on the genre, see: Frye (22, 289–92) and Bakhtin (112–22). For a more recent treatment that reflects the continued influence of Frye and Bakhtin and that discusses many works well known to Barfield, see Weinbrot. As with the role of Kierkegaard, I am interested in affinity, not influence.
5 Roger Poole outlines the reception of Kierkegaard through French and German Existentialism. He also notes that Charles Williams, a prominent member of the Inklings, enlisted Alexander Dru and Walter Lowrie to translate Kierkegaard and thus was directly responsible for the appearance in English during the 1940s of Kierkegaard's major works. See Poole. See also Lindop (243–4).
6 Regarding the Pauline provenance of Kierkegaard's thought, it is perhaps worth remembering that Kierkegaard derives the title of *Fear and Trembling* from Saint Paul: "Wherefore, my beloved, as ye have always obeyed, not as in my presence only, but now much more in my absence, work out your own salvation with fear and

trembling. For it is God which worketh in you both to will and to do of his good pleasure" (Philippians 2:12-13).

7 *Either-Or* has multiple levels of pseudonymous authorship: the book was published under a pseudonym, "Victor Eremita," and each of the book's two parts has a different author. The first, aesthetic, part is a manuscript by "A" that is "discovered" by Eremita, while Part Two, on the ethical, consists of two letters addressed to "A" by "Judge Vilhelm," which attempt to convince the aesthete of his errors. Granting the ethical voice to a representative of the law obviously dovetails with *This Ever Diverse Pair*, satirized in this case by the pedantic and misanthropic Burden. I cite the Swensons's translation, which is no longer standard but was the version used by Barfield.

8 In this respect, Burgeon and Burden also remind one of two characters in Blake's prophetic poems, Los and his Spectre, as well as Prometheus and Jupiter from Shelley's *Prometheus Unbound*, albeit in the mode of satire rather than mythopoeic prophecy.

9 The reference to Goethe's *Faust* recalls the bookplate Josephine Spence made for Barfield that includes the line "Zwei Seelen wohnen ach! in meiner Brust."

10 One is reminded of the distinction Kant and the Romantic generation made, of which Barfield was no doubt aware, between the "agreeable" and the "beautiful," along the sliding scale of the aesthetic.

11 I designate this character as "Owen Barfield" throughout my discussion.

12 When I say that a character says or does something, it is always implicit that "Owen Barfield" arranges the dialogue and describes the action in that way, but it would be too cumbersome to make that observation in every instance.

13 Barfield was well aware, from Steiner's *Christianity as Mystical Fact* and elsewhere, that the conventional period of initiation was three days, at the end of which should occur a kind of "resurrection" into a new way of being, though this was not the invariable result. Barfield's three plays *Orpheus*, *Medea*, and *Angels at Bay* dramatize successful, failed, and ambivalent initiations, respectively. For Barfield's attestation to the importance to him of Steiner's book, see Schenkel (26). See also Steiner (2006, 1–14) for an account of initiation that resonates with Barfield's use of it throughout the Burgeon trilogy.

14 See Barfield (1976) for Barfield's interest in Ficino.

15 It is worth recalling that Barfield does the same when he distinguishes between medieval allegory and the modern symbol: "the essence of symbolism is, not that words or names, as such, but the things or events themselves, are apprehended as representations. But this . . . is the normal way of apprehension for a participating consciousness. *Our* "symbolical" therefore is an approximation to, or a variant of, *their* "literal." Even when they got down to the bedrock of literal, they still experienced that rock as a representation" (*SA* 87). This, we recall, is what Barfield most wanted readers to glean from *Saving the Appearances*.

16 See Harrison (165). See also Copley (95).
17 Barfield's characterization of the increasingly intimate, yet always distinct, thoughts and voices of Burgeon and the Meggid derives in many details from R. J. Zwi Werblowsky's *Joseph Karo, Lawyer and Mystic*, as the narrator himself notes. For example, the Maggid's visits to Karo take the form of question and answer (Werblowsky 53). The Maggid primarily imparts knowledge (Werblowsky 289) and never exceeds Karo's ordinary capacities (Werblowsky 289). The Maggid speaks to Karo "in thy mouth" while he is wide awake (Werblowsky 259) about "the doctrines of metempsychosis (*gilgul*) and of world-cycles (*shemittoth*); there was angelology and demonology" (Werblowsky 189). The Maggid favors early morning visitations (Werblowsky 257) and speaks in a manner tailored to Karo's individual mind (Werblowsky 263).
18 Burgeon would have done well to remember that the Maggid presented itself to Karo as both the Shekhinah (the feminine aspect of the Godhead) and the Logos (Werblowsky 268). Barfield made a careful note of this in the margins of his personal copy of Werblowsky book.
19 Because of this ambiguity, I refer to the voice as both "the Meggid" and "Anthroposophia" throughout this chapter.
20 The importance of this meditation for Barfield is attested by his many fruitless attempts to translate it, deciding in the end that he could not improve on the version by his friend George Adams.
21 The microcosm-macrocosm understanding is true of Karo as well (Werblowsky 59).
22 Werblowsky defines the Shekhinah in a way that resonates with the themes of *Unancestral Voice*: "There exists, of course, also the more usual type of mysticism in which the intense love of the soul for God assumes definitely erotic qualities. Where both motives, that of the theurgic unification of God with his *Shekhinah* and that of a personal communion with God in his personal, accessible, i.e. "feminine," aspect of the *Shekhinah mediatrix*, merge, as they did in sixteenth-century Safed, the result is a mysticism full of dialectical richness" (Werblowsky 134–5).
23 This contradicts a passage about Karo that Barfield scored in his copy: Karo's mystical life did not spill over into his daytime activities (Werblowsky 286).
24 So too, in a passage marked by Barfield, Werblowsky notes that the Maggid speaks words of wisdom *within* Karo (Werblowsky 80).
25 Barfield also refers to Paul's complex use of *energeia* in a lecture given in 1958. See *RM* 256.

Bibliography

Adams, Hazard. *The Book of Yeats's Vision: Romantic Modernism and Antithetical Tradition*. Ann Arbor: University of Michigan Press, 1996.
Adey, Lionel. *C. S. Lewis' 'Great War' with Owen Barfield*. Victoria: Ink Books, 2002.
Bakhtin, Mikhail. *Problems in Dostoevsky's Poetics*. Edited and translated by Caryl Emerson. St. Paul: University of Minnesota Press, 1984.
Barfield, Owen. "Form in Poetry." *The New Statesman*, August 7, 1920a, 501–2.
Barfield, Owen. "The Reader's Eye." *The Cornhill Magazine* 49 (September 1920b): 327–31.
Barfield, Owen. "Ballads." *The New Statesman*, October 2, 1920c, 701–2.
Barfield, Owen. "John Clare." *The New Statesman*, December 25, 1920d, 371.
Barfield, Owen. "Walter de la Mare." *The New Statesman*, November 6, 1920e, 140–2.
Barfield, Owen. "The Silent Voice of Poetry." *The New Statesman* 16 (January 15, 1921a): 448–9.
Barfield, Owen. "George Santayana." *The New Statesman* 16 (March 26, 1921b): 216–17.
Barfield, Owen. "Boswell." *The New Statesman* 17 (August 13, 1921c): 520.
Barfield, Owen. "The Fourteenth Century." *The New Statesman* 18 (October 22, 1921d): 78.
Barfield, Owen. "Some Elements of Decadence." *The New Statesman* 18 (December 24, 1921e): 244–5.
Barfield, Owen. "Idiom." *The New Statesman* 21 (June 30, 1923a): 368, 370.
Barfield, Owen. "Drama." *London Mercury* 8, no. 45 (July 1923b): 326–9.
Barfield, Owen. "Milton and Metaphysics." *The New Statesman* 21 (August 11, 1923c): 524–5.
Barfield, Owen. "Romanticism and Anthroposophy." *Anthroposophy* 1 (Easter 1926): 111–24.
Barfield, Owen. "An Introduction to Anthroposophy." *Anthroposophy: A Quarterly Review of Spiritual Science* 5, no. 1 (Easter 1930a): 58–80.
Barfield, Owen. "Psychology and Reason." *The Criterion: A Quarterly Review* 9 (July 1930b): 606–17.
Barfield, Owen. "Review of Geoffrey West's *Deucalion—Or the Future of Literary Criticism*." *Spiritual Science: A Monthly Review of Anthroposophical Thought and Activity* 1 (November 1930c): 8–10.
Barfield, Owen. "Rudolf Steiner and English Poetry." *Anthroposophical Movement* 9 (May 12, 1932a): 77–9.
Barfield, Owen. "Equity." *Anthroposophy: A Quarterly Review of Spiritual Science* 7, no. 2 (Midsummer 1932b): 134–56.

Barfield, Owen. "Destroyer and Preserver." *Anthroposophical Movement* 9, no. 18 (September 15, 1932c): 145–7.

Barfield, Owen. "The Transitional Seasons." *Anthroposophical Movement* 10, no. 2 (January 26, 1933a): 10–12.

Barfield, Owen. "Style." *Anthroposophical Movement* 10, no. 11 (June 8, 1933b): 83–6.

Barfield, Owen. "The Crisis in Europe." *The Spectator*, September 23, 1938a, 482.

Barfield, Owen. "Betrayal." *The New Statesman*, September 24, 1938b, 452–3.

Barfield, Owen. "An Effective Approach to Social Change." *The Christian News-Letter*. *The Christian News-Letter* Supplement to No. 39 (July 24, 1940a): Unpaginated.

Barfield, Owen. "Panic and Its Opposite." *Anthroposophical Movement*, October 1940b, 1–2.

Barfield, Owen. "The Russet." *The New English Weekly: A Review of Public Affairs, Literature and the Arts* 29, no. 26 (October 10, 1946a): 217.

Barfield, Owen. "Semantics." *The New English Weekly: A Review of Public Affairs, Literature and the Arts* 30, no. 1 (October 17, 1946b): 6.

Barfield, Owen. "Tradition in Poetry." *The New English Weekly: A Review of Public Affairs, Literature and the Arts*. 30, no. 5 (November 14, 1946c): 47.

Barfield, Owen. "Cosmetics." *The New English Weekly: A Review of Public Affairs, Literature and the Arts*. 30, no. 22 (March 13, 1947a): 189.

Barfield, Owen. "The Doppelganger." *The New English Weekly: A Review of Public Affairs, Literature and the Arts* 31, no. 12 (July 3, 1947b): 105.

Barfield, Owen. "The Eurhythmist." *Anthroposophical Movement*, August 1952, 8.

Barfield, Owen. *History in English Words*, 2nd ed. London: Faber and Faber, 1954.

Barfield, Owen. "The Light of the World." *Supplement to Anthroposophical Movement*, February 1954a, 1–10.

Barfield, Owen. "The Art of Eurhythmy." *The Golden Blade*, 1954b, 53–62.

Barfield, Owen. "Israel and the Michael Impulse." *Anthroposophical Quarterly*, Spring 1956a, 2–9.

Barfield, Owen. "Walter de la Mare." *Anthroposophical Quarterly*, Autumn 1956b, 7–10.

Barfield, Owen. *Saving the Appearances: A Study in Idolatry*. London: Faber and Faber, 1957.

Barfield, Owen. "Towards a Science of Man." *Anthroposophical Quarterly*, Summer 1958, 7–8.

Barfield, Owen. "Editor's Preface." In *Anthroposophy: An Introduction*, edited by Rudolf Steiner, 7–12. London: Rudolf Steiner Press, 1960.

Barfield, Owen. "Rudolf Steiner (1861–1925)." *The Contemporary Review*, 1961a, 88–91.

Barfield, Owen. "Meditations and Meditation." *Anthroposophical Quarterly*, Autumn 1961b, 72–4.

Barfield, Owen. "Davy on Snow." *Anthroposophical Quarterly*, Spring 1962, 17–18.

Barfield, Owen. *Worlds Apart*. London: Faber and Faber, 1963.

Barfield, Owen. "The Riddle of the Sphinx." *Arena* 19 (April 1964): 121–8.

Barfield, Owen. *Unancestral Voice*. London: Faber and Faber, 1965.

Barfield, Owen. *Speaker's Meaning*. Middletown: Wesleyan University Press, 1967.
Barfield, Owen. "The Disappearing Trick." *The Golden Blade*, 1970a, 53–66.
Barfield, Owen. "Introduction." In *The Case for Anthroposophy Being Extracts from Von Seelenrätseln*, edited by Rudolf Steiner, 7–23. London: Rudolf Steiner Press, 1970b.
Barfield, Owen. "Coleridge Collected." Review of *Collected Works of Coleridge*, edited by Kathleen Coburn. *Encounter* 35 (November 1970c): 74–83.
Barfield, Owen. *What Coleridge Thought*. Middleton: Wesleyan University Press, 1971.
Barfield, Owen. "A Letter to the Editor." *The Listener*, September 28, 1972, 406.
Barfield, Owen. *Poetic Diction: A Study of Meaning*, 2nd ed. Middletown: Wesleyan University Press, 1973a.
Barfield, Owen. "Poetry in Walter de la Mare." *Denver Quarterly* 8 (Autumn 1973b): 69–81.
Barfield, Owen. "Coleridge's Enjoyment of Words." In *Coleridge's Variety: Bicentennial Studies*, edited by John Beer, 204–18. London: Macmillan, 1974.
Barfield, Owen. "Ficino and the Florentine Academy." *Anthroposophical Quarterly* 21, no 1 (Spring 1976): 14–16.
Barfield, Owen. *The Rediscovery of Meaning, and Other Essays*. Middletown: Wesleyan University Press, 1977.
Barfield, Owen. "Owen Barfield and the Origin of Language, Part 1." *Towards* 1, no. 2 (June 1978a): 1–7.
Barfield, Owen. "Owen Barfield and the Origin of Language, Part 2." *Towards* 1, no. 3 (December 1978b): 13–15.
Barfield, Owen. *History, Guilt, and Habit*. Middletown: Wesleyan University Press, 1979.
Barfield, Owen. "The Concept of Revelation." *VII: An Anglo-American Review* 1 (1980): 117–25.
Barfield, Owen. "Meaning, Revelation and Tradition in Language and Religion." *The Missouri Review* 5, no. 3 (Summer 1982): 117–28.
Barfield, Owen. "Introduction." In *The Meaning of Love*, edited by Vladimir Solovyov, 7–16. West Stockbridge: Lindisfarne Press, 1985.
Barfield, Owen. *Owen Barfield on C. S. Lewis*. Middletown: Wesleyan University Press, 1989.
Barfield, Owen. *A Barfield Sampler: Poetry and Fiction by Owen Barfield*, edited by Jeanne Clayton Hunter and Thomas Kranidas. Albany: SUNY Press, 1993.
Barfield, Owen. "Selections from Owen Barfield's Introduction and Notes." In *Lectures 1819-1819 on the History of Philosophy*, edited by Samuel Taylor Coleridge, 869–92. Princeton: Princeton University Press, 2000.
Barfield, Owen. "Death." *VII: An Anglo-American Literary Review*, 2008, 45–60.
Barfield, Owen. *This Ever Diverse Pair*, 3rd ed. Oxford: Barfield Press, 2010.
Barfield, Owen. *Romanticism Comes of Age*. Oxford: Barfield Press, 2012.
Beaney, Michael, ed. *The Oxford Handbook of the History of Analytical Philosophy*. Oxford: Oxford University Press, 2015.
Beer, Gilian. *The Romance*. London and New York: Routledge, 1970.

Beer, John, ed. *Coleridge's Variety: Bicentennial Studies*. London: Macmillan, 1974.

Behler, Ernst. *Irony and the Discourse of Modernity*. Seattle: University of Washington Press, 1990.

Beiser, Frederick. *German Idealism: The Struggle Against Subjectivism, 1781–1801*. Cambridge, MA: Harvard University Press, 2002.

Berlin, Isaiah. *The Crooked Timber of Humanity: Chapters in the History of Ideas*, edited by Henry Hardy. London: John Murray, 1990.

Berlin, Isaiah. *Three Critics of the Enlightenment: Vico, Herder, Hamann*, edited by Henry Hardy. Princeton: Princeton University Press, 2000.

Berlin, Isaiah. *Liberty*, edited by Henry Hardy. Oxford: Oxford University Press, 2002.

Blake, William. *The Complete Poetry and Prose of William Blake*, edited by David V. Erdman, Rev. ed. Berkeley: University of California Press, 1982.

Blaxland-de Lange, Simon. *Owen Barfield: Romanticism Comes of Age*, 2nd ed. Forest Row: Temple Lodge, 2021.

Blunden, Edmund. "Literary Gossip." *Athenaeum* 4732 (January 7, 1921): 19.

Bradbury, Malcom and James McFarlane, eds. *Modernism: A Guide to European Literature, 1890–1930*. New York: Penguin Books, 1991.

Brooker, Jewel Spears, ed. *T. S. Eliot: The Contemporary Reviews*. Cambridge: Cambridge University Press, 2004.

Brooker, Jewel Spears. *T. S. Eliot's Dialectical Imagination*. Baltimore: Johns Hopkins University Press, 2018.

Bruns, Gerald. *Tragic Thoughts at the End of Philosophy*. Evanston: Northwestern University Press, 1999.

Bryant, Edwin F. and Laurie L. Patton, eds. *The Indo-Aryan Controversy: Evidence and Inference in Indian History*. London: Routledge, 2005.

Cassirer, Ernst. *The Myth of the State*. New Haven: Yale University Press, 1946.

Cassirer, Ernst. *The Philosophy of Symbolic Forms, Volume Two: Mythical Thought*. Translated by Ralph Manheim. New Haven: Yale University Press, 1955.

Cassirer, Ernst. *The Philosophy of Symbolic Forms, Volume Four: The Metaphysics of Symbolic Forms*. Translated by John Michael Krois. New Haven: Yale University Press, 1995.

Castle, Gregory. *Reading the Modernist Bildungsroman*. Gainesville: University Press of Florida, 2005.

Castle, Gregory. *A History of the Modernist Novel*. Cambridge: Cambridge University Press, 2015.

Christensen, Darrel E. and Manfred Riedel, et. al., eds. *Contemporary German Philosophy, Volume 1*. University Park: Pennsylvania State University Press, 1982.

Clark, Elizabeth A. *History, Theory, Text: Historians and the Linguistic Turn*. Cambridge, MA: Harvard University Press, 2004.

Coleridge, Samuel Taylor. *The Collected Works of Samuel Taylor Coleridge Volume 4: The Friend*. Edited by. Barbara E. Rooke. Princeton: Princeton University Press, 1969.

Coleridge, Samuel Taylor. *The Collected Works of Samuel Taylor Coleridge Volume 5: Lay Sermons*. Edited by R. J. White. Princeton: Princeton University Press, 1972.

Coleridge, Samuel Taylor. *The Collected Works of Samuel Taylor Coleridge Volume 7: Biographia Literaria*. Edited by James Engell and W. Jackson Bate, 2 vols. Princeton: Princeton University Press, 1983.

Coleridge, Samuel Taylor. *The Collected Works of Samuel Taylor Coleridge Volume 11: Shorter Works and Fragments*. Edited by H. J. Jackson and J. R. de J. Jackson. Princeton: Princeton University Press, 1995.

Coleridge, Samuel Taylor. *Lectures 1819-1819 on the History of Philosophy*. Princeton: Princeton University Press, 2000.

Collingwood, Robin George. *The Principles of Art*. Oxford: Oxford University Press, 1938.

Collingwood, Robin George. *An Autobiography*. Oxford: Oxford University Press, 1939.

Collingwood, Robin George. *An Essay on Metaphysics*. Oxford: The Clarendon Press, 1940.

Collingwood, Robin George. *The Idea of History*. Oxford: Oxford University Press, 1946.

Collis, J. S. *Farewell to Argument*. London: Cassell, 1935.

Copley, Anthony R. *A Spiritual Bloomsbury: Hinduism and Homosexuality in the Lives of Edward Carpenter, E. M. Forster, and Christopher Isherwood*. London: Lexington Books, 2006.

Corbin, Henri. *The Concept of Comparative Philosophy*. Translated by Peter Russell. Ipswich: Golgonooza Press, 1981.

Diener, Astrid. *The Role of Imagination in Culture and Society: Owen Barfield's Early Work*. Glienicke and Berlin: Galda + Wiilch Verlag, 2002.

Di Fuccia, Michael Vincent. *Owen Barfield: Philosophy, Poetry, and Theology*. Eugene: Cascade Books, 2016.

Dray, William H. *History as Re-Enactment: R. G. Collingwood's Idea of History*. Oxford: Oxford University Press, 1995.

Dupré, Louis. *The Enlightenment and the Intellectual Foundations of Modern Culture*. New Haven: Yale University Press, 2005.

Easton, Stewart C. *Man and World in the Light of Anthroposophy*. Spring Valley: Anthroposophic Press, 1982.

Eco, Umberto. *Faith in Fakes: Essays*. Translated by W. Weaver. London: Martin Secker and Warburg, 1986.

Eliade, Mircea. *Rites and Symbols of Initiation: The Mysteries of Birth and Rebirth*. Translated by Willard R. Trask. New York: Harper Colophon Books, 1958.

Eliade, Mircea. *Images and Symbols: Studies in Religious Symbolism*. Translated by Philip Mairet. New York: Sheed & Ward, 1961.

Eliot, Thomas Stearns. *The Letters of T. S. Eliot*. Edited by John Haffenden. Baltimore and London: Johns Hopkins University Press, 2009–.

Eliot, Thomas Stearns. *The Poems of T. S. Eliot*. Edited by Christopher Ricks and Jim McCue. Baltimore and London: Johns Hopkins University Press and Faber & Faber, 2015.

Eliot, Thomas Stearns. *The Complete Prose of T. S. Eliot: The Critical Edition*. Edited by Ronald Schuchard, 8 vols. Baltimore and London: Johns Hopkins University Press and Faber & Faber, 2021.

Faivre, Antoine and Jacob Needleman, eds. *Modern Esoteric Spirituality*. New York: Crossroad Publishing Company, 1995.

Feinendegen, Norbert and Arend Smilde, eds. *The "Great War" of Owen Barfield and C. S. Lewis: Philosophical Writings 1927–1930*. Inklings Studies Supplements, 2015.

Fischer, Luke. "Owen Barfield and Rudolf Steiner: The Poetic and Esoteric Imagination." *Literature and Aesthetics* 21, no. 1 (2011): 135–57.

Frye, Northrop. *The Collected Works of Northrop Frye*. Edited by Alvin A. Lee, 30 vols. Toronto: University of Toronto Press, 1996–2012.

Goldie, David. *The White Goddess: A Historical Grammar of Poetic Myth*. New York: Farrar, Strauss and Giroux, 1966.

Goldie, David. *A Critical Difference: T. S. Eliot and John Middleton Murry in English Literary Criticism, 1919–1928*. Oxford: Clarendon Press, 1998.

Goodman, Nelson. *Ways of Worldmaking*. Indianapolis: Hackett Publishing, 1978.

Graves, Robert. *Of English Poetry*. New York: Alfred A Knopf, 1922.

Griffin, Nicholas. "Russell and Moore's Revolt Against British Idealism." In *The Oxford Handbook of the History of Analytical Philosophy*, edited by Michael Beaney, 430–50. Oxford: Oxford University Press, 2015.

Groden, Michael, Martin Kreiswirth, and Imre Szeman, eds. *The Johns Hopkins Guide to Literary Theory and Criticism*. Baltimore: Johns Hopkins University Press, 2005.

Hannay, Alastair and Gordon D. Marino, eds. *The Cambridge Companion to Kierkegaard*. Cambridge: Cambridge University Press, 1998.

Harding, Jason. *The Criterion: Cultural Politics and Periodical Networks in Inter-War Britain*. Oxford: Oxford University Press, 2002.

Harrison, Andrew. *The Life of D. H. Lawrence*. London: Wiley Blackwell, 2016.

Hayman, David. *Ulysses: The Mechanics of Meaning*. Englewood Cliffs: Prentice-Hall, 1970.

Heidegger, Martin. *Being and Time*. Translated by John Macquarrie and Edward Robinson. Oxford: Blackwell, 1962.

Henrich, Dieter. "Fichte's Original Insight." Translated by David R. Lachterman. In *Contemporary German Philosophy, Volume 1*, edited by Darrel E. Christensen, et al., 15–53. University Park: Pennsylvania State University Press, 1982.

Kant, Immanuel. *Practical Philosophy*. Translated by Mary Gregor. Edited by Allen Wood. Cambridge: Cambridge University Press, 1996.

Keats, John. *The Letters of John Keats*. Edited by Hyder Edward Rollins, 2 vols. Cambridge, MA: Harvard University Press, 1958.

Keats, John. *The Poems of John Keats*. Edited by Jack Stillinger. Cambridge, MA: Harvard University Press, 1978.

Kelley, Donald R. *The Descent of Ideas: The History of Intellectual History*. Aldershot: Ashgate, 2002.

Kelly, John. "Eliot and Yeats." *The Yeats Annual* 20 (2016): 179–228.

Kennedy, Sarah. *T. S. Eliot and the Dynamic Imagination*. Cambridge: Cambridge University Press, 2018.

Kenner, Hugh. *The Poetry of Ezra Pound*. London: Faber & Faber, 1951.

Kermode, Frank. *Romantic Image*. London: Routledge, 1957.

Kierkegaard, Søren. *Either/Or*. Translated by Walter Lowrie, 2 vols. New York: Doubleday Anchor, 1959.

Kierkegaard, Søren. *Concluding Unscientific Postscript*. Translated by Walter Lowrie and David Swenson. Princeton: Princeton University Press, 1963.

Kierkegaard, Søren. *Fear and Trembling and The Sickness unto Death*. Translated by Walter Lowrie. Princeton University Press, 2013 [1941].

Kojève, Alexandre. *The Religious Metaphysics of Vladimir Solovyov*. Translated by Ilya Merlin and Mikhail Pozdniakov. New York: Palgrave Macmillan, 2018.

Lawrence, D. H. *Selected Literary Criticism*. New York: Viking, 1956.

Lawrence, D. H. *Lady Chatterley's Lover*. New York: Grove Press, 1959.

Lawrence, D. H. *Apocalypse*. New York: Penguin Classics, 1976.

Leavis, F. R. *Two Cultures? The Significance of C. P. Snow*. London: Chatto & Windus, 1962.

Lewis, Clive Staples. *Christian Reflections*. Edited by Walter Hooper. Grand Rapids: William B. Eerdmans Publishing Company, 1967.

Lewis, Clive Staples. *The Abolition of Man*. New York: HarperOne, 2001 [1944].

Lewis, Clive Staples. *The Collected Letters of C. S. Lewis, Volume 3: Narnia, Cambridge, and Joy, 1950–1963*. Edited by Walter Hooper. New York: HarperCollins, 2007.

Lindop, Grevel. *Charles Williams: The Third Inkling*. Oxford: Oxford University Press, 2015.

Lissau, Rudi. *Rudolf Steiner: His Life, Work, Inner Path and Social Initiatives*. Gloucestershire: Hawthorne Press, 2005.

Locke, John. *Essay Concerning Human Understanding*. Oxford: Clarendon Press, 1975.

Longenbach, James. *Stone Cottage: Pound, Yeats, and Modernism*. Oxford: Oxford University Press, 1988.

Lovejoy, Arthur O. *The Revolt Against Dualism: An Inquiry Concerning the Existence of Ideas*. New York: Open Court, 1930.

MacIntyre, Alasdair. "Précis of Whose Justice? Which Rationality." *Philosophy and Phenomenological Research* 51, no. 1 (March 1991): 149–52.

MacIntyre, Alasdair. *After Virtue*, 3rd ed. South Bend: University of Notre Dame Press, 2007 [1981].

Maddelena, Giovanni. "Owen Barfield, the Inklings and Pragmatism." *Journal of Inklings Studies* 2, no. 2 (December 2017): 67–88.

Marcel, Gabriel. *The Philosophy of Existentialism*. Translated by Manya Harari. New York: The Philosophical Library, 1956.

Marksey, R. "The History of Ideas at 80." *Modern Language Notes* 117 (2002): 1083–97.

McDermott, Robert. "Rudolf Steiner and Anthroposophy." In *Modern Esoteric Spirituality*, edited by Antoine Faivre and Jacob Needleman. New York: Crossroad Publishing Company, 1995.

Mead, G. R. S. *Quests Old and New*. London: G. Bell & Sons, Ltd., 1913.

Moran, Dermot. *Introduction to Phenomenology*. London and New York: Routledge, 2000.

Murry, J. Middleton. *Aspects of Literature*. New York: Alfred A. Knopf, 1920.

Norris, Christopher. *New Idols of the Cave: On the Limits of Anti-Realism*. Manchester: Manchester University Press, 1997.

Nussbaum, Martha. *Love's Knowledge*. Oxford: Oxford University Press, 1992.

Perry, Seamus. "Eliot and Coleridge." In *Coleridge's Afterlives*, edited by James Vigus and Jane Wright, 224–51. New York: Palgrave Macmillan, 2008.

Pfau, Thomas. *Minding the Modern: Human Agency, Intellectual Traditions, and Responsible Knowledge*. Notre Dame: University of Notre Dame Press, 2013.

Pittman, Allen. "Saving the Final Appearance: A Visit with Owen Barfield." *Rudolf Steiner Library Newsletter*, 1999, 8–11.

Poole, Roger. "The Unknown Kierkegaard: Twentieth-Century Receptions." In *The Cambridge Companion to Kierkegaard*, edited by Alastair Hannay and Gordon D. Marino, 48–75. Cambridge: Cambridge University Press, 1998.

Pound, Ezra. *Make It New*. London: Faber and Faber, 1934.

Pound, Ezra. *Personae: Collected Shorter Poems of Ezra Pound*. London: Faber and Faber, 1952.

Richards, I. A. *The Principles of Literary Criticism*. London and New York: Routledge & Kegan Paul, 2001.

Richardson, Joanna. *Baudelaire*. New York: St. Martin's Press, 1994.

Ricoeur, Paul. *Time and Narrative, Volume 1*. Translated by Kathleen McLaughlin and David Pellauer. Chicago: University of Chicago Press, 1984.

Rorty, Richard M. Ed. *The Linguistic Turn: Essays in Philosophical Method*. Chicago: University of Chicago Press, 1967.

Rosenbaum, S. P. *Victorian Bloomsbury: The Early Literary History of the Bloomsbury Group*. New York: Palgrave Macmillan 1987.

Schenkel, Elmar. "Owen Barfield: Interview with Elmar Schenkel, September, 1991." *Old Crow*, 1993, no pagination.

Searle, Leroy. "The New Criticism." In *The Johns Hopkins Guide to Literary Theory and Criticism*, edited by Michael Groden, Martin Kreiswirth, and Imre Szeman, 691–8. Baltimore: Johns Hopkins University Press, 2005.

Shelley, Percy Bysshe. *Selected Poems and Prose*. Edited by Jack Donovan and Cian Duffy. New York: Penguin Classics, 2016.

Sheppard, Richard. "The Crisis of Language." In *Modernism: A Guide to European Literature, 1890–1930*, edited by Malcom Bradbury and James McFarlane, 323–36. New York: Penguin Books, 1991.
Skagestad, Peter. "Collingwood and Berlin: A Comparison." *Journal of the History of Ideas* 66, no. 1 (January 2005): 99–112.
Smith, Logan Pearsall. *The English Language*. London: Oxford University Press, 1912.
Smith, Logan Pearsall. *Words and Idioms: Studies in the English Language*. London: Constable & Company, 1925.
Solovyov, Vladimir. *The Meaning of Love*. Translated and Edited Thomas Beyer. West Stockbridge: Lindisfarne Press, 1985.
Steiner, Rudolf. *Theosophy*. Translated by E. D. S. Chicago and New York: Rand McNally & Company, 1910.
Steiner, Rudolf. *Anthroposophy: An Introduction*, Rev. 2nd ed. Edited by Owen Barfield. Translated by V. C. B. London: Rudolf Steiner Press, 1960.
Steiner, Rudolf. *The Philosophy of Freedom: The Basis for a Modern World Conception*. Translated by Michael Wilson. London: Rudolf Steiner Press, 1964.
Steiner, Rudolf. *The Stages of Higher Knowledge*. Translated by Lisa Monges and Floyd McKnight. Spring Valley: Anthroposophic Press, 1967.
Steiner, Rudolf. *The Case for Anthroposophy Being Extracts from Von Seelenrätseln*. Edited and Translated by Owen Barfield. London: Rudolf Steiner Press, 1970.
Steiner, Rudolf. *Anthroposophical Leading Thoughts: Anthroposophy as a Path of Knowledge*. London: Rudolf Steiner Press, 1973.
Steiner, Rudolf. *The Christmas Conference: For the Foundation of the General Anthroposophical Society, 1923/1924*. Translated by Johanna Collis and Michael Wilson. Spring Valley: Anthroposophic Press, 1990.
Steiner, Rudolf. *Truth and Science*. Translated by William Lindeman. Spring Valley: Mercury Press, 1993.
Steiner, Rudolf. *The Four Seasons and the Archangels*. Translated by Pauline Wehrle. Forest Row: Rudolf Steiner Press, 1996a.
Steiner, Rudolf. *Riddles of the Soul*. Translated by William Lindeman. Spring Valley: Mercury Press, 1996b.
Steiner, Rudolf. *The Effects of Esoteric Development*. Translated by Jann Gates and Christopher Bamford. Hudson: Anthroposophic Press, 1997.
Steiner, Rudolf. *Towards Social Renewal*. Translated by Matthew Barton. Forest Row: Rudolf Steiner Press, 1999.
Steiner, Rudolf. *Rosicrucian Wisdom: An Introduction*. Translated by J. Collis. Forest Row: Rudolf Steiner Press, 2000.
Steiner, Rudolf. *Christianity as Mystical Fact*. Great Barrington: SteinerBooks, 2006.
Steiner, Rudolf. *Goethe's Theory of Knowledge: An Outline of the Epistemology of His Worldview*. Translated by Peter Clemm. Great Barrington: SteinerBooks, 2008.
Steiner, Rudolf. *The New Essential Steiner: An Introduction to Rudolf Steiner for the 21st Century*. Edited by Robert McDermott. Spring Valley: SteinerBooks, 2009.

Stern, Robert. "Transcendental Arguments." *The Stanford Encyclopedia of Philosophy*. https://plato.stanford.edu/entries/transcendental-arguments/ (accessed June 1, 2021).

Stough, Christina C. "The Skirmish of Pound and Eliot in 'The New English Weekly': A Glimpse of Their Later Literary Relationship." *Journal of Modern Literature* 10, no. 2 (June 1983): 231–46.

Sugarman, Shirley. "A Conversation with Owen Barfield." In *Evolution of Consciousness: Studies in Polarity*, edited by Shirley Sugarman, 3–30. Middletown: Wesleyan University Press, 1976a.

Sugarman, Shirley, ed. *Evolution of Consciousness: Studies in Polarity*. Middletown: Wesleyan University Press, 1976b.

Surette, Leon. *The Birth of Modernism: Ezra Pound, T. S. Eliot, W. B. Yeats, and the Occult*. Montreal: McGill-Queen's University Press, 1993.

Taylor, Charles. *Philosophical Arguments*. Cambridge, MA: Harvard University Press, 1995.

Taylor, Charles. *Modern Social Imaginaries*. Durham and London: Duke University Press, 2004.

Taylor, Charles. *A Secular Age*. Cambridge, MA: Harvard University Press, 2007.

Valery, Paul. *Leonardo, Poe, Mallarmé*. Translated by Malcolm Cowley and James Lawler. London: Routledge, 1972.

Veeser, H. Aram, ed. *The New Historicists*. New York: Routledge, 1994.

Verene, Donald. "Cassirer's Metaphysics." In *The Symbolic Construction of Reality: The Legacy of Ernst Cassirer*, edited by Jeffrey Andrew Barash, 93–103. Chicago: University of Chicago Press, 2008.

Vigus, James and Jane Wright, eds. *Coleridge's Afterlives*. London: Palgrave Macmillan, 2008.

Ward, Aileen. *The Unfurling of Entity: Metaphor in Poetic Theory*. New York: Garland, 1987.

Weinbrot, Howard D. *Menippean Satire Reconsidered: From Antiquity to the Eighteenth-Century*. Baltimore: Johns Hopkins Press, 2005.

Welburn, Andrew J. *Power and Self-Consciousness in the Poetry of Shelley*. London: Palgrave Macmillan, 1986.

Werblowsky, R. J. Zwi. *Joseph Karo, Lawyer and Mystic*. Oxford: Oxford University Press, 1962.

Wilson, Colin. *Beyond the Occult*. London: Bantam, 1988.

Wittgenstein, Ludwig. *Tractatus Logico-Philosophicus*. Translated by D. F. Pears and B. F. McGuinness. London and New York: Routledge, 1974 [1961].

Woolf, Virginia. *Roger Fry*. London: Hogarth Press, 1940.

Wordsworth, William. *The Prelude, or the Growth of the Poet's Mind*. Edited by Ernest de Selincourt. Oxford: Oxford University Press 1926.

Yeats, William Butler. *The Collected Works of W. B. Yeats*. Edited by Richard J. Finneran et al., 14 vols. Houndsmills: Macmillan, 1991–.

Zaleski, Philip and Carol Zaleski. *The Fellowship: The Literary Lives of the Inklings: J. R. R. Tolkien, C. S. Lewis, Charles Williams, and Owen Barfield*. New York: Farrar, Straus and Giroux, 2016.

Index

absolute presuppositions   60, 62, 65, 67, 71, 73
Adams, George   230 n.20
Adams, Hazard   2
Af Klint, Hilma   108
Ahriman   207–8, 211
Aldington, Richard   13, 220 n.12
alienation   12, 14, 47, 52, 71, 73, 86–7, 98, 126, 157–8, 161, 166, 168, 174, 178, 185, 198
alpha-thinking   130, 133
antecedent unity   13, 29, 75, 79, 85, 90, 93, 101, 107, 114, 132
anthroposophia   200–4, 206, 208, 210–11, 230 n.19
anthroposophy   51, 77, 83–6, 88, 100, 106–37, 200, 213, 224 n.4
anti-historicism   52–9
anxiety   52, 125, 138, 148, 166, 169, 175–6, 210
Aquinas, Saint Thomas   89, 152
Aristotle   22, 83, 116–17, 129, 143, 152, 158, 160, 225 n.1
   De Anima   151
   Nichomachean Ethics   151
Arnold, Matthew   12, 137
Auden, W. H.   2–3
Auerbach, Erich   3, 77, 105
authenticity   144, 175–9
Ayer, A. J.   57, 144, 184

Bachelard, Gaston   1
Bacon, Francis   25, 43, 116–17
Bakhtin, Mikhail   168, 228 n.4
Barfield, Owen
   Angels at Bay   144, 229 n.13
   "The Art of Eurhythmy"   122
   A Barfield Sampler   8
   "The Concept of Revelation"   102–4
   "Cosmetics"   167
   "Danger, Ugliness, and Waste"   137, 139

"Death"   143–7
"Decadence"   16
"Destroyer and Preserver"   143, 147–8
"The Devastated Area"   20
"Dope"   20, 39
"The Doppelganger"   167–8
Eager Spring   137, 190, 221 n.24
"Effective Approach to Social Change"   142
English People   121, 147, 177, 183, 193
"Equity between Man and Man"   164
"Form in Art and in Society"   154–7
"Form in Poetry"   8–9, 16–17
"The Form of *Hamlet*"   219 n.4
History, Guilt, and Habit   64–74
History in English Words   37–51, 69, 81, 83, 108, 118, 166, 220 n.12, 221 n.22
"Israel and the Michael Impulse"   122, 126–9
"Language and Discovery"   100
"The Light of the World"   111, 122–6, 129
"Man, Thought, and Nature"   212
"Matter, Imagination, and Spirit"   100
"Meaning, Revelation, and Tradition"   102, 104–6
Medea   229 n.13
"Milton and Metaphysics"   13, 16, 29, 41
"Of the Consciousness Soul"   120–1
Orpheus   183, 220 n.16, 229 n.13
"Panic and Its Opposite"   164
"Participation and Isolation: A Fresh Light on Present Discontents"   157
"The Philosophy of Samuel Tayler Coleridge"   143
Poetic Diction   15, 18–38, 45, 47, 49, 66–7, 77–8, 81, 83, 89, 118, 121,

188, 193, 199, 219 n.3, 219 n.9, 221 nn.22–23
"Poetic Diction and Legal Fiction"   164, 228 n.3
"The Psalms of David"   164
"The Reader's Eye"   16
The Rediscovery of Meaning   75
Riders on Pegasus   172, 183, 204, 208, 220 n.16
"Romanticism and Anthroposophy"   114–15
Romanticism Comes of Age   225 n.1, 225 n.4, 226 n.7
"Ruin"   20
"The Russet"   166
Saving the Appearances   30, 35, 38, 58, 69, 75, 108, 122, 126–36, 193, 212, 221 n.24, 222 n.2, 223 n.10, 225 n.1, 225 n.18
"Semantics"   166–7
"Seven Letters"   20, 137–8
"The Silent Voice of Poetry"   16–17
"Some Elements of Decadence"   9
Speaker's Meaning   64–74, 90
"Speech, Reason, and the Consciousness Soul"   118–20
"The Spiritual Basis of Fascism"   137, 139
"Style"   143, 148–9
"Thinking and Thought"   116–18
This Ever Diverse Pair   168–79, 181, 183, 192, 198, 206–7, 209–11, 213
"The Time-Philosophy of Rudolf Steiner"   86–9, 169
The Tower   50
"Tradition in Poetry"   166–7
Unancestral Voice   151, 181, 194–213, 230 n.22
The Unicorn   167, 172
What Coleridge Thought   85, 94–100, 103–4, 157
Worlds Apart   138, 180–94, 198, 206–7
Baudelaire, Charles   123, 187–8
Beckh, Hermann   114
behaviorism   21
Behler, Ernst   53
being   52, 63, 79, 92, 99–100, 132, 135, 146, 152

Bell, Clive   7, 16, 219 n.4
Bellow, Saul   3
Bely, Andrei   151
   Kotik Letaev   151
Benjamin, Walter   1
Berdyaev, Nikolai   64
Berlin, Isaiah   3–4, 52–3, 55–7, 60–1, 63, 65–6, 90, 158–9, 222 n.2
   "Historical Inevitability"   57–9
   "The Philosophical Ideas of Giambattista Vico"   222 n.2
   "Two Concepts of Liberty"   159
   Vico and Herder: Two Studies in the History of Ideas   222 n.2
beta-thinking   131, 134
Black, Max   7
Blake, William   3, 9, 11, 17, 20, 29, 34, 36, 109–10, 136, 140–1, 182–3, 229 n.8
   The Four Zoas   151
   Jerusalem   136, 140
   Milton   136, 140
Blavatsky, Helena   108, 195
   The Secret Doctrine   195
Bloom, Harold   2
Blumenberg, Hans   138
Bohm, David   2
Bosanquet, Bernard   84
Boswell, James   40
Bradley, F. H.   7, 84–5, 88
Brentano, Franz   78–9, 223 n.4
Brooker, Jewel Spears   220 n.12
Bruns, Gerald   150
Byron, Lord   9
   Don Juan   9
   Vision of Judgment   9

Campbell, Joseph   2
Camus, Albert   138
Carter, Frederick   195
   The Dragon of the Alchemists   195
Cartesianism   68, 71, 95–8, 101, 105, 113, 149, 155, 161
Cassirer, Ernst   3–4, 75, 77, 89–90, 92–3, 101–2, 105, 186, 193, 222 n.1, 223 n.7, 224 nn.11–13, 224 n.16
   An Essay on Man   90
   The Individual and the Cosmos in Renaissance Philosophy   91

Index

Language and Myth 91
*The Philosophy of Symbolic
    Forms* 90–1, 224 n.12
*The Platonic Renaissance in
    England* 91, 224 n.12
"Spirit and Life" 91
The Theory of Knowledge 224 n.12
Christ 87, 121, 136, 170–1, 200, 206,
    208, 211–13
  as transforming agent 199–200, 204,
    206–9, 211
Cohen, Hermann 224 n.16
Coleridge, S. T. 3–4, 9, 11, 17, 19, 22–5,
    35–6, 38, 41, 43, 49, 75–7, 83,
    86, 89, 102–3, 106, 114, 120,
    138, 143, 145, 151, 153, 156,
    179, 187, 193, 220 n.15, 220 n.17
  Biographia Literaria 154, 227 n.5
  "Essay on Faith" 227 n.5
  metaphysics 83–6, 94–102
  "On the Principles of Genial Criticism
    Concerning the Fine Arts" 154
  Statesman's Manual 104
collective habits 67, 70–2, 74, 95
Collingwood, R. G. 3–4, 13, 52, 55–7,
    60, 64–9, 73, 90
  Autobiography 63
  Essay on Metaphysics 63
  The Principles of Art 66
common sense. *See* collective habits
concrete thinking 22, 30–1, 34, 37,
    50, 112, 117, 119–20, 124, 193,
    199
conscience 46–7, 143, 145, 153, 175, 179
consciousness 7–9, 14–17, 19, 24–6,
    29–30, 34–7, 57, 59, 71, 88–90,
    96, 99, 103, 105, 121–2, 125,
    130, 144, 179, 190–1, 193, 199,
    207
  evolution of 7, 15, 37, 39, 41, 44, 57,
    64–74, 76, 80, 87, 89–90, 95,
    104, 111–12, 114, 116, 118, 121,
    131, 136, 137, 188–9, 198–9,
    202, 205
Corbin, Henri 2, 105, 225 n.18
cosmology 32, 37, 51, 77, 87, 96, 100,
    106–37, 164, 192, 194, 200, 207
criticism 12, 14, 17, 20–3, 25, 102
Croce, Benedetto 61

Darwinism 67–9, 71, 73, 103, 206
Davy, Charles 137–8
  Towards a Third Culture 137
death 143–7
De la Mare, Walter 2, 20
Descartes, Rene 68, 87–8, 95, 113, 157
devotion 46–8
Di Fuccia, Michael Vincent 223 n.3
Dilthey, Wilhelm 76
dissociation of sensibility 13, 15, 24,
    32, 50
Donne, John 13, 15, 220 n.12
Dostoevsky, Fyodor 147
Dray, William 62
dread 147–8, 168–9, 174, 176
Dryden, John 14
Dupré, Louis 138

Eco, Umberto 226 n.13
Eliade, Mircea 181
Eliot, T. S. 2–4, 7, 9–10, 12–15, 20,
    22–5, 27–30, 32–3, 35, 38–9,
    44, 48, 55, 115, 119, 128,
    137–8, 143, 156, 165, 219 n.5,
    220 n.12, 220 nn.18–19, 226
    n.12, 227 n.4
  Ara Vos Prec 9
  "Gerontion" 10
  "The Metaphysical Poets" 13, 28, 30
  "The Perfect Critic" 22
  The Sacred Wood 22
  "Ulysses, Order, and Myth" 35
epistemology 77–8, 82, 118, 129, 135,
    223 n.6
equality 139, 158–62, 228 n.7
equity 161, 164, 172–3, 175, 177–9, 228
    n.7
esotericism 110, 112, 123, 127–9, 131,
    195
eurythmy 122–3, 133
existentialism 3, 77, 86, 88–9, 102, 143,
    164–5, 179, 180, 185

faith 170–2, 174, 213
Fichte, J. G. 78, 91, 101, 159
Ficino, Marsilio 229 n.14
figuration 130–2, 134, 193
France, Anatole 27, 31
Fry, Roger 7

Frye, Northrop 1–2, 109–10, 168, 228 n.4
Funk, Robert 2

Gadamer, Hans-Georg 76
Gilson, Etienne 87, 152
Given, The 78–80, 84, 86, 223 nn.6–7
Goethe, J. W. 3, 9, 38, 75, 77–8, 82–5, 102, 107–8, 113, 147, 190, 224 n.12
   Faust 174, 229 n.9
Goodman, Nelson 76, 222 n.1
   Ways of Worldmaking 222 n.1
Graves, Robert 4, 7, 11, 112, 219 n.7
   On English Poetry 21, 219 n.7

Hardy, Thomas 11–12, 219 n.9
Hegel, G. W. F. 24, 27, 57, 61, 78, 80, 83, 91–2, 95, 101–2, 154, 159–60, 227 n.6
   Logic 92
Heidegger, Martin 1, 3–4, 52, 76, 79, 87–8, 92–3, 105, 107, 116, 138, 144, 147, 223 n.8, 224 n.17
   Die Frage nach der Technik 223 n.8
Heller, Erich 185
   The Disinherited Mind 185
Herder, J. G. 57–8, 160, 222 n.2
hermeneutics 15, 18, 34, 65, 76, 188
history of ideas 52, 55–6, 59–60, 68, 114, 118, 131
Hobbes, Thomas 27
Hume, David 4, 40, 129, 149–50, 158
Husserl, Edmund 79, 87, 89, 93, 223 nn.4–5
Huxley, Aldous 13

Ignatieff, Michael 56
imagination 18–19, 23–4, 27, 29, 34–6, 48, 50, 62, 72–3, 83, 84, 96, 100, 102–3, 106, 107–8, 110, 113–16, 120–1, 125, 134–7, 155, 183, 187, 189, 193, 199, 206–7, 213
   as clairvoyance 37, 83, 107–8
   moral imagination 137–43, 162
initiation 81, 125, 128, 149, 163, 181–2, 185, 191, 193–5, 209, 211–12
inspiration 115, 125, 135, 146
intuition 135

irony 148

Jacobi, F. H. 150
James, Henry 151, 184
   The Golden Bowl 151
Joyce, James 35, 220 n.20
   Ulysses 192
Judaism 127, 133–4
Jung, Carl 115, 186

Kandinsky, Wassily 108
Kant, Immanuel 4, 27, 78, 88, 91, 141, 149, 150, 154, 159–60, 224 n.12, 229 n.10
   categorical imperative 141, 147, 150
Kantianism 24, 27, 75, 78, 80, 90–1, 96, 98, 101, 105, 113, 159, 224 n.15
Keats, John 9, 14, 39
Kenner, Hugh 1
Kermode, Frank 13
Kierkegaard, Søren 147, 165, 169–70, 173–4, 176, 179, 191, 201, 210–11, 213, 228 n.5
   Concluding Unscientific Postscript 210
   Either-Or 169–70, 173, 179, 229 n.7
   Fear and Trembling 169–70, 228 n.6
   The Sickness Unto Death 169, 174, 176
Klee, Paul 108
Kojève, Alexandre 227 n.6
   The Metaphysics of Vladimir Solovyov 227 n.6

Langer, Suzanne 90, 186, 193
law 170
Lawrence, D. H. 3–4, 13, 20, 33, 35, 48–50, 108, 194, 196, 199, 201–6, 208, 210, 221 n.26
   Apocalypse 194–6, 199
   Fantasia of the Unconscious 13
   Lady Chatterley's Lover 195
   New Poems 32
   Women in Love 195
Lehrs, Ernst 226 n.12
Leibniz, G. W. 101, 113
Lewis, C. S. 2, 4, 20, 38, 47, 52–6, 65, 90, 138, 146, 172, 184, 226 n.1
   The Abolition of Man 137, 151, 153

The Allegory of Love 47
Lewis, Wyndham 220 n.12
liberty 158–62
life 10, 16, 30, 32–3, 35, 49, 78, 85, 91–3, 95–6, 99, 101, 111, 113, 132
literalism 70, 110, 112, 133–6, 140, 190–1, 212
Locke, John 27–9, 31, 47, 88, 188
logic 27–8, 85, 87, 97–100, 110, 116, 119–20, 132, 156
logomorphism 15, 67
Logos, The 85–6, 93, 116, 120, 123, 125–6, 132–5, 196–8, 202, 204, 211, 225 n.18
love 47–9, 139, 146, 147, 155, 201, 213, 221 n.24, 228 n.8
Lovejoy, I. A. 4, 52, 59–61, 65–6, 68, 90
Lucifer 207–9, 211
Lukacs, John 2
Lyell, Charles 68–9

MacIntyre, Alasdair 138, 149–51, 154, 158
macrocosm/microcosm 84–5, 87, 113–14, 120–1, 123, 136, 154, 190, 196, 201, 205–6, 213, 230 n.21
Maddelena, Giovanni 221 n.25
Marcel, Gabriel 2–3, 77, 165, 169, 223 n.10
Marvell, Andrew 166, 228 n.3
  "The Garden" 166
Marx, Karl 160
Masefield, John 9
matter 10, 46, 48, 59, 68, 94–5, 100–1, 103, 107, 110, 113, 126, 190
Mead, G. R. S. 108
meaning 7, 21–2, 27, 30, 34–7, 51, 81, 88, 90–1, 104–5, 120–1, 136, 146, 173, 177–80
mechanism 48, 70–1, 85, 88, 111, 133
Merleu-Ponty, Maurice 76, 225 n.17
metaphor 21, 25, 35–7, 43–4, 47, 100, 107, 110–11, 116, 120, 131, 146–8, 155–6, 190
metaphysics 14–15, 25, 33, 51, 56, 63, 67–8, 73, 75–107, 113–14, 116–18, 120, 125, 129, 131, 136, 152, 164, 194, 200, 220 n.15

Milton, John 13–15
Paradise Lost 166
Moore, G. E. 88, 149–50
Principia Ethica 150
moral philosophy 137–57
Muirhead, J. H. 83, 85
Müller, Max 27–8, 31, 66
Murry, John Middleton 4, 10, 12–13, 20
myth 31, 45–6, 81, 93, 132, 187, 189

Natorp, Paul 224 n.16
nature 25, 29–30, 33, 35, 50, 61–2, 65–6, 71, 85–6, 88, 115, 117–18, 121, 128, 132, 145, 167, 184–5, 187–9, 191, 196, 205, 208, 212–13
Nemerov, Howard 2–3
Nietzsche, Friedrich 81, 108, 195
Norris, Christopher 14, 23
Novalis 3, 9, 75, 212
Nozick, Robert 154
Nussbaum, Martha 151
Nuttall, A. D. 1–2

objective idealism 83–6, 94–5, 100, 153, 163, 224 n.15
Ogden, C. K. 21
Orwell, George 148

participation 23, 67, 84, 87, 128, 131–4, 136, 158, 161–2, 210–11
  final 30, 128, 134–5, 180, 185, 190, 193, 198, 212
  original 35, 127–8, 132
Pascal, Blaise 22
Pater, Walter 12, 16
Paul, Saint 169–71, 210–13, 228 n.6, 230 n.25
Peirce, Charles Sanders 16, 221 n.25
Perry, Seamus 219 n.5
Pessoa, Fernando 108
Pfau, Thomas 138
phenomenology 3, 18, 71, 78–9, 82–3, 86–7, 89, 95, 97, 100–4, 121–2, 129, 131, 143–5, 186, 204, 210, 220 n.15, 225 n.18
Plato 94, 132, 159, 192
Platonism 85, 90, 94, 109, 150, 159, 172, 180, 183, 224 n.16
poetic principle 11, 25, 29–34, 37

poetry   17–18, 36, 50
  consciousness and   17
  music and   17–18
  silence and   18–19, 73
polarity   36, 45, 71, 73–4, 85–7, 92, 94–7,
    99–102, 110, 125, 137, 143,
    165–6, 171–2
political philosophy   157–62
positivism   3, 61, 64, 71, 77–8, 80, 86,
    90, 100, 102, 106, 107, 144,
    183–4, 187–9, 192, 206,
    223 n.6
potency   195, 199, 201–2, 212
Pound, Ezra   1, 9–10, 12–13, 48, 55, 108,
    165, 220 n.12
  Hugh Selwyn Mauberley   10–11
Proust, Marcel   115
Pryse, J. M.   195
  The Apocalypse Unsealed   195

Raine, Kathleen   2
Raleigh, Sir Walter   7
rational principle   11, 25–31, 34, 37, 48,
    98
Rawls, John   154
reason   99–100, 106, 142–3, 152–3,
    161–2
revelation   102–8
Richards, I. A.   4, 7, 20–2, 25, 220 n.14
  The Meaning of Meaning   21
  The Principles of Literary Criticism   21
Richter, Jean Paul   108
Ricoeur, Paul   7, 34–5, 75, 105
Rilke, Rainer Maria   108
Rollins, Hyder   39
Romantic Modernism   3–4
romanticism   9, 12, 19–20, 23–4, 39,
    49–50, 56, 77, 112, 114–15, 118,
    155–6, 162
  vs. Classicism   10–12, 20, 116
  ethics   151
Roper, Trevor   55–6
Rorty, Richard   15
Roszak, Theodore   2
Rousseau, Jean-Jacques   159, 224 n.12
Russell, Bertrand   22, 27, 47, 85, 88
Ryle, Gilbert   62, 95, 144, 184

Santayana, George   12, 219 n.10

Sartre, Jeal-Paul   3–4, 77, 88–9, 101–2,
    120, 137, 185, 191, 223 n.10
Schelling, F. W. J.   57, 78, 91–2, 101, 114,
    154, 223 n.10, 224 n.13
Schiller, Friedrich   39–40, 154
Schopenhauer, Arthur   41, 108
Schuchard, Ronald   7, 221 n.22
self, the   11, 16, 32–3, 51, 70, 72, 74,
    85–6, 89, 95, 98–100, 119, 122,
    125, 143–4, 146, 148–9, 152–3,
    159–60, 169, 174–6, 201, 203–4,
    228 n.8
self-consciousness   12, 24, 29, 35–6, 48,
    73, 82, 85, 88–9, 91, 94, 97, 119,
    120, 147, 223 n.7
self-transformation   76–7, 82, 87, 100,
    106, 107, 110, 126, 134, 144–5,
    147–8, 163–4, 171, 190–1, 198,
    209, 213
Shaw, George Bernard   11–12, 219 n.8
Shelley, Mary   174
Shelley, Percy Bysshe   3, 9, 11–12, 14, 23,
    25–7, 30, 33, 35–6, 43, 46, 137,
    139, 220 n.13
  Adonais   9
  "A Defence of Poetry"   46
  Prometheus Unbound   25, 229 n.8
Sheppard, Richard   12
Skagestad, Peter   56–7
Smith, Logan Pearsall   4, 7, 38–9, 48–9,
    219 n.10, 220 n.17
  English Idioms   39
  The English Language   38–9, 41
  "Four Romantic Words"   114
  Words and Idioms   38
Snyder, Alice   83
Solovyov, Vladimir   4, 227 n.6
  The Meaning of Love   139, 153
soul   12, 25, 41, 46–7, 50, 52, 81, 112–13,
    144–5, 170
  consciousness   118–22, 133, 136, 152,
    161
  imaginative   120, 134, 226 n.9
  intellectual   119, 122, 136
  sentient   122, 132
Spengler, Oswald   44, 53, 56
Spinoza, Baruch   13
spirit   26, 31, 37, 46, 49–50, 74, 81, 88,
    90–3, 95, 100–1, 103, 107, 110,

113, 115, 144, 171, 174, 190, 198, 211
spiritual beings   108, 114, 124, 126, 130, 152, 193–4, 204, 206–8
Steffen, Albert   147
Steiner, Rudolf   4, 25, 32, 51, 64, 77, 83–6, 102, 106–36, 139, 142–3, 151, 153, 157, 162, 181, 194, 200–1, 212, 220 n.15
  Christianity as Mystical Fact   229 n.13
  metaphysics   77–83
  Philosophy of Freedom   222 n.2
  The Threefold Commonwealth   156
  Von Seelenrätseln   223 n.4
Swinburne, Algernon   9
symbol   90, 93, 100, 102, 104–8, 110, 131, 152, 163, 165, 180–1, 185, 187–91, 193, 198, 213
synecdoche   84, 100, 104, 107, 110–11, 123, 146–8, 152, 154–6, 162, 201, 206

tautegory   84, 87, 92, 179
Taylor, Charles   138, 224 n.17
  "The Validity of Transcendental Arguments"   224 n.17
Tolkien, J. R. R.   2
Tolstoy, Leo   144
Toynbee, Arnold   53, 56

understanding   98–100, 106, 162
Unger, Carl   114

uniformitarianism   69

Valery, Paul   109–10
Veeser, H. Aram   53
Verene, Donald   75
Vico, Gimambattista   56, 66, 221 n.23
Volkelt, Johannes   78

Ward, Aileen   7, 14
Welburn, Andrew   25
Wells, H. G.   12
Werblowsky, R. J. Zwi   199, 230 n.17, 230 n.22
Wheelwright, Philip   2
White, Hayden   2
Whitehead, Alfred Norht   62
Whitman, Walt   32
Wilbur, Richard   2
Williams, Charles   2, 108, 227 n.5, 228 n.5
Wisdom, John   184
Wittgenstein, Ludwig   54, 224 n.17
Woolf, Virginia   3, 13, 184
Wordsworth, William   9, 17, 115

Yeats, William Butler   7, 9, 12, 35, 107–8, 111–12, 115, 144, 220 n.12, 220 n.20, 226 n.12
  "Leda and the Swan"   221 n.26
  Per Amica Silentia Lunae   9
  The Tower   221 n.26
  A Vision   10, 107

www.ingramcontent.com/pod-product-compliance
Lightning Source LLC
Chambersburg PA
CBHW071820300426
44116CB00009B/1378